GALLIPOLI

GALLIPOLI

The Dardanelles Disaster in
Soldiers' Words and Photographs

Richard van Emden
and Stephen Chambers

BLOOMSBURY

LONDON · NEW DELHI · NEW YORK · SYDNEY

First published in Great Britain 2015

Copyright © 2015 by Richard van Emden and Stephen Chambers

The moral right of the authors has been asserted

Maps by John Gilkes

Bloomsbury Publishing Plc
50 Bedford Square
London
WC1B 3DP

www.bloomsbury.com

Bloomsbury is a trademark of Bloomsbury Publishing Plc

Bloomsbury Publishing, London, New Delhi, New York and Sydney

A CIP catalogue record for this book is available from the British Library

ISBN 978 1 4088 5615 4
10 9 8 7 6 5 4 3 2 1

Designed and typeset by Libanus Press Ltd, Marlborough
Printed and bound in China by Toppan Leefung Printing Ltd

*Half-title page: A French 24cm gun firing at Helles. This gun, abandoned during
the evacuation, rests in precisely the same location today.
Frontispiece: Highlanders in the Helles trenches: a kilted battalion of the
52nd (Lowland) Division.
Overleaf: A Senegalese batman to the French General Ganeval. Ganeval was killed by
a sniper in June 1915.*

Dedicated to

Private Fred J. W. Debenham
Army Service Corps,
Suvla Bay, Gallipoli

and

Sub-Lieutenant Douglas Illingworth
RNAS, Armoured Car Squadron

CONTENTS

Introduction

Oh my God, what a life this is! I shall want a six months' rest cure
if I survive it, and please God no more soldiering for me again.
A garden and the cultivation of flowers is what I look forward to.

Major General Granville Egerton (1859–1951), Commanding Officer
52nd (Lowland) Division, 30 August 1915

―――――

For years after the Gallipoli campaign there existed a belief among some surviving officers that, had scarce resources been better utilised and a concerted 'push' made at the right moment and at the right place, the campaign might have been won and strategic victory secured. It was a view submitted on occasions to Brigadier General Cecil Aspinall-Oglander, appointed to write the Official History of the ill-fated 1915 campaign, and a veteran of that expedition. It was not for the Official Historian to pour scorn on such opinions, but with twenty-first century hindsight they were entirely fanciful. If ever a campaign was doomed from the start, then the year-long slog in the Dardanelles was *the* case in point. Anyone who believed otherwise was blinded by over-optimism and had never stood on the region's baked and arid ground or been privy to no more than could be discerned from a stretch of trench.

'The position occupied by our troops presented a military situation unique in history,' wrote General Sir Charles Monro in March 1916. Monro had been brought in to take a grip on the deteriorating situation on the Gallipoli Peninsula, and he had quickly concluded that evacuation was the only option. Within weeks of his arrival, all Allied troops were withdrawn.

Monro's views, written three months after the evacuation, were blunt. 'The mere fringe of the coastline had been secured. The beaches and piers upon which they depended for all requirements in personnel and materiel were exposed to registered and observed Artillery fire. Our entrenchments

Lieutenant Colonel Charles Ryan: an experienced soldier, but the conditions made this a young man's war.

were dominated almost throughout by the Turks. The possible Artillery positions were insufficient and defective. The Force, in short, held a line possessing every possible military defect. The position was without depth, the communications were insecure and dependent on the weather. No means existed for the concealment and deployment of fresh troops destined for the offensive, whilst the Turks enjoyed full powers of observation, abundant Artillery positions, and they had been given the time to supplement the natural advantages which the position presented by all the devices at the disposal of the Field Engineer.'

The hopelessness of occupying a 'fringe of coastline' with winter on its way was self-evident. Yet Monro's damning assessment was so comprehensive, so irrevocable, that it raises the question then, as it does today: what on earth were we doing there in the first place?

Of all the Great War's campaigns and set-piece battles, those fought on the Western Front have remained uppermost in the public imagination: the Somme and Passchendaele, for example. Even Mons, that relative skirmish, is still a name to be reckoned with. Beyond the borders of France and Belgium, however, nothing is recalled with such alacrity as one name: Gallipoli. The campaign on the Anatolian Peninsula continues to enthral the imagination on both sides of the globe. In Australia and New Zealand, 25 April, the day of the first landings, is a national day of commemoration when both nations stop to remember with reverence the contribution of those who fell and those who fought and survived. It is a day more deeply embedded in the hearts of Australians and New Zealanders than Armistice Day, for 25 April has become inextricably entwined with both countries' perception of national identity.

In Britain, the campaign is remembered as one of waste, yet fought with great heroism and in the teeth of impossible odds. Gallipoli is where tens of thousands of Allied men slugged it out with a tenacious Turkish foe. The drama of the campaign is undeniable, for the Allies were never more than a stone's throw from the sea and, therefore, disaster. Here was a land baked dry by searing summer heat, and where water was in desperately short supply. Illness and disease were rife. But Gallipoli is also where a remarkable escape was concocted and brilliantly executed: and over the years the

British have developed a penchant for great escapes. Gallipoli is also remembered as Winston Churchill's 'brainchild' and his greatest disaster. As First Lord of the Admiralty, he was in a position to pursue his restless ambition to attack elsewhere, away from the stalemate of the Western Front. Churchill was a wily politician and he was to have many fine hours, but this decidedly was not one of them, and the failure at Gallipoli haunted him for the rest of his life. His woeful lack of any strategic awareness in pushing for the campaign found him out, and a lesser man would have been finished on the wider political stage.

First Lord of the Admiralty, Winston Churchill: the campaign was his brainchild but also his greatest disaster.

Over the last twenty years I have written extensively on the 'human' aspect of the Great War, on boy soldiers, on prisoners, and on the families of those who fell at the front. In each case I have been surprised and shocked at the stories I have uncovered, and I have been just as shaken by the gripping narrative of Gallipoli. Most historians agree that the idea of forcing the Dardanelles was an impossible dream, that the land campaign, once begun, was doomed to failure. During the fighting, a number of senior officers took the blame for incompetence and dithering. They were removed from command, sent home, and retired. Some were later castigated for their performance, not least the officer in operational command, General Sir Ian Hamilton, who remained steadfastly over-optimistic as to the certainty of success – if he had the right support. Yet in hindsight, in private correspondence written in 1918, even he referred to the campaign as the 'Dardanelles dustbin'. While there is plenty of evidence to substantiate the popular view of ineptitude, research has led me to believe that the terrible physical conditions that prevailed on Gallipoli must contribute towards tempering the harsh criticism of some, though by no means all, of these men.

Overleaf: After a briefing: a snapshot of General Sir Ian Hamilton, Commander-in-Chief of the Mediterranean Expeditionary Force.

Failure, heroic or otherwise, is always likely to highlight differences among those who held the onerous task of commanding men in the field: disagreements as to the right course of action invariably exist. However, such were the unique conditions of Gallipoli that instances of bitter

interpersonal animosity were frequent and of a viciousness not, to my knowledge, found elsewhere. In revisiting the campaign, both senior and junior officers rounded on one another for 'failure'. But some of the greatest ire, not to say loathing, was reserved for the politicians who sent them to Gallipoli, and especially for Winston Churchill.

'I say from the bottom of my heart,' wrote Major General Egerton, on 22 July, 1915, '"Gott strafe Winston Churchill." I hope he will shortly die of cancer.' A line that even Egerton felt the need to black out follows this extraordinary statement. Could those words have been even more intemperate? Such sentiments are shocking. What, if any, are the extenuating reasons for their unusual violence?

Over the years there has been considerable focus on the failure of command and control on Gallipoli, and deservedly so: 58,000 British, Empire and French troops were killed and a further 196,000 were evacuated wounded or sick. Nevertheless, while this book is not revisionist in its aims, it is important to point out here and now one important theme: endemic disease, coursing through men of all ranks, must have had particularly serious implications for those on whom authority rested more heavily than at any time in their lives.

In 1914, the new Secretary of State for War, Lord Kitchener, launched a campaign for a new civilian army. Such was the response that 1.1 million men had volunteered by Christmas. The army was swamped. In order to infuse professional vigour and fire into these willing recruits, a wise decision was taken to strip out a small nucleus of younger officers from regular battalions deploying overseas to train and inspire the volunteers. This sound principle soon hit an unanticipated problem when high casualties among officers in France and Belgium forced the War Office to re-employ retired officers at home to replace the younger officers now needed abroad. Out of necessity, some of these older men were given command of Kitchener battalions, brigades and divisions. The inevitability of re-employing so-called 'dugout' officers proved problematic. These men were in their late fifties and even sixties and had been enjoying cosy retirement in such places as the Yorkshire Dales and the leafy Home Counties. They had served in campaigns as far back as the Zulu or Afghan wars of the late 1870s and early 1880s and were no longer suited to service abroad, and certainly not in such a harsh climate as that to be found on the rocky, scrub-covered Gallipoli Peninsula.

Those officers chosen for 'higher commands, especially battalions and brigades, were weak' according to an anonymous officer who accompanied the 11th (Northern) Division to the Dardanelles in June 1915. In choosing those in senior command, 'Age and length of service seemed to be almost the only – certainly the principal – qualifications to be considered. The average age of the battalion commanders must have been well over fifty, and the brigadiers about the same. Practically all these officers were recalled from retirement, into which they had gone because they were not sufficiently efficient to be required even in time of peace.'

'Inefficient' does not mean they had once lacked ability, simply that they were no longer suited to command, owing to fitness, or natural redundancy in the length of time elapsed since service. The problem was intractable because of a simple lack of alternatives, according to the officer. 'If an unsatisfactory or aged commander were "outed", there was no guarantee that one more efficient or younger would be sent. Indeed, it is hardly too much to say that the probability was that an older man would be selected; for the only names on the Military Secretary's lists were those of retired officers.'

Gunfire on the Peninsula was almost continual and, given the small, restricted area under Allied control, there was little opportunity for respite. Men could not be withdrawn from the line and into 'rest' twenty miles from the trenches, as they could be on the Western Front. When the deepest point of penetration into enemy lines was little more than three miles, then the entire position at Gallipoli was, in effect, one front line with an adjacent sector slightly more or less dangerous than the next. Officers and men were constantly stressed. The Turks were able to land shells almost anywhere they wished. These were not necessarily aimed shells, but desultory shelling that sapped energy and morale.

As Captain Albert Mure, 1/5th Royal Scots, wrote:

In Gallipoli the so-called 'rest-camp' or reserve-trench was the most dangerous place. The firing-line, so long as you kept your head well down, was really the safest place, except just when you were going over the top; that was hot always. In the support-trenches you usually got shelled, and the snipers paid you their best attention. The shells and the bullets that went over the top of the firing-line (as more did than didn't) found their way to the reserve-trenches. And you were always under fire in every part of the damned peninsula. There was no real cover. In the firing-line you got some of the shots intended for you; out of it you got all the shots intended for you, and a great many that were not.

At the same time, men worked in intense daytime heat in which sickness spread with terrible consequences, leaving men weak and listless. Being 'ill' on Gallipoli included dysentery, enteric fever, jaundice, even malaria. And then there was 'soldier's heart', various cardiac disorders brought on by over-exertion, a desperate lack of sleep and mental fatigue. Dysentery was perhaps the commonest ailment: it robbed a man of any dignity and of all energy. He felt wretched to the point that he might care little for life or death. Feeling ill, in broiling heat, when flies in their billions circulated and irritated, was torture, without the added stresses of command and responsibility, when hundreds, perhaps thousands of lives depended on clear-headed decisions.

It is into this context that we place officers like Major General Egerton and others who were 'found wanting' during the Gallipoli campaign. Is it surprising that these men fell out during and after the war? Is it surprising that their best efforts were not good enough?

In this book, I, along with my co-author Stephen Chambers, have drawn on a large number of memoirs and diaries, most of them not published before. Other books can be found to give blow-by-blow accounts of the campaign, but our intention is to give the reader a more intimate account of the period, looking at the experience as it affected the individual soldier or sailor rather than relying on overviews of strategy and objectives. For this reason, we have chosen to draw on privately written accounts, so that the reader is given the opportunity to 'know' many of the individuals and to follow their progress, rather than moving from one shorter personal extract to another. For too long, the Turkish perspective on the campaign has been sidelined and even ignored. We aim to address this imbalance by using first-hand accounts written by Turkish soldiers to give a sense of what it was like to defend the Gallipoli Peninsula from foreign invasion. In addition we have sought wherever possible to combine the text with powerful and directly complementary pictures taken by the soldiers themselves on privately kept cameras.

For the greater part of the war, the personal ownership of cameras was banned after the army became concerned that such images were appearing uncensored in the national press. The appearance in tabloid and broadsheet newspapers of British and German troops happily fraternising in no-man's-land during Christmas 1914 infuriated the army's senior command and when the press began to advertise openly for images taken at the front, the authorities clamped down, threatening to court-martial anyone caught in possession of a camera. A further order was issued on 16 March 1915 banning private photography across all theatres of war, including Gallipoli, where operations were opening. The survival of albums from the period reflects the decision by many men, particularly officers, to take the risk and ignore the ban.

The majority of this book's illustrations are taken from one of the most comprehensive privately owned collections of photographs known, that of my co-author, military historian Stephen Chambers. A Gallipoli devotee, he has built a superb collection of memorabilia from the campaign. His photographs are some of the most stunning that I have ever seen; the best are shown here, most never previously published.

For the vast majority of the time, men were not fighting but undertaking daily chores: the endless repetition of fatigues to ensure that trenches remained habitable and the men were resupplied for their daily needs. In these respects, Gallipoli was not very different from the Western Front, and yet it was in fact entirely different. At Gallipoli, men continued the monotonous grind, ferrying supplies up and down from the beaches to the men in the trenches, and at Gallipoli war could never have been more than a few hundred yards away. Such was the tiny area in which they operated that there could be no retreat, no rest. Shot at from the front, from the sides and even from the back, men suffered horrors distinct from anywhere else. Gallipoli has its own extreme drama.

Overleaf: Major General Henry de Beauvoir de Lisle takes the salute from the 1/6th Manchester Regiment prior to its departure for Gallipoli.

1 Forcing the Straits

'Saluting's a thing for Pommie bastards – not for Austry-lian boys like us.' But still, we had a great affection for the 'Cobbers' – these wild Australian boys. The only slight resentment we felt … was the fact that their basic pay was 6 shillings as against our 1 shilling a day. But there it is – the wages of war, like the wages of sin, quite often vary.

Private Charles Watkins, 1/6th Lancashire Fusiliers, 42nd Division

———

In the early years of the twentieth century, the once great Ottoman Empire was in decline. Turkey itself was weak and its government, under Sultan Abdul Hamid, was ineffectual. In 1909, a group of army officers and civil servants, known collectively as the 'Young Turks' under its charismatic leader Enver Bey, attempted to overthrow the government with the lofty aim of reinvigorating and modernising the state, which was largely undeveloped and agricultural. Unfortunately, foreign investment was essential, and as a result various other countries, including Germany, had considerable economic interest in Turkey and its future. Enver Bey himself was briefly Turkish Military Attaché in Berlin in the same year, and was highly impressed by the German military machine. From then on, his sympathies were generally with Germany.

In 1912, Turkey's weakness was emphasised again in the First Balkan War, in which she was soundly beaten by an alliance of neighbours known as the Balkan League (Greece, Serbia, Bulgaria and Montenegro) and was forced to cede more land in a treaty negotiated and signed in London. Almost all the remaining European territories of the old Ottoman Empire were partitioned between the victorious allies.

The Balkans were nothing if not unpredictable, and the victors soon fell out over the spoils of war, dissolving the Balkan League, and, in the Second Balkan

52nd (Lowland) Division embarking at Liverpool: Divisional HQ and 156th Brigade on RMS Empress of Britain, 23 May 1915. Major General Granville Egerton wrote: 'At least 50% of these men never returned.'

War, Bulgaria launched an attack on Greece and Serbia, lost, and had to cede land gained in the earlier war, Turkey recovering some of her former losses. However, her population was still fewer than forty-five million, half of whom were not ethnic Turks but Greeks, Slavs and Arabs, and foreign investment was still essential.

By 1913, the Young Turks were the *de facto* leaders in Constantinople, and Enver Bey (now elevated as Enver Pasha) was General of the Army and Minister of War. The Turkish government was divided. Most ministers were inclined to look to Britain for help in modernising the army, but Enver Pasha was convinced that Germany would quickly win any conflict in Europe, and was much more inclined to look to Germany for aid.

At a time when Britain might have reaffirmed an historic friendship with Turkey, her leaders chose to pursue more pressing strategic priorities, devoting their energies to 'allies', France and Russia, and an 'Entente' signed in 1904. Germany, meanwhile, nurtured a nascent friendship with the Turks, making small gestures of no particular value but which in themselves helped foster a feeling of bonhomie between Berlin and Constantinople. One such gesture saw the dispatch of two German cruisers, the *Goeben* and the *Breslau*, to the Turkish capital. These ships underlined Germany's growing naval might, and when the crew of the *Goeben* helped douse a serious barrack fire in Constantinople, the friendship grew firmer still.

While the Germans courted the Turks, the British, like their allies France and Russia, chose to reject Turkish approaches. Growing diplomatic indifference to Constantinople led to incidents of neglect that antagonised the Turkish government which, as a consequence, saw only ever greater attractions of an alliance with Germany. One case concerned two ships under construction in Britain, bought and paid for by patriotic public subscription in Turkey. The ships were near completion when the First Lord of the Admiralty, Winston Churchill, concerned over impending war with Germany, decided to add them to the strength of the British fleet. Churchill had no legal authority to seize the ships when Britain was not at war with Turkey, yet he ordered the shipbuilders to slow work long enough that, should war break out in Europe, the ships could be seized. This happened on 1 August, much to the anger of the Turks.

The assassination in Sarajevo of the Archduke Franz Ferdinand, the heir to the Austro-Hungarian throne, had been the catalyst for an international war.

The killing, in late June, had appeared to be a local crisis but one which had quickly spiralled out of control. The murderer turned out to be a Serbian nationalist and Austro-Hungary, an ailing nation-state, sought to reassert itself with German backing, threatening to invade Serbia. Such a limited war would not upset the Turks – after all, the Serbs had been a member of the Balkan League – but Serbia appealed to its traditional ally, Russia, for support, and Russia was, under the Entente of 1904, friends with France and Britain.

As the war clouds darkened over Europe, and ultimatums were thrown one way, then another, the Turks hoped to remain on the sidelines. But international wars have a nasty tendency to suck in smaller nations, and it soon became apparent that Turkey might be required to choose sides or risk being battered by the uncertain winds of war. Turkey had been impressed by German naval strength and Germany had no obvious territorial aims in the region, unlike the nations of the Entente. A victorious Germany might help reverse Turkey's losses in the Balkans. Yet recent history should have forewarned Turkey that forays into armed conflict were a huge gamble. As Europe lurched towards war, the German Ambassador in Constantinople pressed the Turks to join the Central Powers, while his British counterpart left for a well-earned holiday. Enver Pasha and his close political allies negotiated a secret deal. In exchange for German help to

German cruisers Goeben and Breslau in Constantinople, both gifts to the Ottoman fleet.

recover lost land and a guarantee of her national borders, Turkey would join the Central Powers in the event of a Russian attack against Germany. The Treaty was signed on 2 August. However, before it could be ratified, conflict erupted when Germany declared war on Russia. In Berlin there were high expectations of a quick and decisive victory and therefore no direct pressure for Turkey to join the war. Nevertheless, Germany would keep diplomatic channels open. It seemed more than likely that if Turkey entered the war, it would not be on the side of the Allies.

The early predominance of German forces in Belgium and France gave the Turks confidence that backing the Central Powers was a safer bet than backing the Allies: Britain, with a large navy but a small army, was deemed by Constantinople to be ineffectual in a European war. In a critical decision, Enver Pasha ordered the Turkish navy to join with the *Goeben* and *Breslau* and launch attacks on five Russian ports. Russia declared war on Turkey and Churchill ordered the British navy, with French naval support, to bombard Turkish forts at the mouth of the Dardanelles. The favourable results encouraged the Allies to believe in the effectiveness of naval attacks on forts, while unfortunately warning Turkey that she should improve her defences in the Dardanelles.

In France, British attention remained firmly on the fighting between her small regular army and a far larger Imperial German Army. As the fighting reached stalemate that autumn, and opposing forces hunkered down in trenches, some British politicians looked for alternative strategies, ideally opening up 'softer' fronts that offered the potential for success and at a far lower cost in casualties than those being suffered in France and Belgium. One of those looking elsewhere was the constitutionally restless Winston Churchill, a man full of thrusting vigour and enthusiasm for the bigger picture, but with little grasp of, or interest in, the complexities of detailed strategy. As First Lord of the Admiralty he had the Grand Fleet at his behest and he was keen to use its menacing power. In October 1914 he used the navy, and the men of the Royal Naval Division, in an ill-advised attempt to defend Antwerp from advancing German forces. This was a disastrous adventure ending with a rapid retreat, and the internment of a brigade of men who inadvertently crossed into Holland. Still, never a man to be set back by setbacks, Churchill was keen to try something else and his thoughts, followed by his energies, settled on an operation against Turkey in the narrow Dardanelles Strait.

In January 1915, the Russians asked the British for military support in an attack on Turkey. Given the precarious situation on the Western Front, the British should have refused, but Lord Kitchener, the Secretary of State for War, held out the possibility of a naval assault in the Dardanelles and Churchill immediately saw the opportunity to advance his scheme. The grand idea would be to send a fleet up the Narrows into the Sea of Marmara and threaten Constantinople, forcing Turkey out of the war. Churchill asked the Commander of the East Mediterranean Fleet whether it would be possible to force the Dardanelles by ships alone. The question might as well have been rhetorical, as he was not interested in a negative response. 'The importance of the results would justify severe loss,' he reasoned. Churchill's influence was in the ascendancy and he would ride roughshod over any reservations expressed by senior naval commanders, no matter how sage their advice.

When the War Cabinet met in mid-January, a decision was taken 'to invade and take the Gallipoli Peninsula, with Constantinople as its objective', as if the first act led automatically to the second. The fundamental flaw was that the war would not be won except on the Western Front, where Britain and France could exert the greatest pressure on German forces, using short lines of resupply and reinforcement. Turkey was not a direct military threat to Britain and her defeat, even if achieved, would not necessarily spell defeat for Germany. Britain needed to control the North Sea, blockade German ports and keep the coast of Britain inviolate from invasion. Committing substantial forces to the Dardanelles perversely increased the Allied risk of defeat in the West.

An attack on Turkey was certain. A bombardment against the outer and intermediate forts guarding the entrance to the Dardanelles would be undertaken before the navy's guns could be turned on the batteries that defended the Narrows. This channel, less than a mile wide in places, separated European and Asiatic Turkey, and would, if forced, open a sea route to Russia. The original intention had been to use pre-Dreadnoughts, ships well past their prime. However, newer, more powerful ships, such as the *Queen Elizabeth* with her huge fifteen-inch guns, were added to the fleet. The French would also join the campaign. They saw a need to curb British ambitions in the Middle East and were keen to be involved in the defeat of Turkey and to garner the prestige that would accrue as a result.

The question exercising naval minds was how ships alone were going to

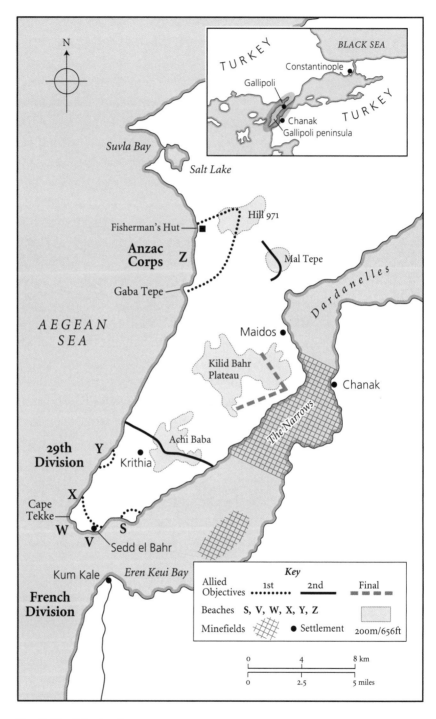

The Gallipoli Peninsula

take and hold the Gallipoli Peninsula. As if already anticipating the need for land forces, the Admiralty sent two battalions of the Royal Marine Light Infantry to the Greek Island of Lemnos, thirty miles from the Peninsula, ostensibly to be used as demolition parties to attack the Turkish batteries in the Dardanelles. The Greeks had captured Lemnos without bloodshed in the First Balkan War but had cooperatively withdrawn so that British Marines could land, thereby not compromising Greek 'neutrality'. The island's harbour, Mudros, was ideal as it was broad and deep enough to accept British and French warships.

In Britain, the Admiralty was not convinced that a naval bombardment of the forts was sensible without further troops being prepared to land if required, so in early February the Royal Naval Division set sail for the region, followed in March by the 29th Division. French forces were also on their way, while the Anzac Corps was already in the area, training in Egypt, as was the 42nd Division. Private Charles Watkins was there. He was proud of his battalion, but he was just a little bit in awe of the Australians training nearby.

The Aussies were under canvas a few miles away at Mena Camp, in the shadow of the Pyramids. They spent their abundant and surplus energy in wild and oft drunken orgies in Cairo some nights. Officers and privates would be seen by shocked British soldiers hobnobbing together, discipline and military etiquette being quite unknown to them. 'Saluting's a thing for Pommie bastards – not for Austry-lian boys like us'. But still, we had a great affection for the 'Cobbers' – these wild Australian boys. The only slight resentment we ever felt – and even that was not their fault – was the fact that their basic rate of pay was 6 shillings as against our 1 shilling a day. But there it is – the wages of war, like the wages of sin, quite often vary.

The indiscipline of these chaps was not so much deliberate as a complete ignorance of King's Regulations and Army Council Instructions, and the Manual of Military Law – those two formidable books that have governed the way of life for the British Army. It was an ignorance so abysmal that British Orderly Room Sergeants from the Regular Army, and well versed in the niceties of the application of discipline, were sometimes attached on to each Australian battalion, to advise and instruct the young Aussie officers. There were many stories about these Aussies that we treasured gleefully – some wildly impossible. Quite a lot of these stories

Private Charles Watkins, 1/6th Lancashire Fusiliers, 42nd Division

'Cobbers', men from the Australian Imperial Force, climb the Giza Pyramids.

were invented, for, to us the Aussies were the fabulous ones – the ones about whom it was natural we should weave stories.

The men of the Australian Imperial Force (AIF) and New Zealand Expeditionary Force were from very varied backgrounds, from cities and the outback, although around a quarter of them had one thing in common: they had been born in another country, mostly in Great Britain; far more were sons of British émigrés. Patriotism drew them to fight, but also the desire for adventure and a chance to see the world. The Anzac forces were on their way to Britain for service on the Western Front when Britain declared war on Turkey, and so a decision was taken to station these troops in Egypt where they could help ensure the safety of the Suez Canal from any Turkish strike. From December, these men had been within sight of the Pyramids, digging trenches and practising assaults in Egypt's sands, after which they were let out on to Cairo's souks and narrow alleyways. There were numerous brawls both with local civilians and Military Police, and incidences of venereal disease were high. On 2 April, in what became known as the 'Battle of the Wozzer', a riot took place in a notorious street, Haret el Wasser, known for its many brothels. At its peak, around 2,000 soldiers of many nationalities were involved, with houses set alight and prostitutes dragged out into the street. Two days later the bulk of the Anzac Corps left for Lemnos and the harbour at Mudros.

The 42nd Division was a territorial unit, and the men who served within each battalion were, in the main, lads who knew one another well; they had worked together in civilian life and had enjoyed their chance to be part-time soldiers.

Private Charles Watkins, 1/6th Lancashire Fusiliers, 42nd Division

Men of my own [42nd Division] Lancashire Division – men of the Rochdale Battalion, my own battalion, the 6th Lancashire Fusiliers. Many, at the start of the war were of spare and poor physique, product of a neat diet of fish and chips and long close-confined work in the mills – but now filled out to more robust proportions after a few months of good army food, fresh air and exercise.

Men of the 5th Battalion – miners and sons of miners most of 'em, more at home with a pick than a rifle, whose clogs had but recently echoed metallically over the flagstones of Wigan and Bury. Pugnacious types of men. Men of the 6th Battalion – the 'officer boys battalion'. Outstanding in their neatness and prissiness, these chaps – recruited from the offices and warehouses of our Northern Metropolis. But valiant youngsters for all their prissiness.

Private Watkins was by nature observant and thoughtful, and there was one man in the battalion for whom everyone had respect, the one man who had always remained somewhat aloof.

A lonely, isolated figure, this Captain Quartermaster of ours, during our training days in Egypt. Seldom would you see him hobnobbing with the other officers. Maybe it's because he was so much older – about 50 I should guess – as against the 20–25 years average of our other officers. Or maybe the very nature of his regimental duties as Captain QM kept him aloof and preoccupied, kept him out of the joyous enthusiasm of the younger and war-ignorant exuberance of the nice young chaps who comprised the general run of our officers. These young boy-officers, they were all more or less of the same social background, sons of solicitors, sons of mill-owners, sons of men who lived in fine houses – and maybe our Captain QM was not out of the same top drawer, socially. Not that there was any lack of respect for him – quite the contrary. After all, a beribboned tunic and a legacy of a battle limp are not things that soldiers can treat with disrespect – especially young and inexperienced boy-soldiers like us who had the usual awe for the old campaigner.

Private Charles Watkins, 1/6th Lancashire Fusiliers, 42nd Division

Above: 'Battle of the Wozzer': firefighters tackling the aftermath of the riot.

Overleaf: In the shadow of the Pyramids: under canvas at Mena Camp.

Every day in Egypt our pattern of training was the same: a long gruelling march in the desert, under the hot sun to build up our stamina. The open-order skirmishing, each section in turn dashing forward some 50 to 100 yards, and their advance covered by the supporting fire of the other sections – supporting fire of lots of exhilarating blank cartridges being fired madly by us. Then finally a bugle call, a fixing of nice, well-polished and shiny bayonets on the end of our rifles, and a dashing charge of glory-mad young boy-soldiers towards a mythical and non-existent enemy, who presumably fled terrified at the very sight of the legendary British bayonet.

Then the bugle would sound the recall and we'd gather together again – like children do after an exciting picnic – 'tired but so happy' – and take about half-an-hour's rest before setting out for the tiring march back to barracks. Half-an-hour's rest, smoking innumerable fags, flushed with victory over our non-existent enemy, swapping stories we'd heard of the might of the British Army. This Captain QM would move amongst us, mostly 'not saying nowt' – his eyes crinkling in amusement – a solitary figure – like a fond old father – and picking his way through the hundreds of reclining figures on the sand, and eyeing us amusedly. Occasionally he'd stop to exchange a few words with some of us. Sometimes gently sarcastic such as 'Be sure to wipe the blood off your bayonets, lads' – and then roar with laughter. Then sometimes genuinely kindly. To a bare-headed lad sitting in the mid-day sun 'Keep your helmet on lad – sunstroke's a bad thing to get'. But we always felt a bit uncomfortable when he was around – like schoolboys who had been too exuberant in their play.

Kitchener had been doubtful of the wisdom of any plan that sent troops away from the Western Front, but he acquiesced and appointed Sir Ian Hamilton to take command of what became the Mediterranean Expeditionary Force (MEF). A drift had begun towards the creation of a land force despite the expectation that the navy would force the Straits without resort to infantry.

On 19 February, the Fleet undertook a slow bombardment of three forts that sat at the entrance to the Dardanelles, Sedd el Bahr, Kum Kale and Orkanie. The British ships were anchored, so as to remain steady. Nevertheless, while firing at these stationary positions appeared straightforward on paper, only a worryingly small proportion of the shells actually hit their targets. Each time the forts appeared subdued, the navy's fire was halted, whereupon the forts burst into life once more in a show of stubborn resistance. Geoffrey Maltby was a seventeen-year-old midshipman from London. This was to be his first time in action.

Friday 19th. 7.15 a.m. Beautiful day. Proceeding at 14.5 knots at all possible speed for Dardanelles. Towards the end of the run, the *Agamemnon* drew ahead of us. At last the funnels and mast of the *Vengeance*, *Cornwallis* and *Inflexible* could be seen behind the west point of Tenedos, and off the entrance of the Dardanelles….

It being so beautifully warm and calm (the sky being wonderfully blue) the fo'c'sle deck was swarming with officers and men. The *Irresistible* could be seen, at about 3 p.m., steaming to the south of Tenedos to coal. It was so clear, and the *Irresistible* could be plainly seen firing for all she was worth, presumably at a fort on the beach. Half an hour later the ship was prepared for immediate action at 3.15 p.m. The boats being thoroughly soaked and filled with a few inches of water, rails taken down, searchlights dismantled, hoses rigged and turned on, and last but not least the gunroom furniture; crockery and other appurtenances struck down below armour

Midshipman Geoffrey Maltby, Royal Navy, HMS *Queen Elizabeth*

Lancashire territorials training in the Egyptian desert.

on main decks. The other ships viz: the *Cornwallis*, *Vengeance* and French ships were having a rare old time with the forts, which could now be plainly seen. But not being required we stopped just astern of the *Agamemnon*, having just passed a flotilla of submarines, French submersibles, destroyers and a light cruiser or two at 4 p.m. We were 25,000 yards from the Asiatic coast and 12,000 yards from the European side. Seaplanes were now visible coming rapidly from the direction of Tenedos; their depot ship the *Ark Royal*, and some colliers being anchored south of Tenedos. The forts did not reply at first. The *Cornwallis* and *Vengeance* were now steaming at about 10 knots concentrating their fire on No. 6 Fort, which was soon a mass of yellow smoke. The forts on the European side and No. 4 Fort on the Asiatic side in particular, now opened fire at 5 p.m. At about the same time attention was turned to the forts on the European side, for the French ships (3 in number) were left to carry on firing at the Asiatic side. While manoeuvring, three consecutive shots fell close to the *Vengeance*, each projectile bursting with such violence as to hide her from view with a huge column of water and fumes; so high in fact that men in her foretop were drenched to the skin. One man was wounded by a shell splinter from a projectile, in the thigh. Otherwise the ship had a miraculous escape.

Lieutenant Harry Minchin, Royal Navy, HMS *Cornwallis*

Five of us were lined up at about 5–7 miles from the Dardanelles in various positions & the signal was made to commence operations. We were told off for Fort 4 on the Asiatic Shore, at 12,000 yards. I was up in the crow's nest, at a height of about 150 feet or so, so I got a good view. At any rate I gave the order to fire the first gun of the whole proceedings & scored a jolly good hit first go. The rate of fire was very slow, about one round every minute, as we were outside their range. This lasted for the forenoon. In the afternoon us and the *Vengeance* got closer, at about 8,000 yards to 5,000 yards & the *Vengeance* was then under quite a heavy fire. So we rushed in to support her and fairly blazed at the fort, every gun in the ship going off together & doing two rounds a minute at least from every gun. We blew No. 1 fort to a perfect inferno, rocks and smoke, flame, dust & splinters all in the air together. We then got under fire from another fort, so we switched on to her then & never in my life have I had such a ripping time. We weren't hit, although we had a few close shaves. I think our rate of fire must have put them off their stroke. 3,000 lbs of shell a minute bursting all round one must be a bit disconcerting.

Strong southerly gales halted further attacks until 25 February when the bombardment was resumed, Allied ships anchoring in a semi-circle around 12,000 yards from the outer forts. The forts replied to Allied fire almost immediately, No. 1 Fort (Cape Helles) hitting one naval ship, the *Agamemnon*, seven times, killing three men, although damage to the ship's superstructure was superficial.

The *Queen Elizabeth* was ordered to fire at No. 1 and continued to fire deliberately with single guns for about an hour. At the end of this time, both guns were put completely out of action, the last 3 rounds fired from the left gun being direct hits. This bombardment made us realise that to put a fort out of action it was necessary to get direct hits on the guns. The Turks fought their guns most gallantly, and time after time we all thought that they would abandon; but the guns, which were on disappearing mountings, invariably reappeared and replied to our fire. When they were eventually put out of action, it was a great satisfaction to see the Turks abandon the fort and run down the side of the cliff. At one o'clock, *Vengeance* and *Cornwallis* steamed in to within 2,000 yards of Sedd el Bahr, supported by our fire, and opened a rapid fire with 6-inch. They were only fired on by howitzers.

Lieutenant Commander Thomas Binney, Royal Navy, HMS *Queen Elizabeth*

Soon afterwards a small party of sailors and Marines were landed to blow up the abandoned guns in the forts of Kum Kale and Sedd el Bahr. These daring raids were continued over the next few days, in order to check the damage wrought and to destroy any guns still operative. Then, on 4 March, a larger raid was undertaken against the same forts.

The raids had alerted the Turkish defenders to the inadequacy of their own defence and efforts had been made by the Turks to improve their response. This did not auger well for this, the latest raid. Sergeant William Meatyard was one of those who took part.

Sergeant William Meatyard, Plymouth Battalion, Royal Naval Division (RND)

I was detailed to land with the force at Kum Kale, and we transferred to HMS *Scorpion* (a destroyer) and when closer in to shore we were again transferred into pulling boats, and towed to shore by a steamboat.

Enemy shells began to fall around the boats, and there were also casualties from well-directed rifle fire. Had the enemy had machine guns I don't think many would have landed. Sergeant [Arthur] Minns was killed by rifle bullet before we got ashore, the bullet having first passed through and wounding Private Liversag who was sitting on his lap.

We got alongside a wooden landing stage that was about 40 yards long, and clambered on to it. Being flat, without rails and clear of obstacles, it afforded no cover. We were subjected to a good deal of rifle fire. On reaching the top we laid down flat until the first boatload had assembled. We were then given the order to stand by, and all rising together doubled for the shore. We were now at the foot of the Fort, and at the commencement

First hours of action and under fire: bombarding the outer forts on 19 February.

of the road that led direct to the village. This road I had been detailed to follow with the advanced patrol which consisted of ten men under Captain Brown. The advance of this patrol was not successful; we had only gone a few yards when we were compelled to lay prone and look for targets to

return fire. Out of the 10 only three remained who were not either killed or wounded. The enemy was well concealed and apparently firing from houses. It was when aiming (having spotted one of the enemy coming up to fire from behind a garden wall), that I got hit by two bullets from the flank, one in the chest and the other in the left foot. I wriggled back round the corner of the Fort and got my two wounds dressed. Fortunately the wounds were not serious and after a breather did not feel much the worse, although lamed. No headway was made up the village road and machine guns were posted at the corner to command it whilst headway was made by another party around either side of the Fort.

The idea was to keep the enemy at bay whilst a demolition party went inside the fort and completed the destruction that the warships had commenced. A section was told off to man the crest of the back overlooking the Fort, and now I joined up with this party, being anxious to get my own back on the enemy, but they still kept well concealed. Meanwhile the party on the right of the fort had made good progress, in fact being too eager they went too far, overstepping the objective.

They must have advanced about a mile up Tennisher Heights and were

outside the Fort of that name. The Turks received reinforcements and, over-whelming our small party, compelled them to retire. During this fighting another company had been landed to reinforce us. A signal was sent to the senior ship asking that the destroyers might close in and open up a covering fire to assist our men's retirement. This the destroyers did with a vengeance, being able to get fairly close in, and it was well for us that they did, other-wise I don't think many would have got back. Steaming single-line ahead, their broadsides of small guns smothered the Turks, who were prevented from following up their successful counter-attack.

The necessary destruction inside the fort having been carried out, we re-embarked at 7 p.m., the wounded going off first, and were put on board HMS *Irresistible*.

Our losses were 19 killed, 26 wounded and three missing.

Although Meatyard's description is dramatic, both raids achieved very little and merely forewarned the Turks, who spent time improving their defences. The men sent in at Sedd el Bahr fort did scant additional damage, not least because they found little to destroy, and this raiding party was forced to pull back under covering fire, the party having suffered a number of casualties.

The naval attacks on the intermediate forts continued but were piecemeal and all but failed in their objective to subdue them. There was another serious obstacle to the navy's campaign. Unsurprisingly, the Turks had laid a series of minefields to protect the entrance of the Straits. This move had been anticipated and twenty-one converted fishing trawlers, with volunteer civilian crews, had been brought to the Aegean to act as minesweepers. These small vessels were never designed for speed and could sail at a maximum of six knots, whereas the current running through the Narrows flowed at four knots; effectively, therefore, the ships appeared to the naked eye to be all but still in the water. As soon as these vessels inched their way forward at night, they were pinpointed by Turkish searchlights and attacked by concealed howitzers from both sides of the coast, something the civilian crews were hardly trained to cope with. When the cruiser *Amethyst* was ordered forward to protect the fishing vessels, she too was quickly targeted as she meandered slowly into view.

Suddenly we were the centre of searchlight glare and all hell broke loose. My gun received a direct hit and all but two of us were wounded. In the forepart of the ship, shells killed many men still in their hammocks. A watch of stokers all together in the bathroom were wiped out and the upper deck looked like a ploughed field.

E. Weaver, Royal Navy, HMS Amethyst

Unless the minefields could be cleared, any attempt to push through the Narrows would not simply be fraught with danger but downright suicidal. It was evident that the Turks were well placed to ward off the Allies' blunt attacks. On 18 March a new assault was launched. The Allied fleet would send forward three lines of ships. First the most modern would batter the enemy's forts again, to be followed by four French ships firing at a shorter distance. A third line of older British ships would then press home the attack while the fishing vessels, now with naval crews, would minesweep under the protection of the navy's big guns. This attack would be renewed the next day so as to overwhelm Turkish defences and force the Straits.

This daring attack was to be thwarted by a brilliant piece of Turkish planning. Over the preceding weeks the Turks had watched Allied ships bombarding the forts before breaking off and manoeuvring round in a natural bay known as Eren Keui. On 8 March a Turkish minelayer, the *Nusret*, had managed to sail out under cover of darkness and lay a series of mines parallel to the bay. On the morning of 18 March the Allied ships made their attack. These ships bombarded the coast with renewed vigour, the attack being continued as directed by the four French ships, two of which, the *Suffren* and the *Bouvet*, sailed up on the Asiatic side of the Straits, close to Eren Keui Bay. Both *Suffren* and *Bouvet* were hit by shellfire but, as they began to withdraw, *Bouvet* hit one of the mines. All that was seen was a small flame and yellowish smoke from the starboard side of the ship.

Overleaf: 18 March 1915: failure again. The photograph shows the damaged wardroom of HMS Agamemnon.

We saw a mass of ships such as we had never seen before. We were amazed, but realising that we should be faced that day with an out-and-out conflict, we completed our supplies and prepared for the attack … The battle developed with considerable violence and at noon the French ships in the second line advanced through the first line and opened a tremendous

General Askir Arkayan, Ottoman Howitzer Battery

bombardment. The batteries replied effectively. Under this fire the *Bouvet* started to withdraw, but at that moment a cloud of red and black smoke arose from the ship, which may have struck a mine. Immediately after this there was a much more violent explosion. We believed that a shell from Mejidiye had blown up the magazine. The ship heeled over at once and her crew poured into the sea. On both sides fire ceased. The destroyers in the rear hastened to save the crew. We opened fire but again firing ceased. Towards sunset the battle slackened and the ships withdrew. Just then the *Queen Elizabeth* opened fire on my battery. She was too far away for us to reply and we withdrew the gun crews without any damage being done.

Midshipman M.
Seyeux, *Gaulois*

For a few seconds the *Bouvet* continued its course then gently, without an explosion, it listed to starboard. The Commander clearly had had no time to stop the engines as we saw it sinking lower and lower without losing speed. A minute after seeing the sheaf of flame, before our astonished eyes, the *Bouvet* turned completely over to starboard and disappeared.

Seaman Sauveur Payro was on *Bouvet*. He had been ordered to get spare shells for the 27cm port gun turret.

Seaman Sauveur
Payro, French Navy,
Bouvet

I was in the right place for the shells when the blow came. The boat immediately listed to starboard. I was completely covered in the coal dust which came from the bunkers. I went to the signal ladder and with the second mate we climbed up. From the bridge I got myself on the funnel, which was entering the water. Then I climbed on to the hull. I believe that the second mate was trapped by the landing keel blocks and that he fell on to a

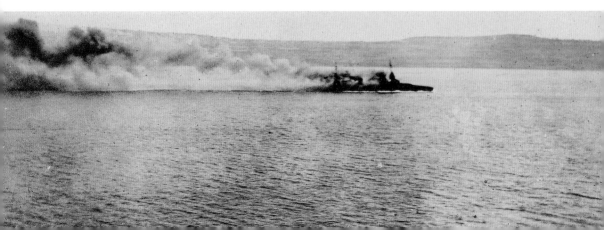

hatchway. From the keel I threw myself into the water. I couldn't rise to the surface because of the tug of the water. I was in the water from some time, then, when the bottom of the ship touched the bottom of the sea, I came straight up, either because the ship touched bottom or the boilers exploded. I couldn't breathe; blood was coming out of my mouth, my ears. When I was on the surface again, if I hadn't found this piece of wood I would have been finished. I managed to grab one of the hammocks and held it between my knees. I saw another chap crying out to me to save him and I told him to come closer to me so that he could be on one end of the plank and me on the other. But when the English came to fish us out of the water I saw that both his legs had been cut off. He died three days later.

The ship's plunge took most of the crew with her. Even those who managed to jump overboard were pulled underwater by the suction: Payro survived only because he was a very good swimmer. In all, the captain and 638 crew died: there were sixty-six survivors. No one yet suspected that this single ribbon of mines had been the cause. Two hours later, as the bombardment of the shore forts continued, another ship, *Inflexible*, already damaged by shellfire, was hit.

We could hear the thunder of the guns above the engines together with the shuddering and the blast showering dust everywhere, but we had no knowledge of how things were going; then there was a thud which shook the ship. It was followed by the silence from our guns. Then we could hear the tread of feet on the deck, meanwhile all electric lights had failed and we lit our secondary oil lamps that gave only a dim light. The engine-room telegraphs rang half ahead and remained at that long enough for us to surmise that we were either through the Narrows or we were retiring. The matter was

Seaman Ernest Bullock, Royal Navy, HMS *Inflexible*

The Bouvet's *last moments: almost 95 per cent of the ship's 704-man crew drowned.*

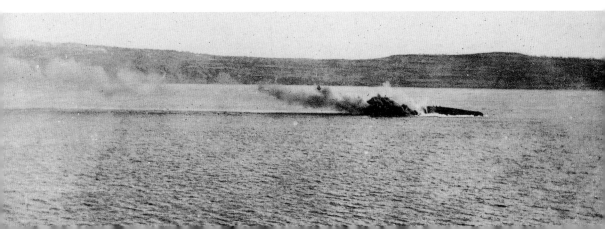

confirmed by a well-meaning voice shouting down the lift shaft, 'Abandon ship stations'. We were still unaware of what had happened until the engineer of the watch received from the bridge a message stating that we had been mined forward, and if possible we would make for Mudros and beach ourselves in shallow water.

Of the watches down below, one should go to his abandon-ship station and the other remain down below till the last moment. Each man tossed up with his opposite number. I won against my friend Wiggie Bennett and in my heart I felt a pang, feeling that all or none should remain down below. We were urged to get a move on as the ship was developing a list and the bows were deeper in the water also. Up we went on the various ladders, groping our way in total darkness [to the mess deck] ... Once outside we were amazed at the shambles. Some of the men were stripped to their underclothes with their lifesaving belts blown up. I noticed that one of the ship's police had a football tied to his waist and as the valve to my lifebelt was missing, someone tied the end with string. Wounded were being placed into the boats. I particularly remember the Master of Arms sitting in a cutter smoking his pipe and making light of his injuries, also the Gunnery Commander being carried on a stretcher to a boat. Though he was soon to die, I heard him say, 'I'm a poor specimen of humanity now'.

The *Inflexible* was able to stay afloat and she limped away to beach on Tenedos island. Worse followed when, three minutes after the explosion on the *Inflexible*, another naval ship, the *Irresistible*, struck a mine. This proved enough and a command was given for all ships in action to pull back. Still no one suspected a line of mines across Eren Keui Bay, and as the *Ocean* went to the aid of the *Irresistible* she too detonated a mine. Destroyers came to the rescue and most of the crew was taken off, but the *Ocean* was eventually abandoned and sank.

The losses precluded any continuation of the assault. The forts were battered but standing and the Turkish minefields guarding the Straits remained more or less intact. The naval assault had failed.

General Sir Ian Hamilton, Headquarters, MEF

I am being most reluctantly driven to the conclusion that the Straits are not likely to be forced by battleships as at one time seemed probable, and that, if my troops are to take part, it will not take the subsidiary form anticipated. The Army's part will be more than mere landings of parties to destroy Forts, it must be a deliberate and progressive military operation carried out at full strength so as to open a passage for the Navy.

Hamilton had arrived in the Aegean the day before the assault and had witnessed at least part of the ill-fated attempts to silence the forts. Four days later, aboard the *Queen Elizabeth*, he met Vice-Admiral John de Robeck, newly installed as Commander of the Allied Naval Forces, and agreed on a combined operation in which infantry would fight their way across the Peninsula to command the Narrows from the European side, allowing the waters to be cleared of mines and permitting access for the navy into the Sea of Marmara. A landing on the Gallipoli Peninsula would go ahead.

Overleaf: Shell stocks being replenished on HMS Agamemnon.

Survivors of the Bouvet *climb aboard HMS* Agamemnon.

2 Narrow-Minded

'I have never spent such a time in my life as I did before the landing, the awful responsibility, for I wasn't just carrying out orders, but carrying through a scheme of my own in which if I failed the consequences might be awful.

Commander Edward Unwin, Royal Navy, SS *River Clyde*

———

There was still every intention of forcing ships into the Sea of Marmara as soon as the infantry had done its job of seizing the high ground immediately to the west of the Narrows, known as the Kilid Bahr Plateau. This area afforded anyone in occupation grand views across the entire area and, crucially, across the water below. The forts guarding the Straits would be rendered inoperable, at least on the European side. There was no thought that such a plan might not succeed; the only questions were where to land sufficient troops to do the job, and how long it would take to seize the plateau.

The campaign at Gallipoli was organised with astonishing speed, not quite on the back of the proverbial envelope but at a pace inconceivable today, when plans are made in great detail and contingencies anticipated. General Sir Ian Hamilton had no such luxury and later conceded that his plans were 'very sketchy' and entirely of his own design. This had one merit, as he recognised. His was the responsibility alone, and he was being given free rein to see 'his' strategy through. The problem facing him was that the Turks held all the land and therefore, geographically, all the best cards. Key to winning the campaign would be the occupation of the high ground, and the Turks sat on every strategically important plot, including the Kilid Bahr Plateau. For the Turkish forces, under the command of General Otto Liman von Sanders, erstwhile head of the Germany military mission in Constantinople, the principal question was to guess correctly where the Allies would land.

Early days and still an adventure: a holed deck as a result of the Turkish shelling.

The Narrows were the obvious objective, so von Sanders had to distribute his forces accordingly. There was a genuine risk to his mind that the Allies might land where the Peninsula narrowed at Bulair, in the north, but while the Peninsula might be cut off from logistical help from Constantinople, it could be resupplied from the Asiatic side. Another perceived threat was to the Asiatic coastline. The Allies could land at Kum Kale and advance behind the Asiatic forts to the Narrows. With this in mind, von Sanders deployed troops to protect against this eventuality. Lastly, there was an invasion of the Peninsula itself. For von Sanders, the best policy was to keep the bulk of his forces in the centre of the Peninsula, ready to move quickly to reinforce any threatened part of the coastline. Holding back an Allied landing would be the job of a relatively small number of Turkish soldiers. Von Sanders' forces, while not well equipped by the fighting standards of the day, were tough men, battle-hardened from the Balkan wars, and now better trained and led than they had been two years earlier. Crucially, they were fighting on their own soil.

As Hamilton worked out his sketchy plans, the Turks concentrated on their own preparations. Von Sanders correctly identified key landing sites, such as Helles and Gaba Tepe, and at both places defensive works were improved at night, with barbed wire strung out along the beaches and trenches dug or strengthened. Troops were prepared and rehearsed, and taken on rapid marches along pre-prepared routes to the identified landing sites.

Although the Turks held the high ground, they were forced to cede the first move to the Allies. The length of the coastline afforded Hamilton some opportunity to deceive von Sanders: Turkish reinforcements held inland would take hours to reach even the closest landing beaches, giving the Allied troops time to dig in if they could land either unopposed or with little opposition. A feint could be used to draw off Turkish forces: an obvious place for such a 'landing' was Bulair.

In considering his options, Hamilton also had to bear in mind the objective: the Narrows. Land too far away and the troops might find themselves unopposed but with a long march across hostile terrain and with increasing enemy opposition. Land near the objective and the Turks were likely to be prepared and in strength.

Hamilton's plans were based on the absolute need to take the Kilid Bahr Plateau. The obvious place to land would be Gaba Tepe and it was here that

Hamilton decided to use the Anzac forces, landing on beaches slightly to the north. He immediately began to speak with General Sir William Birdwood, the Commander of the Anzac Corps, about the forthcoming operation. Birdwood's men would seize the high ground immediately behind the landing beaches, before attacking and taking a prominent hill, Mal Tepe, and then moving on next day to Kilid Bahr. This was the plan; it would now be up to the men themselves to execute it.

We had just finished our divisional training under General Bridges when all sorts of rumours began to go round: we were going soon, nobody knew where or when. Some thought to France, some said Palestine and some the Sinai Peninsula. But the last operation in our training was landing from the open sea and we had to establish ourselves on a supposed beach and drive an imaginary enemy before us. This made some of us think a little and so we drew our own conclusion as to where we were going and sure enough it was true, too true. The men were optimistic and pessimistic in the one breath and so were some of the officers, but owing to the continued preparations for departure it was very obvious that we were going somewhere and very soon. General Sir Ian Hamilton had been given the command and he was making a thorough inspection of both English and Colonial troops. The greatest inspection that ever I witnessed and one of the greatest that has ever taken place was the inspection of our full division one bright morning by General Hamilton. It took place under the cliffs on which a little further back were to be seen the three great Pyramids. It was an inspection pure and simple, there being no spectators, but it must have looked fine to see those thousands of infantry with bayonets fixed, presenting arms to the echoing note of the combined buglers as the General and his staff cantered up. Somewhere about 20,000 bayonets glittering in the bright sunlight from the 'Slope' to the 'Present' and back again, then down to the 'Order' and 'Stand easy', until it was the battalion's turn to be inspected. Sir Ian Hamilton was very pleased with the look of the men, their fitness and keenness and said that he hoped that they would prove themselves shortly.

Lieutenant Edward King, 1st Battalion AIF

In planning the forthcoming operations, Hamilton decided not to use his forces in an all-out assault towards the key plateau of Kilid Bahr, but instead to land the British troops of the 29th Division and a battalion of the Royal Naval Division around Helles to the south, and on a series of beaches designated S, V, W, X and Y. At the same time, it was decided that the French would land at Kum Kale on the Asiatic side of the Narrows, to protect the flank of the British forces from long-range shelling.

The main British effort would be at V and W Beaches, supported by landings at S, X and Y. The aim at Helles was to land, then to march on and capture Krithia village and the heights of Achi Baba that dominated the ground in this southern sector of the Peninsula. The following day, British forces moving north would combine with the Australian and New Zealand Army Corps (Anzacs) moving east for an assault on Kilid Bahr. It does not take historical hindsight to realise that this was, in terms of pace alone, an astonishing timetable, predicated on a high degree of Turkish malleability. Hamilton's optimism was not shared, it is fair to say, by all his commanding officers, including Major General Aylmer Hunter-Weston of the 29th Division, who believed the men were not prepared for such tough objectives when reconnaissance had revealed the preparations made by the Turks at Helles.

The men would land in daylight in open rowing boats, pulled close to the shore by steam launches. At V Beach, the men faced a beach shaped like an amphitheatre, defended by barbed wire and trenches, as well as by two battered forts. The potential for an immediate and serious check here was obvious. At a conference held two weeks before the attack, an experienced sailor, Commander Edward Unwin, voiced his opinion that men rowing in open boats were likely to be easy targets and that a 'specially prepared ship' might be rammed ashore from which the infantry would pour from a series of 'doors' cut into the side of her superstructure. The ship, once beached, could then support the assault with machine guns while also carrying supplies of ammunition, food and water.

The idea was immediately accepted and a ship, a ten-year-old 4,000-ton collier named the *River Clyde*, was handed over for the works to be undertaken. On the decks, casements were made for the protection of machine guns and fired by men under Unwin's command. Of course the ship might run aground before it reached the beach and so a steam hopper and three lighters were to be towed alongside, ready to be drawn forward to bridge any gap between ship and shore.

I have never spent such a time in my life as I did before the landing; the awful responsibility, for I wasn't just carrying out orders, but carrying through a scheme of my own in which, if I failed, the consequences might be awful. The thousands of thoughts that flash through one's head at such a time as to what might happen and how to meet them. And on top of it all the wonder as to how one will behave one's self, as I don't believe any man is quite sure of himself.

Commander Edward Unwin, Royal Navy, SS *River Clyde*

One of those who would be chosen to serve under Unwin was Lieutenant The Hon. Arthur Coke, of the Royal Naval Volunteer Reserve. Before the idea had been broached to beach a ship, Coke had been told by his commanding officer that he would not be needed on Gallipoli for at least a month. 'This was very disheartening,' wrote Coke in a letter home on 19 April, so he and a fellow officer named Wedgewood went to see the General again, to offer their services 'in any capacity'. It worked.

[The General] said he wanted some marines to man the first troopship that lands. Isn't it splendid, we have got the job – Wedgewood, Illingworth, Parker and myself. Forty men were taking ten Maxims and putting them all round the fo'c'sle of the ship and we are to cover the landing of the first troops, who are 2,000 Irish Fusiliers (regulars). Captain Unwin of the navy is in charge of the ship with only twelve men (crew).

The Hon. Arthur Coke, No.3 Armoured Car Squadron, Royal Naval Air Service (RNAS)

He is going to beach her and has cut holes under the fo'c'sle for the men to immediately jump out and land … I cannot think of anything more exciting, also we shall see the whole thing. We shall have the fleet behind us so if the Turks do shell us I don't think it will be for long although she is a pretty big target. Today we have been very busy building shelters over our guns.

All the troops are not here yet. I hear that there are to be 102 Transports here before we start and what with the battleships and colliers etc. it will really be a marvellous sight. I believe we start the landing this week, I think it will be short but sharp to take Gallipoli.

Overleaf: SS River Clyde *being prepared for its epic assignment on 25 April.*

STOP
INSIDE
25

Indeed, not all troops were there yet. For two weeks, Allied forces had been assembling at Lemnos and in the island's harbour at Mudros: it was an impressive sight, with battleships, cruisers, submarines and transport ships at anchor. Behind the harbour were hills, while in the foreground were a small number of houses occupied principally by Greek civilians. The troops were undergoing final intensive training, living under canvas and marching around the island, passing through small villages where agriculture appeared to be almost the sole occupation.

Sapper Thomas Farrer of the New Zealand Royal Engineers was onboard the former German cargo ship *Goslar*. His ship was due to sail for Lemnos but for the moment it was stuck just outside Alexandria, anchored close to the quay. He and his mates were excited at the prospect of going to war, but their ardour was being dampened somewhat by the sight of their new, deeply unpleasant surroundings.

Sapper Thomas Farrer, 1st Field Company, New Zealand Engineers

That afternoon [11 April] I was sent down to the bottom of the after hold where we loaded the wagons of the New Zealand Infantry Brigade Transport. The place swarmed with small brown beetles, with a few black ones as well. We turned in that night on some boards among the coal dust. At 1 a.m. they called us up and we fell in reluctantly after much cursing and swearing. 'Dismiss! We are sorry but there has been a mistake.' So back we went to our quasi beds and turned in again.

Two days later and Farrer was not feeling well; in fact, existing stomach trouble had turned to dysentery.

Sapper Thomas Farrer, 1st Field Company, New Zealand Engineers

13 April: The authorities decided that the *Goslar* was insanitary. The horses were above the men and there were no scuppers, so when they washed down the horseboxes, the water dripped through on to the men who slept below. There was one drip just above my space on the floor so I hung a jam tin below it and was dry. We were crowded in the hold and had reed mats to sleep on. The iron deck was hard and the ship's side was too hot to touch. It was very hot down there and the smell and the flies helped to make it an unenjoyable home.

14 April: Up anchor and back into port and alongside a quay near a supply ship. We took all our gear ashore and piled arms on the sand. I was

told off on a fatigue to clean the decks down. Off went our boots and out came the hose and brooms and to work we set. Starting forward we worked aft down the horseboxes. Lunch on shore and then they all marched away to a camp while I was left that night and the next day. The dysentery was worse and I felt three parts dead. All through the afternoon I lay about on the quay and after tea we went on board and dumped our gear aft by the wheel. A table that was upside down made a good bed but I was not allowed much sleep that night.

Insanitary conditions were not the only problems for those cooped up on board ship. Twenty-four-year-old Captain John Dancy had just arrived at Lemnos.

Below: A welcome wash on deck.

I should mention the age-old hazard that affects the harbour of Mudros, and that is the fickleness of the weather. Intense gales are apt to spring up with no apparent warning, and can make it dangerous for two vessels of differing sizes to lie alongside one another.

Captain John Dancy, Surgeon, Royal Army Medical Corps, Attd. 2nd Brigade AIF

Typically then, when we arrived at Mudros, it was blowing half a gale, and raining sheet upon sheet of water. Helped by two tugs, we nosed our way through the fairway of the entrance, and anchored together just outside the harbour … All night the wind howled and the rain tore against us. The men cursed below while the crew splashed about in their sou'westers on deck. Then in the early morning an extra-violent gust of wind led to a sudden threat of collision, and HMAT *Hymettus* had to weigh anchor although no longer under steam. As a result she was driven by the unabated gale right across the harbour to stick firmly in the mudbank on the other side …

After repeated failures by ocean-going tugs to dislodge the *Hymettus*, permission was given for the ship's company to go ashore for exercise and training. Boulton, Edmunds and I took the stretcher-bearers and hospital orderlies for a brisk informal walk. The wind was still very high, so we carried our pith helmets and aimed north towards where the harbour was sheltered by a collar of hills some 90ft high. The wild flowers were out in profusion wherever they could root, with heather and thyme alone able to survive where the soil was dry and poor. An Australian told me later that, once the short spring was over, everything on Lemnos dries to the colour of a kangaroo pelt.

On the way back to our ship, we stopped to watch the 29th Division practising landing from lighters which were released from a destroyer to be paddled home to shore. In theory they were provided with a gangway, but in practice they jumped out and waded. They had been at it since 12 April, and had got the knack of it; but they were getting very wet and cold, and I doubt if their mothers would have approved.

The men were enthusiastic, and training, though intense, was often carried out in a spirit of fun and high jinks.

Captain Albert
Mure, 1/5th Royal
Scots, 29th Division

A week's hard training had now to be gone in for – training in descending and ascending rope ladders dangling over the ship's side into lighters. This was no easy matter in full marching order, but it had also its humorous side. To me it wasn't particularly funny, because the rifles of the men were

Horse and mule transport proved invaluable to the army on Gallipoli.

in my charge, and though you can fish a man out of the water, a rifle is not so obliging as to give you the chance. We had gunners also on board who did not participate in this form of amusement, but they were not to be done out of their share, which consisted usually in throwing the manure over the side where the ladder was. Even the cooks had to have their look in with the slops.

Tuesday 20th: About 10 a.m. we arrived in Lemnos harbour and anchored there. Every morning we were paraded with everything on. Once we had to climb down the side on a Jacob's ladder and get into a boat and then climb back again. How many boats there were in the harbour I cannot say. We simply could not count them. One hundred to one hundred and fifty is a rough estimate. The *Queen Elizabeth*, 'Lizzie' as we afterwards came to call her, was not far away. TBDs [torpedo boat destroyers] and submarines were constantly coming in and going out. One night it blew from the north and rained and we got some idea how cold it can be in that part of the world. On shore the fresh fields and the beautiful hills beyond looking very enticing and we longed to go ashore. After four months in Egypt we had almost forgotten what grass looked like. Many and various orders were read out to us and we got messages from Sir Ian Hamilton and the King.

Sapper Thomas Farrer, 1st Field Company, New Zealand Engineers

The latter wished us the best of luck and Sir Ian told us we were in for a really rough time; he was confident we should succeed because he knew of our destination.

After the grounding of the *Hymettus* and the as yet unsuccessful attempts to refloat it, Captain Dancy was transferred to a much larger and newer ship, the *Anglo-Egyptian*. Things were beginning to happen.

Captain John Dancy, Surgeon, Royal Army Medical Corps, Attd. 2nd Brigade AIF

The morning of 23 April 1915 broke to reveal an almost miraculous change in the weather. A great calm had fallen, so intense that sleeping men had become aware of it, awakened and called to others. Muffled excitement buzzed below deck, broke loose and gathered momentum until all were awake and at the portholes. One sensed that this agony of waiting had at last found its release, for which in that moment no penalty seemed too high to pay.

By dawn fully half the ship's company were at the rails of the *Anglo-Egyptian*. Spontaneous cheering broke out, with singing and waving from transport to transport. High above us all, beautiful shades of iridescent light were playing about the hilltops. Across the harbour the royal blue of the water, still as a millpond, served sharply to outline the tiers of transports, now more clearly seen to have been camouflaged matt black.

As the day wore on, ship after ship slid down the three lanes of the harbour exit, affording us in our position an especially privileged view of the file past. The cheering and singing were almost continuous, often reaching a crescendo when level with us because of the adjacent French troopships. It was indeed a soul-searching revival of the Entente Cordiale.

Gradually the main plan began to take shape before our eyes. British and French contingents of the 29th Division joined up with the waiting Allied fleets and headed for Tenedos. We ourselves gradually moved out to join a second stream which presently steamed away under escort bearing the Anzac troops in the direction of Imbros and the Gallipoli Peninsula at that level. The third stream comprised those vessels of the Royal Naval Division which had not already gone ahead and these followed a more northerly line leading to the Gulf of Saros, where they were destined presently to put into effect the dummy assault upon the coast at Bulair.

In fact the original landing date, 23 April, was postponed for forty-eight hours. The weather in the Aegean Sea was notoriously fickle and a gale two days before had put paid to any thought of landing under such stormy conditions. Now the weather had changed, the ships could leave.

April 23rd at eight bells in the forenoon watch, we steamed down through the fleet of battleships, English, French and Russian, and also the mighty fleet of transports, cruisers, torpedo-boat destroyers, gunboats and submarines. The send-off was tremendous, bands playing, cheering, singing and messages from all the ships, wishing us success and a safe return. As we passed the flagship *Euryalus* Admiral Wemyss signalled us himself from the quarterdeck using his left arm and telescope. The weather was glorious, and I shall never forget the whole scene.

We reached Tenedos about eight o'clock that night. Arthur [Coke] and

Surgeon Peter Kelly, Royal Army Medical Corps, Attd. RNAS

The invasion fleet gathers: Mudros harbour on the Greek island of Lemnos.

I shared a cabin, I had the top bunk, he had the bottom one and we smoked cigarettes and talked most of the night about all kinds of things from Holkham to Ireland and the reception the Turks had in store for us. We both decided to believe in Commander Unwin and as he had said it would mean death for hundreds, so we believed him. It struck me that night that Arthur had a presentiment that he was not coming back, as his luck had been too great in France for him to get through this time. We both rose at 5 a.m. on Saturday 24 April and the day passed quickly.

On the eve of the landings, the ships had arrived at Tenedos island and were only waiting for permission to proceed. The men could clearly see the Gallipoli Peninsula fifteen miles away and by extension the Turks could see the fleet. Due warning had been given that an attack was imminent.

Captain Clement
Milward, Indian
Army, GSO3 29th
Division

Spent a busy morning. General Hunter-Weston again, in his highly strung way, going through the arrangements for the landing, the naval artillery support of the ships and his oversanguine four phases of the advance to beyond Achi Baba on the very first day. We none of us said what we thought. I was busy, too, with marking maps from the latest Intelligence Aerial Reports, putting in the enemy's guns and trenches north of Achi Baba.

Just before lunch the General and Colonel Wolley Dod [GSO1] went over to the *Eurayalus* in a pinnace. We watched them with amusement as they narrowly escaped falling in the water while getting into the dancing boats; they got an awful tossing going across. It looked like no landing tomorrow. But after lunch the wind suddenly dropped and the sea became calm.

Towards evening we were transferred to HMS *Euryalus*, all the divisional staff, and later the Lancashire Fusiliers came there, too. The South Wales Borderers were put on to the *Cornwallis*, the Royal Fusiliers on to the *Implacable*, the King's Own Scottish Borderers [KOSBs] on the *Talbot* and *Amethyst* and the Munster and Dublin Fusiliers and half of the Hampshires on the *River Clyde*.

The officers and men of the *Euryalus* did all they could for us in the way of dinner and lending us their cabins to write letters. The men lay down on the decks and we slept in cot hammocks outside the ward room, and very comfortable they were.

Late in the afternoon [24th] all hands paraded aft under the big guns, and the ship's padre conducted a short service, which will probably never be forgotten by any man who was there. The bright sunshine and a slight breeze just flecking the blue water with white, the silent, reverent ranks of men in khaki and blue, the mighty guns overhead and the White Ensign flying, made a most impressive sight, and at the end of the service there occurred one of those strange and unexpected incidents which stir the blood of the most stolid and unimaginative.

Sapper Geoffrey Robin, 1st Field Company, Australian Engineers

The Benediction pronounced, the ship's band struck suddenly into a rollicking song tune 'We'll All Go The Same Way Home', and the padre took it up with a shout and roared the joyous carefree words as if they threw their hats in the air in defiance of the gods. 'We'll stick together like the ivy on the old garden wall,' came the last line in a triumphant peal, while the seagulls zoomed away in fright, and the conviction came that these men would

Calming nerves with a concert: on landing, these Australian bandsmen worked as stretcher-bearers.

never be beaten, would never give up the fight, and one thanked the gods for the privilege of being there.

The afternoon faded quietly into dusk and, after consuming an enormous meal, including some magnificent beef steak pudding, rifles were given a final overhaul and ammunition and packs adjusted, and all hands settled down quietly on deck in the gloom of the darkening ship, talking or dozing.

The men who would be charged with taking the Australians into shore were frequently not men at all, but young midshipmen like Eric Bush. Aged fifteen, he was to be handed a great and terrible responsibility.

Midshipman Eric Bush, Royal Navy, HMS *Bacchante*

It is Saturday, 24 April 24 1915, and to keep out of the way I am standing at the after end of the upper bridge watching the captain. I'm his 'doggy'. At the same time I am surveying the scene around me. We are weighing anchor. I can feel the ship trembling as the heavy cable comes in.

Our flagship, the battleship *Queen*, is now leading us out of harbour. Her band is playing 'Fall in and Follow Me'. Next astern come *Triumph*, *Prince of Wales*, *Bacchante* and *London*, in that order. On board three of these ships are 1,500 picked troops who will be the first to land. At the moment they are all on deck cheering and shouting slogans. Someone has found an enormous screen and had painted on it CONSTANTINOPLE.

My job as captain's 'doggy' ends when we are clear of the harbour. I have a feeling he has forgotten me, so I stare at him to catch his eye. Good, he sees me and nods. Off I go.

My immediate destination is the picket boat, resting in her crutches on the boat deck. I have been told to take charge of her at the landings. We shall tow the launch, the first cutter and a merchant ship's lifeboat which we have borrowed for the occasion. These three boats can take about a hundred and sixty soldiers, not a bad command for a midshipman.

Our picket boat has a crew of eight, including myself. We are going to meet on the upper deck to talk things over. Let me introduce them.

First there is Petty Officer William Main, our coxswain. Aged thirty-six, he is short, powerfully built, with jet-black hair. There is character written all over his face. Salt of the earth, I should call him. Leading Seaman Worsley and Able Seaman Bice are our two bowmen. They are both excellent and fine seamen. Then, in the stern sheets, there is Neish, a bearded sailor of the old school, and Hodgson, our youngest seaman. They make a good pair. I can see Stoker Petty Officer 'Bogey' Knight now as he peers out from his engine-room hatch. Tall, hair cropped very short, strong features, he is about the same age as Main. A most reliable man. Finally, there is Stoker J. Bell, a gallant lad who will spend all his time shut up in the boiler room without so much as a clue as to what is going on.

The hands are going to be called before midnight, so the ship's company have been advised to pipe down early. I will have a meal in the gunroom at about 6 p.m. and then turn in. My hammock is on the aft deck with those of the other midshipmen. As I get under the blankets, I feel scared for the first time. I turn over on my side and my hands come together. Soon I am fast asleep – 200 fathoms down.

About six o'clock at night, a big tug drew up alongside and the first of the two thousand troops began to come on board. They were the Irish Brigade, the 1st Dublin and Munster Fusiliers, splendid fellows and some of the best of our crack regular regiments. By 9.30 p.m. the last of the soldiers was on board and the eight big holds were crammed with men packed as close as they could stand. They were mostly the Irish Brigade, but there are also several hundreds of the Hants and Worcesters. These are the first I have seen of our first line regular troops, as fit as fiddles, trained to the inch and splendidly equipped. If the landing can be effected, these men will do it. I have never seen such a collection of splendid manhood, and the very sight of them gives one confidence in our success. These famous regiments have been splendidly chosen for this, the most difficult and hazardous enterprise of the war. When they have cleared the way, lesser men may follow. But I do not envy them their night in the stuffy, uncomfortable holds. The lower ones must be a pretty fair reproduction of the Black Hole of Calcutta, and we have been doing our best to keep them going by making enormous cauldrons of coffee in the galley and handing it round. They are big, rough fellows these, but kindly and generous to a degree and it is a pleasure to be among them. Of a truth the British Tommy has a heart of

Petty Officer David Fyffe, No.3 Armoured Car Squadron, RNAS, SS *River Clyde*

gold under his rough and rather unattractive exterior, and it gave one a queer, choking feeling when one watched these big, light-hearted school-boys and thought of what might be awaiting them within twelve short hours.

Saturday 24 April. This is just a line on the eve of the great landing. We run ashore on this ship at 5.30 tomorrow morning. I only pray everything will go satisfactorily and no shell will strike this ship as we have two whole regiments on board, so it would mean a terrible loss. They are coming on board now off the transport, and are being packed like sardines in the holds. It is all fearfully exciting and I think tomorrow will be the greatest day of my life, as I have got three Maxims on the fo'c'sle and am practically responsible for keeping off any attack while the troops are landing.

The Hon. Arthur Coke, No.3 Armoured Car Squadron, RNAS, SS River Clyde

Despite the optimism, the men could not help wondering what the landings had in store for them. 'On Saturday night when we turned in we wondered if ever again we should go to bed,' wrote Farrer in his diary. Too many would not.

I felt we were for it. That the enterprise was unique and would demand all I was capable of giving, and more. That it was no picnic but a desperate venture. I just longed to get on with it and be done with it. I felt I was no hero and that I had not the pluck of a louse. My nerves were tense and strung up, and yet I never doubted that we would not win through, because I knew the splendid fellows at my back, highly trained, strictly disciplined, and they would follow me anywhere.

Captain Guy Geddes, 1st Royal Munster Fusiliers, 29th Division

About midnight the anchor was weighed and we stood out to sea. Sleep was impossible, such was the crowded state of the ship, not to mention the intense excitement of our mission. It was a glorious night. The big silver moon made fretted silver of the glassy, ink-black waters as we glided slowly between the jutting headland and the island which formed the outer gateway to the Dardanelles. Now we were fairly embarked on our perilous enterprise and one thought with a thrill that dawn would bring our baptism of fire. One felt somehow as if one were clasping hands across the centuries with the great adventurers of ancient times. Was it on such

Petty Officer David Fyffe, No.3 Armoured Car Squadron, RNAS, SS River Clyde

Opposite: Men of 9th AIF climbing down from a transport on to the destroyer HMS Beagle.

a night as this that the Roman fleet put out from the Gallic shore toward the unknown cliffs of Britain? Did Norman William gaze at that same silvery moon when his flotilla set out on their great enterprise? And the old crusaders: were their warlike spirits watching eagerly the start of this new crusade against the ancient foe? We felt, that night, on the old *River Clyde*, that we were living history over again as we forged ahead toward the Turkish coast.

Midshipman Eric Bush, Royal Navy, HMS *Bacchante*

It is now 11.30 p.m. and the gunroom is full of midshipmen but surprisingly quiet. We are all completely dressed. I am sipping from a bowl of cocoa and munching ship's biscuits. There is other food on the table but I am not hungry. From my pocket I pull out the orders and start studying them all over again. 'Cap covers are not to be worn', I read. 'Tows are to be 150 yards apart', 'When approaching the beach, boat-hooks are to be used for sounding, and directly the water shoals pickets boats are to cast off their tows, boats astern sheering off to port'. And so on. But there is no time to finish as I am wanted. 'Midshipmen of the picket boat,' someone shouts at the gunroom door.

Petty Officer David Fyffe, No.3 Armoured Car Squadron, RNAS, SS *River Clyde*

About two o'clock a.m. we slowed down to a mere crawl and we knew that we were near our goal. But now the moon had set and the night was black as pitch. We could see nothing save the streak of creamy foam at our bows and the myriad stars that studded the velvety blackness of the sky overhead. My duties now took me below decks and I was busy at the Maxim belt-filling machine when the dim thunder of guns brought me up on deck. It was about 3.30 a.m. and the pearly-grey light that precedes the dawn was chasing away the night. Clearly now could we hear the guns, although as yet we could see nothing of the ships. The dull thudding drew nearer and nearer and more distinct as we slid slowly ahead, until, all on a sudden, away to starboard, we saw a red flash through the murk, and the rolling boom that followed told us we were nearing the fleet and that the bombardment had begun. Now as we clustered on deck watching the dim flashes that came and went at frequent intervals on both our bows and straight ahead, and listening to the dull thudding and rumbling of the bombardment, there loomed up suddenly out of the grey obscurity the long black shape of a battleship, silent and motionless. Hardly had we passed it when a long low destroyer, her knife-like bows slicing the water into two great foaming rolls that surged along her sides, slid alongside and a hoarse megaphone bawled orders from the dim bridge. Almost at once the *Clyde* began to speed up and soon we were forging ahead toward the booming guns.

Overleaf: A moment caught in time: the view from the deck of the River Clyde *after beaching. Ahead, hundreds of men crouch under a low sandy ridge, the only shelter from deadly Turkish fire.*

3 Opposed Landings

One's first sensation of being under fire was of feeling remarkably naked and uncovered, you felt you would like to have anything between you and the shells – even an umbrella!

Private Charles Duke, 4th Battalion, Australian Imperial Force

––––––––––

Anzac forces were expected to disembark in near darkness halfway along a stretch of coast named Brighton Beach, at a headland known as Hell Spit. Landing there, a mile north of Gaba Tebe, a well-defended headland, was entirely sensible and reduced the risk of heavy casualties from enfilade fire. The ground behind Brighton Beach was reasonably flat and there appeared to be few immediate obstacles. In the event, the troops did not land as planned, but a mile further north between Hell Spit and another headland, Ari Burnu. In between lay a curved beach, 1,000 yards in length, known to posterity as Anzac Cove. Behind this cove were cliffs and severely broken ground rising to a series of ridges, some climbable, some perilously steep. These ridges ran in different directions: anyone mounting a direct attack would undertake not one but a series of challenging climbs.

Making a landing at night against an enemy whose numbers were unknown and whose defensive positions were ill-defined was an immediate and obvious hazard. Once ashore, the men would advance inland over ridges, along gullies and up winding, narrow valleys. If that were not difficult enough, they would cross ground thick with thorny scrub, dense enough in places to made progress difficult without endless minor detours. Even where men persevered, vicious thorns clung to uniforms and webbing, making extraction difficult, time-consuming, and intensely aggravating. This vegetation hid perilous sudden drops; twisted knees or ankles were but the least of the possible injuries.

Morning of 25 April 1915: a naval party from HMS Agamemnon *carries 1st Lancashire Fusiliers, 29th Division, into shore.*

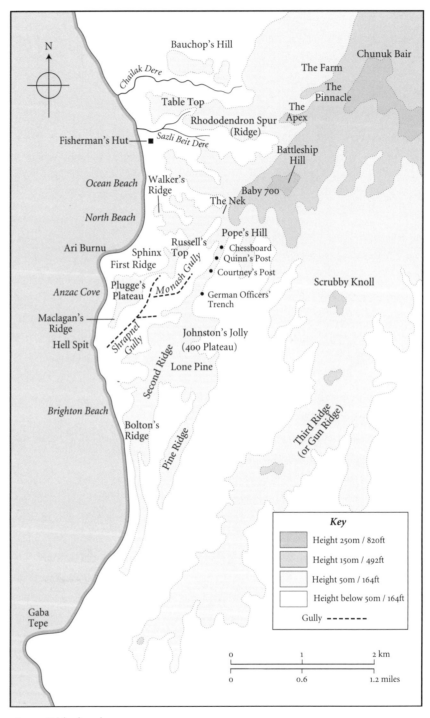

Anzac Bridgehead

Overambitious plans envisaged the Anzacs climbing the cliffs, then advancing over the high ground and on to the prominent position of Mal Tepe, cutting the Turkish supply line to Helles and severely hampering communications on the Peninsula. First ashore would be six companies of the 3rd Brigade, 1st Division, around 1,500 men in all. They would be tasked with advancing deep inland to take the heights overlooking the beach and protecting 2nd Brigade's disembarkation. 2nd Brigade would advance, securing more ground, while 1st Brigade made its way to shore. Only when everyone was ready would a general advance be made on Mal Tepe. Facing the Anzacs were a few hundred Turks spread out over several miles, The role of these men was not to prevent a landing but to contain the Anzac troops while reinforcements were brought up. Within a four-hour march of Anzac Cove there were a further four Ottoman regiments ready to move, comprising nearly 12,000 men in all. Yet the presumption made by the Allies remained steadfastly optimistic. The Turks would not stand and fight.

During the night of 24/25 April, the Anzac forces sailed towards the Peninsula. One of those attached to 2nd Brigade was civilian surgeon John Dancy of the Royal Army Medical Corps.

At about 1 a.m. we drifted slowly to a standstill. The moon was just short of full. Wind and water were dead calm. We rested motionless for a few minutes, and then, with a sudden silence more arresting than any noise, the engines ceased …

A sergeant checked in the personnel by name and rank, but passed the six of us over to the major, who asked us to show what papers we had. He perused these and then looked up and told us that we six – and he read out our names – were posted to be temporarily attached to the Australian Army Medical Corps. The major then read us out a concise briefing. 'You are detailed to land with the assault parties,' he said. 'Once on the beach-head you will join in maintaining whatever emergency dressing stations you may establish or find ready-made for you, until such time as a casualty clearing station with its fuller equipment can move up to displace you further forward. Until then, you don't go beyond the beach-head. The Australian battalions are taking along with them what few MOs they have, and they have at least plenty of stretcher-bearers …'

Captain John Dancy, Surgeon, Royal Army Medical Corps, Attd. 2nd Brigade AIF

Our kit was then double-checked and we were issued with sundry additions. I had already taken off my badges, and one of the orderlies had fixed the RAMC badges on to the wretchedly coarse texture of the 'issue' tunic, which incidentally had already chafed my neck until it fetched blood. Mother would no doubt have sewn some silk in it.

Lieutenant Edward King, 1st Battalion AIF

We dressed and put our equipment on in the dark. Looking out the port-hole one could see the grim dark shapes of destroyers. We were steadily approaching the shore at a distance of about five miles, the sea was like glass and a slight mist covered the waters and everything seemed so peaceful. There were several of us officers just having breakfast in the dining saloon, after having seen that the men were ready in every detail when suddenly we heard it, a dull faint echoing 'boom'. 'They're at it,' we cried and rushed up on deck where it was just glimmering light. [4.30 a.m.] On our right was the cruiser *Bacchante* and even as we were looking at her she suddenly disappeared in a sea of flame and smoke – she had started with six-inch guns and they were directed at the fort of Gaba Tepe, just discernable.

Sapper Geoffrey Robin, 1st Field Company, Australian Engineers

Soon the troops were fallen in and the rum ration issued. The night was warm and still, and very peaceful. Then down the rope ladders and into the boats brought alongside – no easy journey with rifle and full kit and box of gun cotton. As the boats filled they were taken in tow by the pinnaces and moved out clear of the ship and lay in parallel lines headed for the shore like runners on their mark waiting for the pistol.

It was now close to dawn and the moon had set. One could just make out the outline of the other boats on each side, and the old [HMS] *London*, looking like a haven of peace and security further away. Suddenly a square of light showed in the side of the ship as a port was opened and a quiet, drawling voice came across the water, 'Carry on.' The light disappeared, and the pinnaces leapt forward with their tows of boats.

There was a little talk in undertones, but most of us were busy with our thoughts. Most of us hoped we would get ashore before any trouble started. Loaded as we were, any man going overboard knew his number was up, but there was a quiet confidence in the support and assistance of the navy.

On land, from his position near Ari Burnu, Lieutenant Faik was looking through binoculars out to sea when he spotted a large number of ships. It was not clear whether they were stationary or moving, but he immediately reported what he could see to his company commander.

I went to a new observation point and kept watching. This time I saw them as a great mass which, I decided, seemed to be moving straight towards us. In the customary manner, I went to the phone to inform Divisional Headquarters. That was about 2.30 a.m. I got through to the second-in-command, Lieutenant Nuri Efendi, and told him of it. He replied, 'Hold the line. I will inform the Chief of Staff.' He came back a little later and said, 'How many of these ships are warships and how many transports?' I replied, 'It is impossible to distinguish them in the dark but the quantity of ships is very large.' With that the conversation closed. A little while later the moon sank below the horizon and the ships became invisible in the dark. The reserve platoon was alerted and ordered to stand by. I watched and waited.

Lieutenant Faik, 2nd Battalion, 27th Regiment, 9th Ottoman Division

Australians from 9th AIF in readiness: HMS Beagle *heads towards Anzac.*

Captain John
Dancy, Surgeon,
Royal Army
Medical Corps,
Attd. 2nd Brigade
AIF

About 3 a.m. a long space was cleared to reveal lines painted upon the decks so as to divide off a number of sections, each with its number boldly inscribed at all four corners. The troops fell in upon these sections in companies and a quick roll-call was taken. They then climbed over and down into the darkness of the boat below, followed by their officers and afterwards by any allocation of medical services. When our lot went over the side I noticed that we had drawn a full colonel as senior officer on the boat, and I wondered suspiciously whether this had any significance . . .

My first impression on reaching the boat was that it was full up already and they would have to leave me behind. Still, the Anzacs moved over, moved up and moved over again, until finally they stood locked together by their own equipment. By this I mean not only the pack and rifle, bayonet and bandolier, but also twin water bottles of 1½ pints each (one for the wounded), those two tubular linen bags round the waist with their load of iron rations filled with bully beef, biscuits, sugar and tea. So much so that the cluster of all these made it impossible quickly to get at the real needs of the occasion, which everyone knew to be the fags and the matches; and buried for all time was the talisman that so many soldiers carry, that photograph, that lock of hair or last letter, destined only to be revealed in case of capture or unwittingly in death.

Once filled, the boat pushed off to the limit of her moorings, and we were left to wait in the darkness for the unknown. There were seats for the few; the rest were left to stand. Sleep was long overdue for most of us, though few were able to accept it easily. However, as if by common consent, voices died down to a whisper; standing men began to sag at the knees and settle to the bottom of the boat. The first to go down were able to stretch to some purpose, but the last few could only sit or kneel among the network of limbs. I found a somewhat uneasy attitude in which I was able to lose myself in snatches despite an Australian who was overlapping me. He told me he came from Melbourne and was 'just a cockie' (farmer). We took it in turns to lie still while the other dozed, but presently we both dozed off together and I was awakened by a knee driven hard into the pit of my stomach.

'Sorry, Sport, waking you up like that!'

I made it to be about 4.15 a.m. when three picket boats chugged into position and took the fifteen boats in tow. The first movement brought most of the men to their feet again.

To begin with, our five boats dragged together as one clump, but as we gathered way they fanned out, and we took up our position as the most northerly tow of the three with our boat at the top end. The temptation to call across from boat to boat was at first agonising, but we soon separated.

The shore is now about two miles away. The moon has set, and it's one of the darkest nights that I can ever remember. The ships have all left us to take up their stations, and we are alone: twelve picket boats with their tows, steaming east in line abreast. We're the spearhead of the invasion. May God be with us.

I'm finding this last run a bit exacting. It is not easy to keep station in the pitch dark or to prevent tell-tale sparks from coming out of the funnels.

Midshipman Eric Bush, Royal Navy, HMS *Bacchante*

Australians from an early wave, preparing to row ashore in cutters.

The line concertinas sometimes and then opens out again. Worsely and Bice are keeping a good lookout for'ard. It has gone 4 a.m. and the sky ahead seems to be getting a little lighter and the stars less distinct. Yes, there is no doubt about it, dawn is breaking. In a moment or two, Worsley comes aft to say that he thinks he can see land ahead. I go for'ard with him. Yes, there's land there all right.

My heart beats faster. I look starboard and then to port. We seem to be pretty well in station. Bow waves all along the line are bright with phosphorescence. I hope this won't give us away. I look aft. One tow seems all right, too. The men have already tossed their oars without waiting to be told. It's 4.20 now. Soon it will be all over.

Inky darkness masked the presence of the tows of 3rd Brigade as they approached the Peninsula. Each tow was supposed to be 150 yards from the next but in the gloom they drifted towards one another, contracting the beachfront over which they would land. The inexperienced officers on board each boat tried to ascertain where they were meant to land, and when the outline heights of Gabe Tepe were seen in the first glimmers of dawn, one officer, concerned he would land too close to the promontory, turned in two manoeuvres a full 40 degrees to the north. As the distance between this boat and its neighbour narrowed, so this too conformed to the change of direction, followed by almost every other boat.

Sapper Geoffrey Robin, 1st Field Company, Australian Engineers

All was quiet, and presently the shoreline appeared dimly in the half-light, and the faint line of the high ground at the back, with still no sign or sound of the enemy, until a voice from one of the leading boats shouted, 'Tell the colonel the –– fool's landed us a mile too far north!' That sounded a bit unpleasant, and on the instant came a rifle shot and the thought 'That's fired at us!' Then came a regular crackle of fire and the nasty tat-tat-tat of a machine gun which providentially ceased after firing a dozen rounds, apparently jammed.

Lieutenant Faik, 2nd Battalion, 27th Regiment, 9th Ottoman Division

In a little while, the sound of gunfire broke out. I saw a machine gun firing from a small boat in front of Ari Burnu. Some of the shots were passing over us. I immediately ordered the platoon to occupy the trenches on the high ridge which dominated Ari Burnu and sent only two sections under Sergeant Ahmed to the trenches on the central ridge overlooking the beach. At the same time, I wrote a report to the Battalion Commander stating that the enemy was about to begin landing and I was going to a position on the far side with a reserve platoon.

The next few minutes seem to drag. Then Worsley indicates that he can touch bottom with his boat-hook. We stop engines. Our heavily laden boats carry their way better than we do and forge ahead. Our launch, the heaviest of them all, comes right up alongside for a moment. One of the soldiers holds out a watch for me to send home to his mother, but it is too late to help him. Our engines are going astern, and we are out of reach.

Oars, muffled to prevent any noise, are being lowered carefully, without making a splash. The men are startling to row. Some of the soldiers are helping with the oars, others are adjusting their equipment, tightening their chin-stays, slinging their rifles. I take all this in at a glance, but what stirs my imagination is the look on the men's faces.

Midshipman Eric Bush, Royal Navy, HMS Bacchante

Behind the 3rd Brigade, the 2nd was still some way out at sea just as the first gunfire was heard.

We continued in this way over smooth water till dawn broke and the earliest light began to reveal a dim silhouette of land ahead. As we drew nearer, we heard the subdued crackle of rifle fire and the distant hum of machine guns. Smoke was slowly rising and we caught an occasional pinpoint of flashing light. Nearer again, and deeper throated notes began to echo towards us over the water coming from the howitzers of Gaba Tepe and field guns lurking in the olive groves.

'Sounds like Maclagan's boys are there already' [meaning 3rd Brigade]. We pressed on towards the shore, and behind us passed the *Queen Elizabeth* coasting in silence …

As the shore drew nearer, so we seemed to be quickening our pace. The rattle of fire grew more continuous; heavier explosions drowned one

Captain John Dancy, Surgeon, Royal Army Medical Corps, Attd. 2nd Brigade AIF

Overleaf: Covering fire of the Royal Navy supports the Anzac landing.

another, the smoke and the acrid fumes of cordite began to reach us, and the water was popping under a hailstorm of shrapnel.

I did not require to 'lie low'. Several good men were lying low already and I was needed to stoop and do what I could for them where they lay.

Colonel Ewan Sinclair-Maclagan, CO, 3rd Brigade, was landing with his 'boys'. The Turks had not spotted the approach of the tows until they pulled on to the beach. Then in the half-light, they began to make out the shapes of boats and men jumping ashore and they opened fire. It was not coordinated, and, from surviving images taken of the landings, not initially effective. The Turkish infantry were hampered by the narrowness of the beach and the protective height of the cliff. In a photograph taken that morning in almost full light, the body of one man can be seen on the beach and even he may not have been in the first rush ashore. Nevertheless, the Australians were under fire and they climbed the cliffs just as fast as they could, the fire increasing as they did so.

Private Albert Perry, 10th Battalion, 3rd Brigade AIF

Crack-crack! Ping-ping! Zip-zip! Trenches full of rifles upon the shore and surrounding hills open on us, and machine guns, hidden in gullies or redoubts, increase the murderous hail. Oars are splintered, boats are perforated. A sharp moan, a low gurgling cry, tells of a comrade hit. Boats ground in four or five feet of water owing to the human weight contained in them. We scramble out, struggle to the shore, and rushing across the beach, take cover under a low sandbank.

'Here, take off my pack, and I'll take off yours.' We help one another to lift the heavy, water-soaked packs off. 'Hurry up, there,' says our sergeant. 'Fix bayonets.' Click! And the bayonets are fixed. 'Forward!' And away we scramble up the hills in our front. Up, up we go, stumbling in holes and ruts. With a ringing cheer we charge up by roots and branches of trees; at times digging our bayonets into the ground, and pushing ourselves up to a foothold, until, topping the hill, we found the enemy had made themselves very scarce.

Corporal George Mitchell, 10th Battalion, 3rd Brigade AIF

A torrent of voices. A torrent of men that rises and rushes forward, and upward. I pick the line where the hill towers highest above … The slope is terrific. Bushes break in my hand as I haul myself upward. It is half-light. It is full light. A clay abutment stands on my left. A clay wall stands before me. I think I can climb it. My equipment is tugged, a bullet through it. The whine of a bullet fans my forehead. I am being fired on by someone hidden in the cliff a hundred feet to my left. I must keep going, though the slope becomes steeper. Bullets strike about me with sounds as of pick-blows. I lie down in a little gutter, sand-bedded. A bullet strikes against my cheek, showering me with a stinging spray.

He can see me. It is only his excitement and unsteadiness that has saved me thus far. Now he will dwell on his aim and make sure and I will be dead before I have a chance to fire a shot. Anything but that! I leap up and run downhill, steadying myself by the bushes. There to the right the shore ridge is lower. Up and on, I must rejoin my section …

What had caused them to fly from a position from which they should have driven us back into the sea every time? A few scattered Turks showing in the distance we instantly fired on. Some fell to rise no more; others fell wounded and, crawling into the low bushes, sniped our lads as they went past. There were snipers in plenty, cunningly hidden in the hearts of low green shrubs. They accounted for a lot of our boys in the first few days, but gradually were rooted out. Over the hill we dashed, and down into what is now called 'Shrapnel Gully', and up the other hillside, until, on reaching the top, we found that some of the lads of the 3rd Brigade had commenced

Private Albert Perry, 10th Battalion, 3rd Brigade AIF

Australians from the 2nd Brigade landing at Anzac.

to dig in. We skirted round to the plateau at the head of the gully, and took up our line of defence.

As soon as it was light enough to see, the guns of Gaba Tepe, on our right, and two batteries away on our left opened up a murderous hail of shrapnel on our landing parties.

The second wave of tows arrived perhaps ten minutes after the first and came under much heavier attack, with men being hit before they left the boats.

Lieutenant Faik, 2th Battalion, 27th Regiment, 9th Ottoman Division

We arrived at Yuksek Sirt [Russell's Top] and occupied the trenches opposite the northern beach of Ari Burnu. I ordered firing to be opened from 1,300 metres. The 2nd Platoon in the Haintepe [Plugge's Plateau] trenches a little way in front of us had been drawn into the fighting from the start. Torpedo boats towed the enemy craft and as they approached the shore they slipped the tow rope and quickly abandoned the craft. The torpedo boats then withdrew, firing continuously. The craft at which we were firing remained far from the shore because the coastal waters were shallow. Some of the enemy troops were hit and stayed in the craft. Those who were not hit jumped into the sea and only five or ten men escaped by getting into our 'dead' area.

Captain John Dancy, Surgeon, Royal Army Medical Corps, Attd. 2nd Brigade

The tow was cast off and the boatmen urged us forward in a frenzy of last-moment sculling. One or two men stood fixing their bayonets, but most just stood measuring the distance to the beach. One man jumped too soon, and did not reappear again. After a minute another one followed and was seen to be standing up to his armpits on firm bottom. Then the rest jumped, one after the other, and struggled forward through the shallows. Several fell as they ran; and on the beach I saw even more men lying untidily, some quite still and others making an occasional movement.

I turned to cast my eye round the boat. The boatmen had ceased rowing when the exodus began, because they could no longer ply their oars among the men in the water. Boulton was not there: I had not seen how he went. The colonel had gone, too, so who was now in charge of the boat? There was one boatman left standing, and an Australian with a damaged leg who was insisting on rising and going ashore with the boys. He was deathly pale and bleeding.

'If you were a dinkum Ozzy,' he said angrily, 'you'd carry me in.'

There was a second boatman, but he was hanging over the side, trapping his oar under his own dead weight …

Then I jumped over into two feet of water and waded heavily ashore. The lapping edge was already pink and frothy with fallen men. Almost at once the boat beached behind me: I could as easily have waited for it. Through moving my cramped legs I seemed suddenly to recapture my fuller faculties. Shrapnel was flying in all directions save mine. It was a blind gamble with it; because in the dense smoke and dust up-beach, few men could easily sight a chosen target. I now began to run to the cliff-side for cover, almost tripping over a man who was sitting in the sand and trying to stop the bleeding in his leg. I seized him by both shoulders of his tunic and dragged him backwards to my left, where I sensed a space under the overhanging face of the cliff. On the way we had to avoid others; among them I spotted my companion of the boat, and stooped over him.

'That you, Sport?' 'I feel real crook,' he said hoarsely. 'Been watching you from here. Reckoned you were taking a return ticket on the boat.'

We completed the journey, and I roughly fixed the leg. Then I went back to my bedfellow. But this time he did not answer.

There were three orderlies under the cliff with me, and it was a happy choice of site. In retrospect it seems quite clear that, as end boat, we had stood furthest to the north. And, since our only instruction was to follow any landing that had taken place already, we also had found our way into Anzac Cove.

Moreover we were at the Cove in one of its more favourable moments, when the first wave of the Anzac troops had, if only temporarily, blazed their way to the inland heights, from which we could hear the bulk of the rifle fire still continuing.

Corporal George Mitchell was blazing a trail above the cliffs at Anzac Cove, fighting his way inland while, simultaneously, trying to keep some semblance of order amongst the men in his section.

Two Hours After Landing

Corporal George
Mitchell, 10th
Battalion, 3rd
Brigade AIF

*Above: Two hours
after landing: further
waves of the
Australian Division
come ashore.*

Trailing blood drips from a smashed hand: a man of my own company is coming towards me. 'A Turk stepped out of the bush in front of me,' he laughed. 'We fired together. His bullet smashed my rifle and hand. Mine got him.'

I find two men pressed against a bank, bullets striking about them. 'What are you doing?' I ask airily.

'Taking cover,' they reply.

'Your cover is no good,' I answer. 'The bank is the wrong way round. Come on.'

Upward and onward again. Bodies of friend and foe lying about. I find my platoon standing and sitting in little groups. They are laughing, high on exultation. 'Next stop Constantinople,' they greet me cheerfully. I assemble my platoon. In spite of the success of our first hammer blow in the dark, there seems a sinister air over the scrubby valley beyond. The little red instruction book tells of counter-attacks.

'Dig in. He will come back at us soon.' I don't think he will, but that is the right thing for a young and earnest NCO to say. Big McConnachy seats himself restfully. 'Be hanged to your digging in. I'm going to have a cig first.' The hard-baked gravel flies under the strokes of our entrenching tools. Not a bullet disturbs our labour. This is the perfect hour.

It passes. A spray of bullets whistle and ricochet around us. Laughing, each man flattens into his cover. 'We want a better field of fire,' calls our officer. 'Prepare to move forward.' Reluctantly I get ready. Bullets are now coming over in a sustained stream. 'Advance!' Up high and naked to the squall we run. Pounding on iron-shod boots. Sprays of gravel that rise and sting. A man who shouts and folds up in mid-stride crashes and rolls. Another, still another.

'Down!' Bare, naked hillside. 'Enemy in scrub on hillside left front. Rapid fire.'

All about us is the swift thudding of our weapons. The familiar reek of cordite swirls about us. Heavier and heavier beats the fire upon us. A smack on my left. Crowther gleefully shows me his cap – a black-edged hole through the brim. 'Not born to be shot.'

Up and down the line comes the smacking of bullets striking flesh, shouts of stricken men. Strings of machine-gun bullets sweep round and over us. The man besides me dies horribly. I try to press into the very soil.

We came under fire from the enemy who were climbing up to the ridge where we were from a slope 100 metres to our left. We began to engage them on this side. In this fighting Sergeant Suleyman was wounded. Some of the private soldiers were also hit. I too received a severe wound in the groin and was reduced to a state where I could no longer command the platoon.

Lieutenant Faik, 2nd Battalion, 27th Regiment, 9th Ottoman Division

The number of wounded making their way down to the beach was growing rapidly. Under Anzac Cove's cliffs, Captain Dancy began to treat them while making sure that as many as possible were out of immediate harm's way from bursting shrapnel.

There was a choice of three good sites at the base of the cliff, all of which should be immune from rifle bullets, and at least one safe from shrapnel. It was a sort of void, or dead space. So we concentrated on filling this one first. There were two stretchers only, but we soon abandoned them. The wounded

Captain John Dancy, Surgeon, Royal Army Medical Corps, Attd. 2nd Brigade AIF

were sunk too deeply in the thick prickly scrub, or lost in crevices in the ground out of which they could only be manhandled and then carried to cover. Some of them were impaled upon this double-gauge barbed wire that no 'issue' cutters could hope to sever.

I enquired whether Boulton had been seen anywhere. Apparently he had disobeyed orders and started off up the heights with the rest of the boys.

By now it was about 6.30 a.m. We had achieved a great deal in the time and I had no dressings left. The wounded were piled up in our safest alcove virtually on top of one another, many of them groaning despite their incredible toughness, and I had used all my morphine. So now I looked round for our boat, only to find that it had floated away from the water's edge, boatman, wounded and all.

However there were other boats that had just emptied, and the comparative lull in the firing seemed to be holding out. So we got our wounded down to the first boat to hand, carrying most of them for the sake of quickness with what is known as a 'hand-seat', and dumping them with what I fear must have been rough ceremony. We then went back for two cases of fractured femur and brought them on the two stretchers. Fortunately my orderly was a most powerful chap.

News of the landing had reached the Turkish reserves, but as reports came in, it was not always clear which required the most urgent response.

Captain Zeki Bey, 1st Battalion, 57th Regiment, 19th Ottoman Division

My battalion was on parade when the news of the landing came to us. It chanced that there had been ordered for that morning an exercise over the ground, especially towards Koja Chemen Tepe [Hill 971]. The commander of our division had received about dawn a report that a landing had occurred at Ari Burnu. The Turkish staff and commanders concerned did not expect a landing at Ari Burnu because it was too precipitous. The message then asked the commander of the 19th Division to send one battalion from Boghali against Ari Burnu. The regiment was assembled when the order came. Mustafa Kemal came himself, and ordered the regiment and a battery of artillery – mountain guns – to intercept the 'English' who had landed. He reasoned, 'If this force has gone in the

Opposite: Early casualties: the wounded make their way back to the beach.

direction of Koja Chemen Tepe, the landing is not a mere demonstration – it is the real thing, the landing of a main force.' For that reason he took, not one battalion, as the commander of the 9th Division had asked, but the whole regiment. They went at once straight across country towards the south of Koja Chemen Tepe towards Chunuk Bair – Kemel himself leading.

Finally, the third wave of troops began to arrive: the Australian and New Zealand Division. By this time the men in the open boats were being subjected to heavy rifle and shrapnel fire.

Lieutenant Edward King, 1st Battalion AIF

Turkish reserves awaiting the order to move.

We did not waste time on the beach but went straight for them … We threw off our packs and swarmed to the crest where we were met with a deadly machine-gun fire; men were falling in all directions, but the advance was not stopped. Down the other side of the ridge into the valley where the fighting was short and sharp and then up the second ridge about twice

as high as the first. When I got on that ridge of death with reinforcements I was almost paralysed with the terrible sights I saw. Billy was dead. Steen was dead. Dead men lying in grotesque attitudes … Three devils were raving mad – badly wounded – singing songs and cursing the Turks.

In the valley our company had been split up, the major and several of the company were cut off from us. He and his party went to one part of the fighting line while the captain and the remainder of us drifted to another part of the line. I never saw him again.

Despite his good work, Captain John Dancy's surgical skills were of considerably more use on board ship than on the beach, where he merely patched up those who had filtered back to the shoreline. When an opportunity arose to go out to the *Queen Elizabeth*, he took it.

On board they had some 200 wounded and it was everybody's job to press forward with urgent surgery, even of the most major kind. So I fell into the swing with all the others, and was directed with my most urgent casualties to a large deck cabin. There I found the surgeon to be a middle-aged New Zealander named Halliday, who told me at once that he had spent the last twenty years as a hospital anaesthetist and was completely lost with a scalpel. Even as I arrived he was rummaging about inside an abdomen for a large piece of shrapnel, which, to his evident amazement, he suddenly found in his hand. Meanwhile the anaesthetic was being administered by a nervous orderly who had plainly been warned to go easy with the ship's supply of chloroform and ether. I washed up quickly and rushed to the rescue by putting in a row of stitches in double-quick time while the victim came round sufficiently to take an almost intelligent interest in the proceedings …

Captain John Dancy, Surgeon, Royal Army Medical Corps, Attd. 2nd Brigade AIF

The fighting was confused as the Anzacs clambered their way to the top of First Ridge, including Plugge's Plateau, Russell's Top and Walker's Ridge. Most Turks sensibly fell back, outnumbered. There was little point in going toe-to-toe with the invaders; it was much better to use the tortuous natural terrain to the Turks' advantage and snipe at an enemy who had no knowledge of the landscape. The Australians had to climb, then slide or slip down on their backsides into gullies and valleys before climbing again, hauling themselves up with heavy, often sodden equipment, carrying boxes of ammunition or tripods for the machine guns. As the men pushed forward they became strung out and disorientated, necessitating halts so that they could be reorganised. All this took time. Given the firm objectives of 3rd Brigade, it was imperative to take and hold as much of the enemy's high ground as possible, but this was much easier said than done, and the understandable hesitancy on the part of the CO, Colonel Sinclair-Maclagan, meant that progress slowed. Turkish resistance, initially light, stiffened as the morning wore on and reinforcements were brought up to protect Third Ridge. Those Australians who reached this far were too few to hold their position and they were pulled back to Second Ridge by Sinclair-Maclagan, worried that his brigade would become overextended. The Australians never reached the Third Ridge again.

Lieutenant Colonel Mehmet Sefik, Headquarters, 27th Regiment, 9th Ottoman Division

We guessed that the enemy was advancing slowly and cautiously in order to capture the ridge where we were, which dominated all sides – namely Chunuk Bair to Gaba Tepe. We set about our task of throwing the enemy back and we felt a moral force in ourselves for performing this task. All the signs indicated that opposing our 2,000 armed men was a force of at least four or five times that size – or even bigger. We had to prevent the enemy from reaching and occupying the dominating line of Chunuk Bair–Gaba Tepe and had to gain time until the 19th Division arrived.

From the ships, many more men watched myriad gun flashes on land and were exhilarated by what they saw.

Sapper Thomas Farrer, 1st Company New Zealand Engineers

We all crowded into the bows and tried to make out what was going on. Close to Gaba Tepe a cruiser was bombarding what seemed to be a fort inland. A captive balloon which looked like a giant yellow sausage was directing the fire of the naval guns. Through a pair of glasses I could see that the beach of what was afterwards called 'Anzac Cove' was crowded with men. Further to the left, among the sandy bluffs, there seemed to be a zigzag road up the hill and some men were cutting a road up the side of the cliff. We were all getting very excited; our water bottles were filled with tea and we fell in on deck in full marching order. My equipment weighed 45lbs with fifty rounds. We took no blankets but had our waterproof sheets.

If the infantry were going to get some support, it was imperative that light artillery, and the horses that pulled the guns, were landed. Other animals were needed, too, to carry forward ammunition, so donkeys were taken ashore. Midshipman Charles Churchill was given the unenviable task.

The last trip I had involved the taking of donkeys. The launch was a big boat and would hold over a hundred men and I was ordered to take four pack donkeys. The gunwhale must have been at least three foot six above the bottom boards and so I said to the reserve lieutenant who had ordered us to do this, 'How am I going to land them? There are no piers or decks or hoisting gear ashore.' His reply was, 'You do as you are told, little fool, and don't ask stupid questions' – from which I deduced that he had not any helpful suggestions in his mind. So I said, 'I can't do it with six sailors, I must have more men.' 'Well, here are six soldiers for you and stop your damned arguing.' The donkeys were hoisted into the boat on slings and off we went shorewards. On the way I instructed the sailors and soldiers. 'When the boat grounds, one on each leg, one on each ear, one on each tail and one each side with hands clasped under the belly. When I say 'Heave' you all heave and over the side goes the donkey. If any of you fails to pull his weight you will all get kicked.' One sailor said, 'Supposing they don't swim towards the shore, sir?' To which I replied, 'Even donkeys aren't as bloody stupid as that.' And the operation worked.

Midshipman Charles Churchill, Royal Navy

Sapper Farrer and the men of the 1st Company New Zealand Engineers were warned that they would land at 4 p.m. Just as the troops had been before them, the engineers were towed towards the beach and then ordered to row.

Sapper Thomas
Farrer, 1st
Company, New
Zealand Engineers

Taylor was sitting on my seat facing the bows ahead staring vacantly up at the cliffs. The end of my oar caught against him but he took no notice. Fox and Goodman had the oar in front of me and Woodhall was rowing no. 7. We tried to keep together but it was not a great success [and we] managed to run our boat against the stern of a boat full of wounded. Then we started to get ashore. Abbey got excited and shouted to us to go quicker. So, like a fool, I made a dash for it. Stepping on to the boat with the wounded in it, I jumped, but instead of landing in shallow water I caught my foot in a rollock and fell face downwards into deeper water. Luckily I was out before water got into my rations. My tunic and cardigan were wet, but my shirt was dry enough …

We climbed up the hill and sat down just below the crest of the ridge, to the right of a bit of Turkish trench. There we fixed bayonets, put some ammunition in our pockets and took off our wet equipment. There was an Australian 18-pounder just over the other side of the hill which was making a terrific noise. We all had picks and shovels and with these and our rifles we were marched over the ridge. There we were set to work to dig a fire trench. A line was worked out with picks and then we set to work with a will. The ground was hard and stony, very different to the sands of Egypt, and my hands were soft. We were right in front and a bit to the left of the Australian gun. It was firing every few minutes. I was beginning to feel a bit jumpy and every time the gun went off I thought it was a Turkish shell bursting. We had not been at work long before shrapnel began to come over from the north. Some fell in the bushes close to the trench and Friedlander was hit in the neck. He thought someone had thrown a stone at him.

Up on Second Ridge, Lieutenant Kings' men were under severe pressure. He was gratified to watch as an Indian Mountain Battery come into action, hurling shells at the Turks. But then his captain was hit and King, the last officer in the company, was ordered to take the reminder of the men, around fifty with several NCOs, 'half-right' in order to stop a flank attack. He was, he estimated, about a mile inland and here 'with a fair field of fire' he halted and entrenched as the sun began to set.

We had lost an enormous number of men during the day and we were very fatigued, but we expected no rest that Sunday night. The Turks tried all they knew to toss us back into the sea, but our men's blood was properly up, with the result that the Turkish dead lay heaped up in front of our trench in the morning. The Turks made one fatal mistake that night. Just as they prepared to charge they began to make a frightful noise and to shout out 'Allah-Allah', and so giving their position away, an advantage that we were not slow to make use of.

Lieutenant Edward King, 1st Battalion AIF

The wounded suffered terrible privations. Many could not be retrieved and others lay for hours waiting for water and basic medical help. After delivering the first wave of Australian troops into shore, fifteen-year-old Midshipman Eric Bush was heading back out to the destroyers to pick up more men. In his launch were wounded from the beaches.

Second ridge: Australians establishing a rough trench line. Unknown to them, these lines would remain static for the remainder of the campaign.

Unfortunately there is nothing we can do to help them. One Australian is wounded in the wrist and is clutching his arm in a desperate endeavour to check the flow of blood. Another sits in the bottom of the boat with a

Midshipman Eric Bush, Royal Navy, HMS Bacchante

bullet sticking out of his cheek. More wounded are there, but I can't see them properly.

As we round the stern of the nearest destroyer, I notice that they are having casualties too. Some wounded are being carried along the upper deck by sailors to a place of safety. As we turn to recover our other two boats, I see fresh troops clambering down into our launch. There is no time to take out the wounded, so they, poor chaps, have to make another trip inshore, in fact several more before anyone can attend to them …

Able Seaman Hodgson has been hit and is lying in the stern sheets where he fell. I leave Petty Officer Main's side for a moment, and with Able Seaman Neish drag him on to one of the seats in the after cabin. He can't speak and looks in a bad way. We have his jumper off him and his singlet too. Ah, there is the wound – a tiny red mark just under his right shoulder blade shows where the bullet went in. We make him as comfortable as we can, and leave him.

Unloading from the destroyers is finished, and we are now on our way to the transports for more troops, stores and ammunition. They are anchored rather far out. It is not their fault. A heavy Turkish gun has made them keep their distance. A Turkish battleship, too, has been potting at them from across the Straits, but *Triumph*, with one of the balloons to help her, has driven her off.

We managed to persuade one of the transports to take poor Hodgson's body. He is dead.

Those fortunate to be taken off the Peninsula crowded on to the decks of ships to be tended by medical orderlies and doctors who were worked to exhaustion. On board ship, Captain Dancy treated one wounded man after another with hardly time to think, making an instant diagnosis as to whether treatment was even worthwhile. As he worked, another case arrived, seemingly beyond help. Dancy recognised the man.

Captain John Dancy, Surgeon, Royal Army Medical Corps, Attd. 2nd Brigade AIF

I had seen him first on the beach at Anzac, and had left him for dead. The poor chap had a wound of entry over the heart, and a corresponding wound of exit at the back of his chest. Not unnaturally, he was collapsed to the

point of being pulseless. I had taken a quick glance at his mortal-looking wounds and passed on to someone else, pausing only to indicate him to a courageous chaplain who had appeared from nowhere and was flitting from body to body with very little semblance of hurry.

Men wounded from the landings lie on the deck of HMTS Franconia *awaiting medical attention.*

Many men succumbed to wounds long before they received effective treatment. However, occasionally apparent miracles did occur.

This same man appeared before me on the hospital ship several days later. By then, what he had to show was a painful track abscess at least one foot in length, and visibly only skin-deep. In fact the explanation had become obvious: his rifle bullet had ricocheted off his fifth rib over his heart, and, continued merely by the elasticity of his skin, had described a half-circle round his chest wall, finally breaking through the skin at the back to

Captain John Dancy, Surgeon, Royal Army Medical Corps, Attd. 2nd Brigade

continue in its original direction. Naturally, this was a one in a million chance, but by no means beyond the vagaries of a rifle bullet.

The Aussie recognised me at once, and indeed held out his hand and seemed delighted to renew our acquaintance. For my own part, I must confess, I felt a trifle abashed.

'You didn't reckon I needed an operation, did you, Doc?' he said. 'And you were bloody right. When you turned me over to that old Bible-basher, he cottoned on to that pretty much straight away. And he was bloody right, too …'

Many of the wounded came from Second Ridge. The fighting there was vicious and closely fought, with Turkish reinforcements sent in to halt the Australian and New Zealand troops' push onto Chunuk Bair. Turkish artillery was becoming effective and individual Turkish soldiers picked off Anzacs who appeared above the skyline, targeting men holding rank. But the Turkish troops were also suffering, and but for the swift, decisive actions of commanding officers, such as Lieutenant Colonel Mustafa Kemal, the Anzacs might have made greater progress. This officer was to become the living symbol of Turkish resistance, and through his courage and ingenuity he was largely responsible for frustrating Anzac progress onto the heights of Chunuk Bair. It was during the fighting that he comprehended the seriousness of the Turkish situation. Halting and turning back men who were running away, he issued the order for which he gained immortality in Turkey: 'I don't order you to attack – I order you to die.' Kemal committed his reserves to the fray, the Turkish troops attacking down the ridge towards the Anzac troops, who had not anticipated such an assault.

Lieutenant Colonel Mustafa Kemal, Headquarters, 19th Ottoman Division

A line of skirmishers of the enemy approached Battleship Hill and was advancing completely unopposed. Now just consider the situation. I had left my troops, so as to give the men ten minutes' rest. It meant that the enemy was nearer to me than my troops were, and if the enemy came to where I was, then my troops would find themselves in a very difficult position. Then, I still do not know what it was, whether a logical appreciation or an instinctive action, I do not know, I said to the men running away,

'You cannot run away from the enemy!' 'We have no ammunition!' 'If you haven't got any ammunition you have your bayonets!' I said. And, shouting to them, I made them fix their bayonets and lie down on the ground. When they fixed their bayonets and lay down on the ground the enemy also lay down. The moment of time that we gained was this one …

Turkish field artillery battery: shrapnel fire often proved lethal to those not properly entrenched.

To my mind there was a more important factor than this tactical situation – that was everybody hurled himself on the enemy to kill or die. This was no ordinary attack. Everybody was eager to succeed or go forward with the determination to die.

The ferocity of the Turkish counter-attack forced the Australians to retire. Corporal Herbert Hitch heard the order to fall back, retreating 350 yards and stopping to fire as he went.

Corporal Herbert
Hitch, 11th
Battalion, 3rd
Brigade AIF

The order was passed along, 'Re-form left, Turks advancing on the left!' They were a fine-looking body of men. They weren't running but were walking very quickly. As they came under our fire they ran back and I had two shots at a running man and missed him each time – I thought my rifle must have had the barrel bent. Then suddenly down from the sky as if by magic came the shells – their artillery observer had put them on to us. Providentially they were bursting late and the shrapnel was shredding the scrub behind us.

Hitch did not so much fall back now, as tumble.

Corporal Herbert
Hitch, 11th
Battalion, 3rd
Brigade AIF

I burst through the scrub and found myself on the edge of a steep ravine. I broke through so suddenly I had to grasp a sapling to save going over. There seemed no way of getting out from there. I thought, 'I'm going to get across here somehow!' and I threw my rifle down into this ravine and jumped. I sailed through the air about 25 feet and landed on a slope of 1 in 1. As I jackknifed I felt as though I had landed on a couple of bayonets. I pitched over, head first, and seemed to be heading for a precipice, but I was lucky enough to grab a root with my left hand and swing round and down feet first. I went over two or three vertical falls of about 8 to 10 feet and landed like a sack of spuds each time until finally I reached the breakaway with a drop of about 30 feet and I managed to stop there with about 6 feet to the next drop. As I stopped, the earth I had dislodged came tumbling after me.

The Turks regained the initiative and the Anzacs were pushed back to within 2,000 yards of the beaches. In places, the Turks came within an ace of retaking ground that, if held, would have dominated Anzac positions so as to make their entire bridgehead untenable.

All elements of command and control appeared to be failing even as more men landed. Reinforcements were simply ordered to push up the valley between Plugge's Plateau and Second Ridge without any clear idea of what they were doing, being sent wherever the loudest plea for troops was made. As dusk fell, credible rumours circulated that re-embarkation was likely.

The Turks are counter-attacking with the greatest vigour. The scale of the attack and the noise of the firing worries us a lot. Our anxiety increases when we are told to collect as many boats as we can and bring them inshore ready for an evacuation. Instinctively, we know that if such a drastic step becomes necessary, only a few will get away.

Midshipman Eric Bush, Royal Navy, HMS *Bacchante*

Lieutenant General Birdwood was shocked at reports from his senior officers that there was demoralisation among the troops, and that Turkish shellfire was taking a heavy toll which, if repeated the following day, might lead to disaster. Birdwood believed that the men should remain and fight, but he wrote to Hamilton suggesting that, if evacuation were deemed necessary, it should be undertaken immediately. The weather had begun to turn, and leaving under such circumstances, with Turkish forces bearing down on the beaches, would have proved much harder than remaining where they were. Hamilton agreed with Birdwood. The Anzacs had discovered that the Turks were tough opponents and would not cut and run. The Turks in turn discovered that they had worthy opponents who would not be pushed back into the sea. After just one day's fighting, the ingredients of a stalemate were in place, and all Allied ideas of reaching Mal Tepe were dispelled. Sporadic, localised fighting resumed next day.

We looked a dirty and terrifying lot. Some of the men had been hit and their blood was on their faces and tunics mixed with sweat and dirt, but we had no time to think of appearances. We had to fight, attack, repel and counter-attack through what seemed an eternity, yells and groans and curses mingling with the crack of rifles and revolvers, and men stabbing and clubbing each other for all they were worth. Might was right in that 'do' and we hacked our way through them and back again, no time to see to the wounded. It was kill or be killed and we killed.

Lieutenant Edward King, 1st Battalion AIF

For three or four days what anxieties we endured God alone knows! ... Above Ari Burnu there is a fairly high hill called Koja Chemen Dagh [Hill 971] that completely overlooks the Straits. The enemy's intention was to seize this hill but [a] force held in this neighbourhood arrived in time to

Lieutenant Colonel Fahrettin Altay, Chief of Staff, 3rd Ottoman Army

occupy the hill before the enemy, and to force the latter into a steep, very rough and rather narrow ravine between the hill and the sea. Although three attacks were made to throw the enemy into the sea, they were foiled by naval and machine-gun fire and by the ruggedness of the land and the enemy's defences. We suffered great losses, but those of the enemy were even greater, and he had not achieved his purpose. That he has a few troops on land is of no importance. He can land troops wherever he likes, but his main purpose is to seize the Straits and for that great self-sacrifice is required. Of this, however, there is no sign … These fellows will eventually have to embark their troops at Ari Burnu and remove them one of these nights. They cannot advance one step further but it will be a bit harder to chase them from Seddul Bahr.

While the Allied landings at W and V Beaches would be the main event at Helles, Hamilton was keen to launch diversionary attacks north and east of the Peninsula. By landing to the west of Krithia, at Y Beach, Hamilton hoped his forces would join up with those landing at X Beach to threaten Turkish communications while protecting the left flank of the landings at W Beach. Had Y Beach been defended, the British troops would never have left their landing boats, as sheer cliffs, the best part of 200 feet high, faced the men, with just two narrow tracks leading to the top. As it was, the area was undefended, the landing unopposed.

After the earlier landing at Kum Kale, Sergeant William Meatyard had spent six weeks in hospital undergoing a minor operation on his foot before being pronounced fit and returned to his unit on the *Braemar Castle*. He was the first among the wounded to be returned and he was besieged with questions about mutual comrades. 'How's Nobby getting on? Did Hooky lose his leg? We heard you'd lost your big toe.' Sadly, while on board Meatyard received news from England that his sixteen-month-old daughter Beryl had died, 'and that was worse than any flesh wound', he wrote in his diary.

Meatyard returned just in time for the landings on the Peninsula. His battalion, with the 1st Battalion King's Own Scottish Borderers (KOSBs) and a company from the South Wales Borderers, were to be involved.

We had a cliff to climb before us, the part that we scrambled up being called the 'Gully'. The scouts went on ahead and actually reached the outskirts of Krithia, a small village that we saw but never reached again during the whole campaign. Our scouts came in contact with one or two Turkish scouts during their advance, two were shot dead and one brought in as a prisoner. He looked very depressed. His equipment consisted of a civilian overcoat, and from his size he wore plenty of underclothing, a soldier's headdress, and a white haversack full of loose ammunition and a rifle. His boots were in a very bad state, and rags took the place of puttees.

Sergeant William Meatyard, Plymouth Battalion, RND

Owing to entirely avoidable error, there had been confusion as to who was in overall command on Y Beach, Lieutenant Colonel Matthews of the Plymouth Battalion or Lieutenant Colonel Koe of the KOSBs, and as a result there was no concerted effort to move inland. The vast majority of the landing force remained close to the cliffs. Only a half-hearted effort was made to dig in and when the Turks began to turn up later that afternoon, a defensive line was dug under severe harassing fire. At no time was an effort made to march towards Krithia or to link up with the men who had landed around the corner at X Beach.

Having established a signal station on the side of the cliff to communicate with HM ships, I proceeded with the CO, having sent two signallers with the advanced line of skirmishers. I was ordered to make the signal 'Retire to your original positions', a blue flag being necessary and advisable. They retired, pressed by the Turks to the position that our CO had decided to take up. This all happened within a very short time and the trenches were far from being deep or completed in any way, and it was now necessary to bring fire to bear on the advancing enemy. I should say the distance of our frontage was no more than 800 yards from flank to flank, with the cliffs behind us.

By lying on the reverse slope of the cliff it was possible to use a large flag and keep communication with the ships. It was necessary to lie on my back as bullets passed over from each flank and dropped somewhere inside our semi-circle. Men on each flank complained that their own men were firing at them, but it was the indirect fire of the enemy that passed over the heads of the men on our one flank and so caught the men on the other flank.

Sergeant William Meatyard, Plymouth Battalion, RND

Y BEACH

GULLY BEACH

X BEACH

HILL 114

HILL 138

CAPE TEKKE

W BEACH

CAPE HELLES

An aerial photograph showing the entire French and British front at Helles.

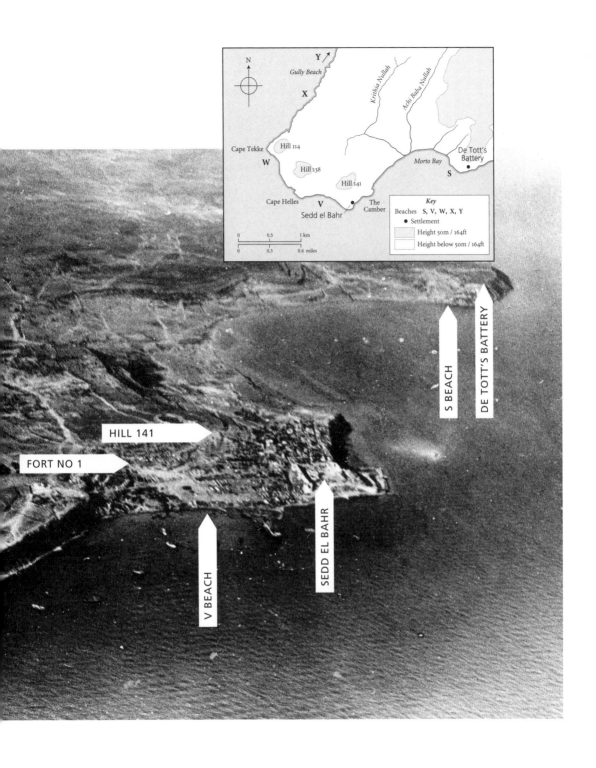

Y ↗

N

Gully Beach

X

Krithia Nullah

Achi Baba Nullah

Hill 114

Cape Tekke

Hill 138

W

Hill 141

Morto Bay

De Tott's Battery

S

Cape Helles

V

The Camber

Sedd el Bahr

Key
Beaches S, V, W, X, Y
● Settlement

Height 50m / 164ft

Height below 50m / 164ft

0   0.5   1 km
0   0.3   0.6 miles

S BEACH

DE TOTT'S BATTERY

HILL 141

FORT NO 1

V BEACH

SEDD EL BAHR

Dummies used as part of the feint landing at Bulair in the Gulf of Saros.

At X Beach, the landing by the 2nd Royal Fusiliers was almost unopposed. A cliff-top bombardment by HMS *Implacable* lying 500 yards offshore put paid to any minimal resistance the Turks might have put up with the few men they had in the area. This meant that the battalion landed without loss and the beach was secured before a bayonet attack was launched on Hill 114, an attack cheered on by sailors on the *Implacable*. The objective was seized and contact made with the forces landing nearby at W Beach. Yet, as the men moved inland there was a counter-attack by a strong force of Turks and they were pushed back almost to the cliffs before reinforcements halted the Turkish attacks. With reports of increasingly hostile fire near Y Beach, a decision was taken to halt the Fusiliers; they were to remain where they were.

By late afternoon, things had become increasingly difficult at Y Beach. No signal lamps had been taken to shore during the landing, and, as darkness set in, Meatyard had been ordered to use the CO's pocket lamp to send important messages to the ships offshore, including an appeal for 30,000 rounds of small arms ammunition and a boat to pick up the wounded. As hostile fire increased, Meatyard recalled sending further, far more alarming messages, including 'can't hold on without reinforcements of at least one battalion' and 'we are in a serious position' and finally 'send boats for us to re-embark'. A message was also sent at dawn appealing to the warships to fire on the Turks, for the commanding officer of the Plymouth Battalion was expecting an attack that might wipe out his diminishing force. HMS *Dublin* opened fire with great accuracy.

By the morning, platoons were ordered to form a rearguard as re-embarkation commenced. Yet the Turks appeared to have no appetite to pursue the men as they retreated down the cliffs, although there was considerable sniping. By 2 p.m. the first evacuation of the campaign had been successful, although Meatyard estimated that each battalion had lost around 25 per cent in casualties. In the excitement to go, a few more men were wounded, for as they clambered aboard HMS *Goliath*, a number still had rounds in the breech, and four men were wounded by accidental discharges.

Two miles away on the other side of the Peninsula, the 2nd South Wales Borderers were to land on S Beach, on the eastern side of Morto Bay and on the right flank of the troops at V Beach. The idea was to take a redundant battery known as De Tott's and hold it while the main force established themselves on W and V Beaches. At S Beach there were delays in landing and the boats, when they appeared, came under sustained rifle fire. The infantry would be supported by the guns of HMS *Cornwallis* and HMS *Vengeance*, the latter taking up 'Action Stations' a mile east of De Tott's Battery.

I took up my position in the lower foretop of the *Vengeance*. Our orders were to shell De Tott's Ridge, and if possible, clear out hostile forces that might be in ambush. At 5 a.m., as if the very heavens had been rent asunder, every ship opened fire simultaneously on its allotted area. One was too engrossed with one's own duty to notice what was happening in other areas; we simply hammered away for all we were worth.

At 5.30 a m., the landing was to be attempted, and all boats, lighters, etc., were filled with troops from the transports and proceeded towards the beaches. Trawlers and boats, which had been secured to the ship astern of us, now crowded with the South Wales Borderers, made for the end of the sandy patch just inside Morto Bay. They were met by a hail of bullets which killed a number of men, and therefore they withdrew for a short time, during which we increased our rate of fire. The trawlers then came round

Lieutenant Robert Seed, Royal Navy, HMS *Vengeance*

the south part of De Tott's; at 6.30 a.m. another attempt was made, and in spite of heavy fire, the men landed and climbed up the side of the cliff. It was splendid to see them with their bayonets flashing in the sun, making the ascent – a sight never to be forgotten.

De Tott's Battery was taken within the hour. The South Wales Borderers had successfully carried out their orders. However, Hunter Weston had given no further instructions that these men could press on and so they stood their ground while fighting raged just around the corner on V Beach.

At W Beach the ships carrying the men of the 29th Division waited on a dead calm sea close to Cape Tekke, at the very western tip of the Peninsula. On HMS *Euryalus*, Captain Clement Milward climbed onto the deck and looked below.

Captain Clement Milward, Indian Army, GSO3 29th Division

The Lancashire Fusiliers were already seated in the tows of cutters and pinnaces alongside. All was deadly still and silent, the engines of our ship hardly made a sound. One couldn't help pitying the men sitting there in

87th Brigade Headquarters coming ashore on X Beach. 'The landing differs from some others. I recollect a bright sunny morning, dead calm sea, not a shot fired. I had a bag in one hand, coat over my arm, and was assisted down a plank from the boat by an obliging sailor, so that I should not wet my boots. The only thing missing was the hotel,' recorded Brigade Major Cuthbert Lucas, who took this photograph.

Brigadier General William Marshall (far right), commanding 87th Brigade, with Headquarters Staff on X Beach. Marshall was wounded during the day but refused to go sick. For two days he commanded all British troops at Helles.

their boats. It was indeed a hush before the storm. There lay the Peninsula with not a sign of life on it, but the Turks were there all right in their trenches watching our every movement.

At 4.30 a.m. we all went to the bridge and the bombardment began. The sight now was wonderful – never to be forgotten. A beautiful sunny morning, a glassy sea, on one side of the Peninsula and Asia Minor, apparently uninhabited, being pounded to bits, and in every other direction ships and ships and ships – British battleships round Helles, all the best of the pre-Dreadnought era, cruisers, destroyers, French battleships off the Asiatic coast, like top-heavy walnuts, all bumps and excrescences, the five-funnelled Russian Cruiser, the *Askold*, and, in the background, the newest and mightiest, yet so symmetrical as to look quite small and low, 'Queen Bess', one funnelled and one masted with her eight 15-inch guns. All these ships had their allotted areas to bombard, some the coastline, some searching up the valley behind and some dropping their 12-inch and 15-inch shells which burst with mighty columns of smoke on Krithia and on the summit of Achi Baba.

The Turkish defensive efforts at W Beach looked formidable. Anticipating a landing, they had dug trenches behind the beach and draped belts of barbed wire along the sand and in the water; landmines, too, had been laid above the shoreline. On the cliffs at each end of the beach were two well-defended redoubts. Despite all this, the Lancashire Fusiliers were expected to wrest control of the shore from the Turks and then move inland to link up with troops on X Beach, before meeting the men landing just around the corner on V Beach. The sight of the navy's shells bombarding the coastline was undoubtedly reassuring, but for many the explosions were too far inland. Krithia and Achi Baba were objectives, but not immediately, and the men rowing towards the shore would have preferred to see the shoreline a horizon of dust and smoke.

Major George Adams, 1st Lancashire Fusiliers, 29th Division

As the boats touched the shore, a very heavy and brisk fire was poured into us, several officers and men being killed and wounded in the entanglements, through which we were trying to cut a way. Several of my company were with me under the wire, one of my subalterns was killed next to me, and also the wire-cutter who was lying the other side of me. I seized his cutter and cut a small lane myself through which a few of us broke and lined up under the only available cover procurable, a small sand ridge covered with bluffs of grass. I then ordered fire to be opened on the crests, but owing to submersion in the water and dragging rifles through the sand, the breech mechanism was clogged, thereby rendering the rifles ineffective. The only thing left to do was to fix bayonets and charge up the crests, which was done in a very gallant manner, though we suffered greatly in doing so. However, this had the effect of driving the enemy from his trenches, which we immediately occupied.

Major Harold Shaw, 1st Lancashire Fusiliers, 29th Division

On the right of me on the cliff was a line of Turks in a trench taking potshots at us, ditto on the left. I looked back. There was one soldier between me and the wire, and a whole line in a row on the edge of the sands. The sea behind them was absolutely crimson, and you could hear the groans through the rattle of musketry. A few were firing. I signalled to them to advance. I shouted to the soldier behind to signal, but he shouted back, 'I am shot through the chest.' I then perceived they were all hit. I took a rifle from one of the men with me and started in at the men on the cliff on my right, but could only fire slowly, as I had to get the bolt open with my foot as it was clogged with sand. About this time Maunsell was shot dead next to me. Our men now began to scale the cliffs from the boats on the outer flanks, and I need only add it was a capital sight. They carried the trenches at the top at the point of the bayonet: there was some desperate work up there. In the trench I had been firing at, the enemy touched off a land mine just too soon, but the people near it, I hear, are deprived of speech, and are deaf.

Shaw's description was part of a letter written to his brother days after the landing. 'I hate even thinking about that scene of carnage,' he continued, 'but, to oblige you, I will unburden myself for the last time while I have the chance.'

Major Shaw was killed six weeks later. By then Major Adams was already dead.

The Lancashire Fusiliers had been confronted not by enemy machine guns, as many believed, but by the accurate rifle fire of perhaps 100–150 Turkish infantrymen, more than enough to give those advancing over exposed ground the impression of intense fire. The Brigade Commander, Brigadier General Stuart Hare, who was leading the second wave into shore, witnessed the Fusiliers' plight. He could see that a further landing on W Beach was senseless and, thinking quickly, he ordered the boats to row to the left, around the corner under the cover of the cliffs. The Turks did not have the numbers to counter this outflanking manoeuvre. Hare and his men scrambled up a steep slope where, in conjunction with a few Lancashire Fusiliers who had reached the top of the beach, they attacked Turkish positions. By 8 a.m. W Beach was tentatively secured and further progress was made as more men were landed in the early afternoon. These men helped to support the attacks on Hills 114 to the west and 138 to the south-east. With a perimeter established above W Beach, Brigadier General Hare then reconnoitred in the direction of X Beach in the hope of meeting men of the Royal Fusiliers, but he was wounded and evacuated. Preparing to land, Captain Albert Mure watched the drama as it unfolded.

We could not tell how the day was going. Indescribable noise we could hear, indescribable flame and confusion we could see, indescribable carnage we could infer, but we could not piece together or interpret the awful confusion of detail. There was a green field to the left on the top of the cliff, and we could see men rushing across it, then coming back, then advancing again,

Captain Albert Mure, 1/5th Royal Scots, 29th Division

as if a stiff fight were going on. Towards Sedd el Bahr there seemed to be no progress, and we, watching and waiting, began to feel nervous, and imagined that all was not well.

Wilson suddenly turned to me and said, 'There are the stretcher cases going aboard the hospital ship. Some poor devils have got it in the neck already.' Of course, a great many had – we knew that – but this was seeing it. A pinnace dashed past us, and we yelled to the officer. He shook his head, and that finished us. Anxiety turned into absolute, craven dumps.

The fighting above W Beach lasted until weight of numbers forced the Turks back, and objectives such as Hill 138 were taken. Even then it proved impossible for the men above W Beach to link up with the men at V Beach.

The landing at V Beach proved the hardest fought of all the engagements that day. Once again barbed wire and defensive trenches threatened to disrupt severely any advance from the shoreline, while Turkish soldiers lodged in the castle of Sedd el Bahr and Fort No. 1 had a clear field of fire from which to make V Beach a death trap. The wide, gently sloping beach offered an inviting place

An historic photograph of the 1st Lancashire Fusiliers rowing to shore at W Beach. Six Victoria Crosses were won that morning.

to pull boats ashore, but it was also overlooked. If the Turks put up a stiff defence, then a sandbank yards from the beach and around five feet high would provide the only shelter. The first men due to land would be the 1st Royal Dublin Fusiliers, brought into shore on strings of rowing boats pulled by steamboats. Behind them would come the *River Clyde*. In its hold were men of the Royal Munster Fusiliers and the 2nd Hampshire Regiment. Petty Officer David Fyffe was on the *River Clyde* as it neared the coast.

It was now light enough to discern the black shapes of warships lying on both sides of us and ahead, and soon we could dimly make out a darker grey line along the horizon that showed the land. Nearer and nearer we grew, passing between lines of great ships that flashed and smoked and thundered, and all of a sudden the dawn ran along the eastern horizon in streaks of scarlet and gold and we saw that we were almost in the midst of the fleet. And there, away to port, was a line of shore, undulating in rows of round-topped hills, that was spangled with sudden flashes of scarlet flame … It was the Turkish coast and the guns of the fleet were preparing our way. Now we were right in the midst of the battleships and the thunder

Petty Officer David Fyffe, No. 3 Armoured Car Squadron, RNAS, SS *River Clyde*

of their guns seemed to rend the firmament. Once we passed close under the quarter of the *Lord Nelson* just as she loosed off both the 12-inch guns of her fore barbette. There was a sheet of scarlet flame that spurted fiercely from the grey muzzles, a great cloud of yellowish smoke that drifted slowly over our decks, and a terrific ear-splitting roar that seemed to burst one's head …

The old castle [Sedd el Bahr] and the village were receiving full attention and it was fascinating to watch the fountains of stones and dust that shot into the air as the big shells burst against the already battered walls of the fort, or demolished the few remaining houses of the ruined village that nestled at its base. It was just as we came opposite Sedd el Bahr, steering slowly up the channel through the lines of ships, that we on the *Clyde* got our first surprise in the shape of a big splash in the water a few yards astern. A friend and I, by virtue of our position as 'bargees', were now on the poop along with two sailors, standing by the hawsers that were towing the barges alongside and we had scarcely time to mark the spreading rings that circled in the water close to our stern, when on a sudden there were two more 'plops' in the water a few yards short of the ship, and we were now fully conscious that shells were being fired at the *Clyde* from somewhere or other and falling uncomfortably close too. We ducked hastily behind the flag house on the arrival of two more visitors that shrieked

1st Essex Regiment lands on W Beach. This beach, soon renamed 'Lancashire Landing', would become the main British disembarkation beach and base at Helles.

close overhead and splashed into the water on the far side of the ship … We had now passed Sedd el Bahr Bay and turning round, the ship steered a diagonal course toward the Asiatic side. When once more opposite the destined landing place, the ship was turned round and, with safety valves screwed down, headed at full speed toward Sedd el Bahr. Never had the old ship attained such a speed, and with her whole hull quivering under the straining engines, and the smoke pouring in oily black clouds from her funnel, she dashed towards the little bay. Nearer and nearer she grew, and as she approached the land the ships ceased firing and an uncanny silence reigned.

The tows carrying the Royal Dublin Fusiliers were meant to land at 5.30 a.m., but embarkation delays, and a strong current running out of the Straits, delayed the Fusiliers' approach and the *River Clyde* had overtaken them. Even the best-laid plans rarely survived first contact with the enemy, but this one appeared to be unwinding even earlier. Commander Unwin had no idea if the tows had landed or not so he had turned the *Clyde* around. He was concerned that there would be hellish confusion if the both forces landed simultaneously. With so many ships close by, this manoeuvre proved extremely difficult. Still he couldn't see the tows, so he decided to head straight for shore.

There was a soft jar that quivered from end to end of the ship, and she was aground. All was now excitement on board and we had our work cut out to ease off the hawsers quickly enough as the train of barges was jerked forward by the collision. Hardly had the ship come to rest when the little steam hopper with her tow of barges rushed out from under the *Clyde*'s quarter and made for the sandy shore some eighty yards distant. Up till now not a shot had been fired from the shore, and indeed we had begun to wonder whether the landing was to be unopposed, but hardly had the hopper's bow appeared beyond her huge consort when the whole slope leapt into a roar of firing, and a tempest of lead poured down upon the devoted craft and her gallant crew. Disaster overwhelmed her in an instant. Nothing could live in such a torrent of lead and in a moment the middy at the wheel and every sailor on the deck of the little ship was shot down.

Petty Officer David Fyffe, No. 3 Armoured Car Squadron, RNAS, SS River Clyde

Overleaf: Sub-Lieutenant Arthur Coke (far left) and Petty Officer David Fyffe (second left) pose for a photograph shortly before landing. In the background is one of the River Clyde's Maxim gun steel emplacements.

Devoid of guidance, the hopper went astray and beached side-on while the barges all went out of line, the connecting ropes broke under the strain, and they came to rest in a hopeless muddle with the farthest barge lying helplessly in deep water about twenty yards from the shore. The bridge of boats had failed and the officers hastily met to construct a new plan.

Minutes after the *Clyde* beached, the rowing boats appeared crammed with the Dublin Fusiliers. As they approached the shore and shallower water, they were cast off by the steamboats. Immediately six oarsmen began to pull towards the shore but the dead weight in each boat made progress painfully slow. Huddled together and unprotected, the men were easy targets.

Petty Officer David Fyffe, No. 3 Armoured Car Squadron, RNAS, SS *River Clyde*

Out of six boats that formed one tow, only one reached the shore and beached side-on, and out from among the crowded benches only about a dozen men leapt into the water and rushed for the sand. Their comrades still crouched upright in the boats but they were strangely still, shot dead where they sat. The other four boats never reached the shore. One by one the oars fell from the dead hands of their occupants and drifted slowly away, and the big white boats lay rocking idly on the shot-torn water many yards from the shore, with not a movement amid the huddle of khaki figures that filled them to the gunwales. As we watched in wordless horror, one of the boats floated slowly past us, bumping along our side, and we could look straight down into her motionless cargo. It was a floating shambles. A mass of corpses huddled together in the bottom of the boat and lying heaped above one another across the crimson benches. Here an arm and hand hung over the gunwale, swaying helplessly as the boat rocked on the waves. There a rifle stuck upright into the sunlight out of a mass of shapeless khaki figures. And everywhere crimson mingling with the brown, and here and there a waxen-white face with draggled hair staring up into the smiling heavens. Slowly the ghastly boat scraped along our sides and slowly drifted out to sea leaving us frozen with a nameless horror and an overpowering dread. Such was our introduction to the glories of war, and when one big fellow turned his drawn white face to us with a slow 'Good God!' as we stared at the vanishing boat, we could only look at him in a queer tight-throated silence and wonder what in Heaven's name it all meant.

The Dublins' commanding officer was dead, the second-in-command mortally wounded. A few of the Dublin Fusiliers managed to make a dash for the shore and the sandbank. Those lucky enough to reach it lay low with no opportunity to hit back, while just yards behind them men were cut down in the water and drowned, pulled under by the weight of their equipment. Between the drowning men, boats floated helplessly in the water with their dead and dying crews. Only where one or two boats had been taken into shore below Sedd el Bahr Fort was a landing effected without catastrophic loss. These men gradually fought their way into the village, where they met with stiff resistance and were pushed back, though at least they had distracted some Turkish riflemen from firing at those lying prostrate on the shore.

Minutes before the landing: SS River Clyde and her tows approach V Beach.

Private Robert
Martin, 1st Royal
Dublin Fusiliers,
29th Division

There were twenty-five in my boat, and there were only three of us left. It was sad to hear our poor chums moaning, and to see others dead in the boat. It was a terrible sight to see the poor boys dead in the water; others on the beach roaring for help. But we could do nothing for them. I must have had someone's good prayer for I do not know how I escaped. Those who were lying wounded on the shore, in the evening the tide came in and they were all drowned, and I was left by myself on the beach. I had to remain in the water for about three hours, as they would fire on me as soon as they saw me make a move. I thought life was up every minute.

None of the infantrymen from the *River Clyde* had landed. The grounded ship was powerless, and the bridge of boats had to be formed manually if the men were to run down improvised gangways and over the boats to the beach. It was intended that the steam hopper accompanying the *Clyde* was to move to the ship's port side and move lighters into position. It was a Heath Robinson idea and, given the circumstances, impossible to execute. The hopper was commanded by Midshipman George Drewry who had been placed in charge of six Greek volunteer crewmen. Understandably, this was not the job for which they had signed up, and they took cover in the hopper's bows. Drewry and an able seaman named Samson were stuck. From the deck of the *Clyde*, Unwin appreciated the hopelessness of the situation and acted. Followed by Able Seaman William Williams, he jumped overboard and got hold of the lighters and pulled them underneath the bow of the *Clyde* and began to connect them up. The closest piece of dry land was a rocky spit thrusting into the sea, and it was towards this rock that the men steered the boats. There was no way to hold the boats together, other than by grim determination, so Unwin and Williams clung on while the call was made for the infantrymen to leave the ship. Immediately the men of the 1st Royal Munster Fusiliers opened the doorways cut into the superstructure and began to run down the gangways towards the lighters.

Petty Officer David
Fyffe, No. 3
Armoured Car
Squadron, RNAS,
SS *River Clyde*

We could hear splash after splash as the gallant fellows fell dead from the gangway. A few however reached the nearest barge, raced across her open deck and crouched for shelter in the adjacent open boat. One after another the devoted fellows made the dash down the deadly gangways until a considerable number gathered in the bottoms of the open boats or were lying prostrate on the deck of the barge. Then the order was given and up they leaped and rushed for the rocks while a hail of rifle and machine-gun fire beat upon them. Wildly they leaped from boat to boat in that gallant rush while we on the ship cheered wildly at the sight, until they reached the last boat when they leaped down into the water and started wading towards the rocks that were their goal, holding up their rifles high above their heads. But to our horror we saw them suddenly begin to flounder and fall in the water, disappearing from view and then struggling to the surface again with uniform and pack streaming, only to go down again never to reappear as the hailing bullets flicked the life out of the struggling men … We almost wept with impotent rage. Nonetheless some fifty or more survivors had reached the edge of the rocky point and were crouching up to their necks in the water behind this slight shelter waiting for a chance to rush over the rocks to the beach.

I took a last look around the hold and then made a dash down the rickety gangway, the rusty sides of the old collier towering above me on my left hand, the open sea on my right, and I landed with a crash on the first barge, bullets spluttering all over the place as our fire had not silenced all the rifles and machine guns on the shore. I lay down flat on my tummy and looked around to get my bearings and a terrible sight met me as the barge was crowded with men who had died and lots of wounded men whom we could not help as we had to push on owing to the other fellows coming on behind. Eventually, after crawling along three barges, I came to the place where I could push my face over the gunwhale of the last barge and make up my mind to jump into the sea. I managed it all right, clutching my explosives – I had lost the shovel somewhere – I managed to get to a place where no bullets could reach me and lay down under cover of a small sandbank and at last I was for the first time on the enemy shore.

Lance Corporal George Smith, 1/1st West Riding Field Company, Royal Engineers, 29th Division

We all made, Dublins and all, for a sheltered ledge on the shore which gave us cover. Here we shook ourselves out, and tried to appreciate the situation, rather a sorry one. I estimated that I had lost about 70% of my Company … Seeing that Sedd el Bahr and the beach to our right was

Captain Guy Geddes, 1st Royal Munster Fusiliers, 29th Division

unoccupied, and fearing the Turks might come down, I called for volunteers to make a dash for it, and make good the right of the beach. The men responded gallantly. Picking Sergeant Ryan and six men, we had a go for it. Three of the men were killed, one other and myself wounded. However we got across, and later picked up fourteen stragglers from the Company of the Dublins who had landed at Camban Bay. This little party attempted to get a lodgement inside the Fort but we couldn't do it so we dug ourselves in as well as we could with our entrenching tools.

As Geddes made his dash to the right, Unwin and Williams remained chest-deep in the cold water, securing the boats, but they were exhausted. Unwin asked Williams if he could hang on, but he replied he could not. Moments later a shell landed and Williams was wounded. If Unwin was to rescue his friend he would have to let go of the ropes holding the boats together. He swam back to a lighter with Williams. Surgeon Peter Kelly was treating the wounded on the *Clyde*.

Below: Dead and dying: a lighter breaks loose from the shore with its human cargo.

Surgeon Peter Kelly, Royal Army Medical Corps Attd. RNAS

Leading Seaman Williams was drowning and Commander Unwin had collapsed in an attempt to save him. I rushed down to render some assistance, but before I got off the ship a bullet glanced off my right shin – stinging like the very devil, almost within a second, and before I had got another yard one entered my left foot obliquely and I fell on my face. [I was taken] to cover and just then a large shell entered the top of the boiler casing at the root of the ship's funnel and the result was awful, fearful fumes which were choking myself and several others close by. I tried to get away but fell down a hatchway as we could not see and then I remember no more until I was roused and coming round found Commander Unwin in a dying state. Shortly afterwards Drewry was carried in covered with blood and comatose …

Making a dash for a better position: Captain Guy Geddes and his volunteers (bottom right, below Sedd el Bahr Fort) attempt to break out from the beach.

After about two hours both seemed out of danger. I remember Arthur [Coke] coming in very cool about everything for a few moments to talk to us all. The saloon was full of wounded officers and some dead ones and he cheered us all up and put his hand on my shoulder and said 'Will I kill a Turk for you?' and then went off smiling but very sympathetic. He very nearly lost his life as he went out of the saloon as a bullet missed his head by inches and entered the pantry from the port side, wounding the captain's servant.

In Unwin's absence, Drewry had taken over, and with the help of two other men a third lighter had been brought round from the *Clyde*'s starboard side and a bridge of sorts completed to the beach. Further attempts were made to land men and three further strings of boats, packed with infantrymen, made for the shore. This time more were able to land but a number were cut down by the burst of three shrapnel shells overhead. More men were sent from the beached collier, and more arrived on lighters, but all were forced to head for the sandbank so that by 9 a.m. a few hundred men were huddled there for protection.

The extent of the disaster unfolding on V Beach was unclear to Major

General Hunter-Weston and his staff onboard the *Euryalus* and a second wave of assault troops were on their way, including one platoon of the 4th Worcestershire Regiment. These men met with a similar fate, and the dead included men of all ranks, among them the Brigade Commander, Brigadier General Napier, who had personally led the assault, and his Brigade Major, who followed him.

Petty Officer David Fyffe, No. 3 Armoured Car Squadron, RNAS, SS *River Clyde*

The price to be paid was too awful and at slightly less than two hours after the *Clyde* had run ashore, operations were suspended and it was decided to wait till nightfall before a further attempt at landing should be made. Word was sent to the fleet of the failure of the operations and the ships recommenced with increased vigour their bombardment of the slopes above the beach and the old castle and village of Sedd el Bahr …

Captain Clement Milward, Indian Army, GSO3 29th Division

10 a.m.: We received depressing messages telling us of the death of General Napier, killed on the lighters, and shortly afterwards of the death of Costeker, his Brigade Major. Colonel Carrington Smith, a fine soldier, of the Hampshires, had taken command, but he was killed on the bridge in the afternoon. Truly the casualties were staggering. General Marshall, too, was slightly wounded. They told us too of how 1,000 men of those on board the *River Clyde* had attempted to get ashore. About half had been hit in the attempt. Twice, a naval lieutenant [John Morse] managed to get away in a pinnace from the *Clyde* to tell us how they stood and his tale was not inspiring … So great was the depression that we had great difficulty in dissuading General Hunter-Weston from going himself to V Beach to lead the men to the attack.

Petty Officer David Fyffe, No. 3 Armoured Car Squadron, SS *River Clyde*

Opposite: 1/5th Royal Scots, with Captain Albert Mure, make their way towards the shore.

Our huge protectress [*Queen Elizabeth*] turned her attention to the old castle on the right. There, in a chamber in the walls, a Maxim gun was spluttering busily through a small window, and not all our painstaking efforts could get at that gun. It was situated opposite my gun position on the forecastle and Lieutenant Coke was devoting all his energies to putting the nuisance out of action. But although the bullets from his gun were knocking little spurts of dust off the walls all around the look-hole, the aperture was too small and the belts rattled through the breach all in vain. Then suddenly one of the 'Lizzie's' six-inch presents blew the top off the wall just above the

hated window and with a fervid 'At last', Coke crawled out of his steel cubby-hatch and crouched behind the rail, glasses glued on the spot. Again the 'Lizzie' fired and again the battlemented parapet dissolved as if by magic above the window. 'Too high, you blighters, too high!' came in muttered accents from the officer, now flat on his face on the deck, for the air was full of whining bullets. Again came the crash behind us, again the shell groaned over our heads and this time the whole face of the wall disappeared in a cloud of flying masonry and dust and yellow fumes. For a second nobody spoke, and then suddenly 'Got him! Got him clean! Beautiful oh beautiful!' came in cries of ecstasy from behind the rail, and our worthy lieutenant danced upon the deck as the dust blew away and we saw that a huge hole gaped in the wall where before the window had been.

But nothing the fleet could do seemed to daunt the defenders. The village with its huddle of partially ruined houses was a very nest of snipers and from behind the tree-clad garden walls and the corners of the narrow streets came a never-ceasing hail of deadly fire … Such of us as were not engaged working the guns, would crouch with ready rifle waiting to catch a snap-shot from behind the bulwarks at the dim figures that flitted from house to house as the shells smashed and wrecked the buildings. And that was all we saw of the enemy that day. A dim figure scuttling out of a falling house and disappearing again as swiftly as it had come. One curious little sight I well remember; a big stork standing on one leg on its nest on the roof-ridge of a high house among the trees. All around it the houses were collapsing in flame and smoke and the infernal din of bursting shells and falling masonry. But still it stood, motionless and imperturbable, the emblem of home and happiness in the midst of ruin and desolation.

Any idea of the Lancashire Fusiliers at W Beach linking up with the men at V Beach was scotched, at least for the time being. The Lancashire Fusiliers and the Worcestershire Regiment had made progress and were with spitting distance of V Beach, but still not close enough, although communication of a sort was made.

Staff Captain Harold Farmar, 1st Lancashire Fusiliers, 29th Division

At Brigade Headquarters [directly above Cape Helles] there was doubt as to the exact situation at Sedd el Bahr. By running from the lighthouse and then slipping over the edge of the cliff, a position could be reached from which the *River Clyde* could be seen; and visual communication was established with the 88th Brigade Signal Section, who worked behind iron plates on the bridge of the collier. By gingerly picking a way, it was possible to reach a point above some men who had landed from the ex-collier and to shout to them. They could get no further, and the cliff was unclimbable. There were very few and almost all wounded. There appeared to be a line of men holding a ridge across the beach, but who made no progress. It transpired later that they were dead, cut down by machine-gun fire as they made a rush. The messages, which came by helio[graph], gave the impression that great difficulties were being encountered.

On the *River Clyde*, Commander Unwin made a miraculous recovery, having appeared to be near death's door. Although there was stalemate on the beach, there were scores of wounded lying in the open, some close to the water's edge and at risk of drowning from the small but perceptible rise in the Aegean tide. Undaunted, Unwin went into action again.

I got a boat under the starboard quarter as far from the enemy as I could get. Taking a spare coil of rope with me, I got some hands to pay out the rope fast to the stern of the pinnace I was in, and paddled and punted it to the beach, eventually grounding alongside the wounded. They were all soaking wet and very heavy, but I cut off their accoutrements with their bayonets or knives and carried two or three to the pinnace, but as her side was rather high out of the water, I'm afraid they were none too gingerly put on board. Still they were very grateful. I could not pick up any more, so I got on my hands and knees, they got on my back and I crawled along to the pinnace. Four more, I managed like this. I found a man in his trousers only, alongside me, he had swum ashore to help me, his name was Russell and he was one of the RNAS. We carried one man down together and then he was shot through the stomach. I tore up my shirt and bound his wound a bit and got him into the pinnace. I was again beginning to feel a bit dickey so I got into the pinnace and told them to haul me aboard. On the way across somebody came alongside in the water and wanted to know why I was

Commander Edward Unwin, Royal Navy, SS *River Clyde*

going back. I replied because I could do no more – and I really couldn't. I was fifty-one!

For these extraordinary acts of self-sacrifice, Unwin was awarded the Victoria Cross, one of five awarded that day at V Beach. Other men now took up the mantle and continued the rescue work well into the afternoon, and under fire until all such work was suspended. All day the surviving infantrymen huddled under the sandbank while the navy blazed away at the Turkish positions. The attack made by the Lancashire Fusiliers along the ridge had put the Turkish defenders at risk of being cut off, and occupied men who would otherwise have maintained their attention on V Beach. Only with approaching darkness could both sides take a breather and the wounded on V Beach be attended to. As night finally fell, the men who had been pinned down all day long got up. Officers began to collect their men, and more troops, bottled up in the *River Clyde*, groped their way down the swinging gangways and across the body-strewn barges to the shore.

Lieutenant Commander Josiah Wedgewood, No. 3 Armoured Car Squadron, RNAS, SS *River Clyde*

For three hours I stood on the end of the spit of what had been rock in two feet of water helping heavily laden men to jump ashore on to submerged dead bodies. This is what went on monotonously: 'Give me your rifle!' 'Your shovel!' 'Your left hand!' 'Jump wide!' 'It's all right, it's only kits!' 'Keep clear of that man's legs, can't you?' Trying to persuade the wounded over whom they had to walk that we should soon get them aboard. Wounded men were brought to the end of the spit and could not be got aboard, because the other stream was more important and never-ending – there they slowly sank and died.

To help the landings, as well as the recovery efforts, the navy had one more trick up its sleeve.

Petty Officer David Fyffe, No. 3 Armoured Car Squadron, RNAS, SS *River Clyde*

Suddenly the higher slope of the shore sprang into a blaze of dazzling light as the searchlights of the attendant battleships thrust their blinding fingers through the gloom, and every stick and stone upon the terraced rise that bore the concealed enemy trenches stood out in fullest detail. By contrast, on the beach at the water's edge, on to which the men were now defiling, the *Clyde* and the awful barges were in pitch darkness, and only the glare from the burning village cast splashes of crimson on the inky water. The enemy, dazzled by the searchlights, and unable to discern anything in the solid blackness that sheltered the *Clyde* and the beach, were helpless to hinder the progress of the landing, and by midnight over two thousand men had reached the stretch of sand with hardly a casualty. The moon rise was late that night and even when the silvery orb did climb into the midnight sky, the shadows cast by the frowning walls of the castle were so long and dense that little could be seen of what was going on on the beach.

We entrenched ourselves on a line from X Beach across the corner of the Peninsula some 600 yards inland to Hill 138. On W Beach they were working feverishly getting water, ammunition and supplies ashore and rigging up piers. The enemy were still in strength in Sedd el Bahr and in the trenches round V Beach.

Captain Clement Milward, Indian Army, GSO3 29th Division

After dinner I accompanied General Hunter-Weston to visit Sir Ian Hamilton on HMS *Queen Elizabeth*, which had gone off halfway to Tenedos. We had a glass of wine with Admiral de Robeck, Sir Ian and General Braithwaite. All were much elated by the wonderful feat of arms by which the 29th Division had gained immortality – the landing safely accomplished. But at what cost? One could not help wondering if all was well …

On our return to the *Euryalus*, the General sent me in the pinnace to V Beach to find out the situation there. As we approached the *Clyde* the midshipman took shelter at his wheel low down behind his armour-plated box.

They were busy collecting wounded off the beach and lowering them on stretchers end downwards into lighters some 10 ft below – a most painful process. I climbed on to the ship and found it full of wounded. I talked to all the officers on the deck and great depression was apparent. They had had a nerve-shattering experience. Colonel Carrington was still lying dead on the bridge and General Napier and Costeker on the lighters below.

Overleaf: New Zealanders making their way down from Quinn's Post while stretcher-bearers walk by.

4 Impasse

Tommy 'has his feelings'. There were pictures of sweethearts (they said so on the back), pictures of wives, and pictures of kiddies dressed in their best. But what touched me most, and gave me a new and nobler view of Tommy, were the pictures of Mother.

Captain Albert Mure, 1/5th Royal Scots, 29th Division

The Australians and New Zealanders held a small bridgehead running from Bolton's Ridge in the south all the way up Second Ridge close to the head of Monash Gully, then back on itself, over towards Walker's Ridge. The line was fragmented and was, in places, identified by infantrymen with rifles rather than by any physical line hacked into the ground. This tenuous plot of land was barely a thousand yards from the sea at its deepest point but it would become impervious to every attempt by the Turks to force the issue and decisively break through. After the landings, the Anzac forces were under orders to dig in. Consolidation was vital, and the wounded were left to stretcher-bearers and the motor launches.

It is daylight again and we are concentrating on landing water and ammunition, and evacuating wounded from last night's battle. We are just beginning to wonder how much longer our boats' crews can keep going. Some of us can hardly keep our eyes open from lack of sleep. We try stuffing ourselves with bully beef and biscuits, washing the mixture down with cups of strong tea. This helps to keep up our strength and makes us more wide awake. If anyone asked me now what I would like best to eat I should reply: 'New bread and butter with brown sugar.' I cannot think why.

Midshipman Eric Bush, Royal Navy, HMS *Bacchante*

Six-inch howitzers being landed: the 1st Heavy Artillery Battery provided vital fire support to the men at Anzac.

Sapper Thomas
Farrer, 1st Field
Company, New
Zealand Engineers

We had our lunch and fell in again with all our gear and two tools each. Along the beach, round the point at the northern edge of the cove and along by the sea till we turned to the right and went up the track leading to Walker's Ridge. The way was narrow and steep and we sweated some going up that hill. When we got to Headquarters about halfway up, we took off all our gear and went on again with only our rifles and tools. At one place we had to run in threes because the sniping was so bad. We came to where the track was very narrow. On the left was a fire trench. Wounded men were lying about and just beside me there was an Australian shot through the leg who was moaning and crying out in an agonised voice that it was murder at the top of the hill. We waited there for a while and then they put us to deepen and widen the track. I was put where there was a precipice on my right; in front, to the left, the ground was covered with bushes about 4′ 5″ high and sloped upward slightly.

The confusing nature of the terrain ensured that neither side was entirely confident as to who was directly in front, on the flank, or even behind. Sniping took its toll, with men picked off from every conceivable angle. In such a cauldron, the Anzacs were extremely jumpy, unsure whether the Turks might reappear in force at any moment.

Sapper Thomas
Farrer, 1st Field
Company, New
Zealand Engineers

I was just starting on my job when two or three men rushed into me from the front. They were in a panic and seemed to be frightened out of their lives and shouted, 'Look out, they are coming'. I lost my head for a moment and ran down the hill with them to where I had left my rifle. It was gone and I began to search feverishly for another and soon picked up an Australian rifle. I threw everything except my paybook out of my pockets and filled them with ammunition and taking a bayonet from a wounded Australian I fixed it on my rifle. There was an officer standing there who asked me if I had a rifle and when I said yes, he said, 'Well then, go up to the top of the hill and stay there.' So I went up the track and got into the flat ground among the bushes fully expecting to meet the Turks straight away but none appeared. When I had gone about 100 yards I came to a crowd of New Zealanders lying on their bellies, so I lay down too. The fire was pretty hot and the bullets were exploding all round us and singing through the bushes. I could not see where the firing line was or where the Turks were. A New Zealander was shot through the head alongside of me and went over like a shot rabbit.

The wounded and the exhausted dribbled back from the front line, some giving their account of bitter engagements. Others were simply shocked, and offered no more than a few words. Sydney Powell was at 4th Battalion headquarters and watched the slow, sad procession of men as they passed by, first a wounded man who had narrowly escaped being bayoneted, then shortly afterwards a lieutenant of the 3rd Brigade.

He had lost his battalion and seemed to be greatly afflicted in mind. He was inexpressibly haggard – grey and ghastly. He sat for a minute with his chin in his hands. He had landed, he said, with the first landing party, and had been fighting through the whole of yesterday. He had then gone with a message to another battalion and had lost his way in returning. The colonel told him where he was likely to find his battalion, and he dragged himself to his feet and tottered off ... Our wounded were dribbling past in no great numbers. Most of them were walking, but we heard of a good many men who could not be moved, on account of the shortage of stretchers. Among these was the commander of my platoon, who had been badly wounded in the groin. He passed us about midday, suffering cheerfully, and died on his way to Egypt.

Private Sydney Powell, 4th Battalion AIF

Until the line could be consolidated, the navy gave covering fire, the shells seeming to tear the air just over the heads of the Anzac infantry, close enough, according to one, to give him painful tremors when they exploded a short distance ahead. Small, localised attacks were made to straighten the line forward, although to the men who took part the plan behind such attacks was not always clear. At 3 p.m. on 26 April, the 4th Battalion AIF were ordered to advance across 400 Plateau.

Private Sydney
Powell, 4th
Battalion AIF

*Above: Out of the
line: New Zealanders
resting off North
Beach. Note Plugge's
Plateau in the
background.*

There was something very queer about that order. It was vague to the last degree. I am not sure if the order was 'advance' or 'attack,' but I am pretty sure that no objective was mentioned. The colonel appeared not to understand it, but his hesitation was summarily cut short by the discovery that the troops were leaving their trenches! Seemingly the men had received the order before it reached the colonel. We at once hopped out after them.

My memories of the next hour or so are clear but incoherent. I have never been able to form a rational picture either of what we were doing or of what we were intended to do. I found myself with the Colonel, the Adjutant, the Signalling Officer, several signallers and others … Owing to the broken nature of the ground, we had lost sight of the troops; but their cheers as they charged told us of their whereabouts. Twice or three times we heard those thin, high cheers. We passed a great many dead. The majority were Australians. In one spot were half a dozen. Though last night's rain must have washed them, they looked curiously dusty. One man was kneeling on one knee; his head was slightly bowed over his rifle, which he still grasped; its butt rested on the ground. Until I looked at his face I thought that he was alive.

Imperceptibly, our small party disintegrated, and at last I was alone with the colonel. A man wearing the colours of the 5th Battalion joined us. He seemed to spring up from nowhere. The air sang with bullets, and in running we crouched as low as we could, and lay on our bellies frequently.

I had some strange fancies. The most persistent of them was that this was a field-day; that presently the 'Cease Fire' would sound, and we should march back to camp and the canteen.

Powell reached the top of a rise where he found himself with a number of men from mixed units. As they lay there, the Turks spotted them and shells landed with increasing accuracy, while snipers, one of whom Powell glanced at momentarily, opened fire. Then came a crash.

Something hit me with stunning force on the head. I believed that I was killed, and my thought was: 'Well, that's the end of it!' I had no fear. In the very presence of death there is no room for fear, no room for any emotion.

Then I realised that I was not dead; and I became at the same time aware of a great pain in my right wrist. I forgot all about my head wound; the pain in my wrist absorbed me. I lifted my arm. And the pain increased to agony. The hand hung like the end of a broken stick; it was almost severed. The corporal rummaged for my field dressings. When the wound had been roughly dressed, the colonel said I had better get back to the lines, and pointed out my route to me …

I was in a dip between the little hill and the rise we had crossed when I heard shouts of 'Unfix your bayonet!' The sun was shining, and the glittering bayonet made me a mark; and no doubt the men behind me saw that I was drawing fire. But with one hand I could not unfix my bayonet as I ran; to stop would have been suicidal; and the idea of dropping my rifle never entered my head …

I had to cross a comparatively level expanse. I have said that the air sang with bullets as the colonel and I went forward; I can find no word to express what the fire was like now. It appeared to come from every direction

Private Sydney Powell, 4th Battalion AIF

but that I was taking. I could no more than walk, and I could not crouch or I should have fallen. A bullet creased the bridge of my nose, and another banged on my trenching tool. My haversack was shot through and my hat knocked off again. This time I let it lie. I was not concerned with hats. But I still held on to my rifle.

I had one idea in my mind: to reach a dressing station. I was in such excruciating agony that I hardly considered my poor chance of reaching anywhere. The whanging, wailing devil's orchestra became a conglomerate of sound and nothing more; it failed to penetrate to my fear-consciousness. Its intensity increased, as the roar of a mob dies down into the sound of single voices. I heard bullets. In front of me I saw trenches and men. Men standing, walking about, walking up to the trenches. As I came nearer to them I recognised men of my own company. They were on rising ground, which put this part of the field out of the fire zone.

The machine-gun officer, my platoon sergeant and several others spoke to me, and I passed on. I had picked up the lie of the land and I knew the way. It did not occur to me then to wonder why my company was back, and my colonel and his second-in-command still out there: but from this and the fact that the rest of the battalion was retiring or had already retired, you can judge how this stunt had been conducted.

The losses among the 4th Battalion had been heavy, a quarter of the battalion's men, according to Powell. He reached Anzac Cove and was fortunate to be swiftly removed from the Peninsula: his short war was over. The Australians were paying dearly for experience. 'But in this first couple of days they had proved two things conclusively: that they could fight and that they could take punishment. Of the cunning and skill they were later to show, they had given scarcely a sign.' Powell acknowledged with evident sadness that the Colonel, Onslow Thompson, never regained 'our lines'. Thompson was killed during his battalion's withdrawal. His body was not recovered until men digging a trench found it and brought him back for burial two weeks later.

Midshipman Eric Bush, Royal Navy, HMS *Bacchante*

It is 10 p.m., but we need not worry any more about our fatigue. We have our three boats in tow and are steaming back to the ship. We can see the

Bacchante ahead of us. She is completely darkened but makes a perfect silhouette against the night sky.

I am lucky. Lieutenant Tom Phillips has lent me his cabin. It is on the upper deck just by the quartermaster's lobby. As I go in, I notice the time; it is midnight. We have been on our legs for seventy-two hours. No wonder we feel weary. My gear has been put out for me and some hot water, too, but I'm too tired to wash, so tip the water away and close the basin.

I cannot sleep for the moment. My mind is too full of thoughts. Visions come back to me of Anzacs cheering and charging up the beach. I see wounded coming out of the water and crawling to safety. I hear the noise of rifle and machine-gun fire and the occasional crump of a heavier shell. I see bronzed faces of soldiers all around us.

I wake up to find that it is still quite dark and it takes me a minute or two to remember where I am. I hear voices, so get down off my bunk and go over to the cabin door to investigate. I await my opportunity and sing out, 'Quartermaster, what's the time, please?' The talking stops, and a sailor appears, smiling. 'It's close on midnight, Mr Bush,' he says.

It is my appearance, I wonder, which amuses him? I must look a sight. No, of course it isn't, I see what's happened. I've slept the clock around.

Midshipman Eric Bush was awarded the Distinguished Service Cross for his work during the landings. He is the youngest-ever recipient, aged 15.

·

At this time the weather had improved, but we were living in a good deal of discomfort. We were not yet properly supplied with stores, the water was brackish, occasionally one had to shave in salt water, and all one's ablutions had to be done on the beach, with the permission of the Turkish artillery.

The beach produced a profound impression on almost all of us, and has in some cases made the seaside distasteful for the rest of our lives. It was, when we first landed, I suppose, about 30 yards broad, and covered with shingle. Upon this narrow strip depended all our communications, landing and putting off, food and water, all came and went upon the beach – and the Turkish guns had got the exact range. Later, shelters were put up, but

Lieutenant Aubrey Herbert, Attd. New Zealand Infantry Brigade

life was still precarious, and the openness of the beach gave men a greater feeling of insecurity than they had in the trenches.

Our hair and eyes and mouths are full of dust and sand, and our nostrils of the smell of dead mules. There were also colonies of ants that kept in close touch with us, and our cigarettes gave out. Besides these trials, we had no news of the war or of the outer world.

Friday, 7 May. This morning a shell burst overhead, when I heard maniac peals of laughter and found the cook frying up, hit in the boot and his kitchen upset; he was laughing like a madman. It's a nuisance one has to sit in the shade in our dining place and not in the sun. They have got our exact range, and are pounding in one shell after another. A shell has just burst over our heads, and hit a lighter and set her on fire.

The mules, most admirable animals, had now begun to give a good deal of trouble, alive and dead. There were hundreds of them on the beach and in the gullies. Alive, they bit precisely and kicked accurately; dead, they were towed out to sea, but returned to us faithfully on the beach, making bathing unpleasant and cleanliness difficult. The dead mule was not only offensive to the army; he became a source of supreme irritation to the navy, as he floated on his back, with his legs sticking stiffly up in the air. These legs were constantly mistaken for the periscopes of submarines, causing excitement, exhaustive naval manoeuvres and sometimes recriminations.

Later that afternoon Aubrey Herbert made his way up Monash Valley to the most exposed position in the Anzac bridgehead, Quinn's Post, high up on Second Ridge, for 'special duties', as he called it. Quinn's Post, named after an officer, Major Hugh Quinn, was overlooked by the enemy and to be seen, even for a moment, meant probable death. 'Men passing the fork in Monash Valley,' wrote the official historian Charles Bean, 'used to glance at the place (as one of them said) as a man looks at a haunted house.' The Turks were as little as seven yards away, and constantly launched bombs across with only wire netting above the trenches to deflect them. The fighting was frequent. It was into this maelstrom that Herbert was sent. A linguist and fluent Turkish speaker, one of his jobs as liaison officer on General Birdwood's staff was to counter the common belief among Turkish soldiers that the Allies did not take prisoners. At one of the most dangerous places in the world, he would attempt to fraternise with the enemy.

I went up the slope to Quinn's Post, with an escort, running and taking cover, and panting up the very steep hill. It felt as if bullets rained, but the fact is that they came from three sides and have each got about five echoes. I got into the trench, and found [Major Hugh] Quinn, tall and open-faced, swearing like a trooper, much respected by his men. The trenches in Quinn's Post were narrow and low, full of exhausted men sleeping. I crawled over them and through tiny holes. There was the smell of death everywhere.

Lieutenant Aubrey Herbert, Attd. New Zealand Infantry Brigade

In conversations with the Turks across the trenches, I generally said the same thing: that we took prisoners and treated them well; that the essential quarrel was between us and the Germans and not between England and the Turks; that the Turks had been our friends in the Crimea; and I ended by quoting the Turkish proverb 'An old friend cannot be an enemy'.

Our lines were very close to the Turkish lines, and I was able to speak clearly with and without a megaphone, and the Turks were good enough to show some interest, and in that neighbourhood to keep quiet for a time. I got through my business quickly, and went back to the beach. It was then

Alive or dead, the mules gave a good deal of trouble. Carcasses were towed out to sea but often floated back in.

Overleaf: Anzac Cove: this bank-holiday appearance belied reality.

There was a smell of death everywhere: the terraces at Quinn's Post.

that the consequences of these blandishments developed, for the places from which I had spoken were made the object of a very heavy strafe, of which I had been the innocent cause, and for which others suffered. When I returned two days later to make another effort at exhortation, I heard a groan go up from the trench. 'Oh, Lord, here he comes again. Now for the bally bombs.'

The Anzacs were clinging on 'by their eyelids', as one soldier put it. Their main route of resupply through Shrapnel Valley leading to Monash Valley was overlooked, not everywhere, but the dual threats from snipers and machine-gun fire from the head of the valley ensured that the momentarily careless soldier was likely to be hit: the beaches behind were under speculative artillery fire around the clock. The survival of the small posts along Second Ridge ensured that the entire Anzac position remained viable – just – but nothing more. After the fighting of the first few days, four battalions of the Royal Naval Division were brought in to temporarily relieve 1st Australian Division. These men would be directly in the firing line when the Turks, bringing up reinforcements, launched their first significant effort to drive into the Allied positions. These night attacks failed. Birdwood ordered a response, and an assault by Anzac troops was made but this, too, failed, despite the support of a heavy bombardment. And then the Turks attacked again, but this attack, too, was repulsed. In the meantime, both sides strengthened their defences so as to ensure that the next attack, when it inevitably came, would be even less likely to succeed. A stalemate had occurred in a matter of a week, although this did not mean that men would now ride out the storm. Aggressive patrols were sent out to capture prisoners or to raid and attack enemy positions deemed too threatening to be allowed to remain.

One of the perennial weaknesses bedevilling the entire Anzac position was the lack of security. During the landings, but also in the weeks that followed, a number of senior officers became casualties, and that added to the overall sense of precariousness. On the second day, Private Powell had seen the divisional commander, Major General William Bridges, walking in Shrapnel Valley looking very 'ungeneral like'. Bridges was dressed in 'slacks and shirt and a plain cap', and carrying nothing but a haversack and field glasses. 'His height and the very plainness of his outfit made him a conspicuous figure.' He was also known for his disregard of danger, a trait too common among some officers. Many of these men were undoubtedly brave but they took unnecessary risks when their first duty was to remain fit, uninjured and in command of their men.

I walked with General Godley and Tabu Rhodes, his ADC, up the height to the plateau which was afterwards called Plugge's Plateau. The gullies and ravines were very steep, and covered with undergrowth. We found General Walker, General Birdwood's chief of the staff, on the ridge that bears his name. Bullets were whining about through the undergrowth, but were not doing much harm, though the shelling on the beach was serious … The Generals all behaved as if the whole thing was a tea-party. Their different staffs looked worried for their chiefs and themselves. Generals Godley and Walker were the most reckless, but General Birdwood also went out of his way to take risks.

Lieutenant Aubrey Herbert, Attd. New Zealand Infantry Brigade

Overleaf: Queueing for brackish water: the limited water supply was a perennial problem.

It was only a matter of time before a very senior officer was killed. On 15 May, Major General Bridges and a party of officers were making their way up Monash Valley. The men were met by Captain Horace Viney of the 3rd Light Horse Regiment, who impressed upon the General the necessity for caution at several points while walking up the gully, particularly where there were gaps in the barricades, and where Turkish snipers waited for the unobservant. 'I had noticed that General Bridges was becoming less and less inclined to dash across the gully at those places where it was necessary to do so. I think that he was of the opinion that I had exaggerated the danger.'

Major General Bridges was shot in the thigh by a Turkish sniper and seriously wounded. He lost a considerable amount of blood, and although his wound was dressed and he was taken aboard a hospital ship, he died three days later. He, like other officers, was dealing with one crisis after another, with incessant appeals for reinforcements being delivered to his headquarters. With his death, his division was robbed of an able and brave commanding officer.

Bridges was mortally wounded the day before the enemy received a huge fillip when a division of reinforcements reached the front line, giving them significant numerical superiority. On the heights of Second Ridge, the Anzac line could not afford to bend, let alone break, and the Turks knew that one massive assault could unlock the whole position, driving the Anzacs into the sea. A bombardment preceded an attack by a total of four Turkish divisions, ninety minutes before dawn on 19 May. The Anzacs had one advantage. They were aware from Royal Naval Air Service reconnaissance that the attack was imminent, and they had prepared. Private Paterson was in an outpost when he heard a murmuring and rustling just ahead of him.

Private Walter Paterson, 11th Battalion, AIF

I woke up my mates and we got ready. Presently, about fifty yards in front over a sky line I saw moving figures coming towards me. We sent back word to the firing line … In another minute a form rose up out of the low scrub about fifteen yards in front of me and started giving orders. I had him covered as he rose and although pretty nervy I do not think I missed. It seemed as if my shot was the signal, for immediately the machine guns opened with a roar and with another roar the Turks rushed forward. We darted back to our lines and got in just as they came up in dense masses about fifty yards behind.

The Turks were mown down in their thousands right along Second Ridge. Turkish officers exhorted their men to greater efforts, with bugles blowing and shouts of 'Allah, Allah'. Every available Australian machine gun and rifle was trained on the enemy. Anzac gunners were firing on pre-prepared lines and only had to open and close the breech, as one shell followed another. The risk was that the sheer weight of numbers would eventually tell, and that critically important posts such as Quinn's and Courtney's would be overrun, but even when some Turkish infantry got into Courtney's they were assailed by the extraordinary efforts of one man, Acting Lance Corporal Albert Jacka, who, with the diversionary help of others, outflanked, attacked and overwhelmed the Turks. Jacka was awarded the Victoria Cross.

The Turkish attacks failed comprehensively, so that by dawn the principal fighting was over. The Turks lost an estimated 10,000 men, killed, wounded and prisoners. The Australian firepower was such that it had proved impossible for the Turks to cross the open ground without severe losses, while the undulating, winding front line had enabled the Australians to help one another with flanking fire. The Australian positions had appeared vulnerable, but they were, in fact, nigh impregnable if the men in defence were prepared.

Turkish prisoners await evacuation from the beach.

Private Ken Hamilton, 5th Australian Light Horse, takes aim as Private Allan Duke stares at the camera.

The Turkish dead and wounded lay everywhere, even on the Australian parapets. Coupled with the dead of the previous weeks, the vile, putrid smell became unbearable and a tentative offer of a ceasefire was made to the Turks, negotiations for which were accepted. Aubrey Herbert was called upon once more. 'Rightly or wrongly,' wrote Herbert, 'we thought that GHQ, living on its perfumed island, did not consider how great was the abomination of life upon the cramped and stinking battlefield.' General Birdwood sent Herbert to Imbros to receive official sanction. He returned to discover that talks were already under way. During the negotiations, Herbert would be used as a hostage while the Turks sent a representative to agree a ceasefire. Herbert was 'exchanged' for a Turkish officer, Kemal Bey. Before Kemal Bey was taken behind the lines he was blindfolded in order that he did not see the Anzac positions or the paucity of barbed wire. This caused some amusement, as the Turkish officer was helped to lift his legs 'enormously high' into the empty air as though he were crossing thick belts of barbed wire. Aubrey Herbert was also blindfolded before he set off into Turkish lines.

Lieutenant Aubrey Herbert, Attd. New Zealand Infantry Brigade

I mounted a horse and rode off with Sahib Bey. We went along by the sea for some time, for I could hear the waves. Then we went round and round – to puzzle me, I suppose – and ended up in a tent in a grove of olives, where they took the handkerchief off, and Sahib Bey said: 'This is the beginning of a lifelong friendship.'

We had cheese and tea and coffee, Sahib Bey offering to eat first to show me that it was all right, which I said was nonsense. He said: 'It may not be political economy, but there are some great advantages in war. It's very comfortable when there are no exports, because it means that all the things stay at home and are very cheap.' He tried to impress me with their wellbeing. He said he hated all politicians and had sworn never to read the papers. The Turks had come sadly into the war against us, otherwise gladly. They wanted to regain the prestige that they had lost in the Balkans … He said, after I had talked to him: 'There are many of us who think like you, but we must obey. We know that you are just and that Moslems thrive under you, but you have made cruel mistakes by us, the taking of those two ships and the way in which they were taken.' He asked me a few questions, which I put aside.

An armistice would last from 7.30 a.m. to 4.30 p.m. Each side would provide working parties of no more than 200 men who would undertake the job of collecting the bloated, blackening corpses, placing them by nationality in a line so as to be handed over to the opposing side. The men would be unarmed and would go forward with water, shovels and stretchers. A dividing line was marked out and maintained by white flag-bearers. All weapons would be collected and handed over. So as to avoid the possibility of misinterpretation of intentions, recovered rifles would be carried on stretchers. Neither side would be allowed to undertake any improvements to their lines while the treaty was in force. The Australians unfortunate enough to be chosen for the task were ordered to shave and tidy themselves up so as to impress the enemy by their appearance. No one remained unaffected by the sights and smells, and many men retched throughout the job.

Home, sweet home: dugout life on Gallipoli.

Lieutenant Aubrey Herbert, Attd New Zealand Infantry Brigade

I was afraid something might go wrong, but it went off all right. [Lieutenant Colonel Andrew] Skeen offered me breakfast but, like a fool, I refused. He put some creosote on my handkerchief. We were at the rendezvous on the beach at 6.30 [a.m.]. Heavy rain soaked us to the skin. At 7.30 we met the Turks, Miralai Izzedin, a pleasant, rather sharp, little man; Arif, the son of Achmet Pasha, who gave me a card, 'Sculpteur et Peintre', and 'Etudiant de Poésie'. I saw Sahib and had a few words with him, but he did not come with us. Fahreddin Bey came later. We walked from the sea and passed immediately up the hill, through a field of tall corn filled with poppies, then another cornfield; then the fearful smell of death began as we came upon

'The stench was unimaginable.' Anzac and Turkish troops temporarily halt the bloodshed to clear hundreds of dead during the 24 May truce.

scattered bodies. We mounted over a plateau and down through gullies filled with thyme, where there lay about 4,000 Turkish dead. It was indescribable. One was grateful for the rain and the grey sky. A Turkish Red Crescent man came and gave me some antiseptic wool with scent on it, and this they renewed frequently. There were two wounded crying in that multitude of silence. The Turks were distressed, and Skeen strained a point to let them send water to the first wounded man, who must have been a sniper crawling home. I walked over to the second, who lay with a high circle of dead that made a mound round him, and gave him a drink from my water-bottle, but Skeen called me to come on and I had to leave the bottle.

On 28 June, during an assault on Sniper's Ridge, Second Lieutenant Stanley Jordan (left, arm in sling) and a number of his men were captured. One was Private Daniel Creedon (right), a clerk from Mayborough, Queensland. During the attack, he was slightly wounded and trapped in no-man's-land. In a diary written during captivity, he recalled: 'I knew that someone was moving near me. I thought it was some of our lads, but on looking up I found that to my horror I was looking down three Turkish rifles.'

Creedon was taken with four other ranks, Privates John O'Callaghan, William Allen (kneeling centre), George King and Charles Matthews, to a dressing station in the Turkish lines. 'After our wounds had been attended to, we were placed on mules and sent to a General. On arriving here we were taken into the General's dugout and were again given cigarettes.' Creedon recalls that Jordan was asked a number of questions and the photograph was taken at this time.

Stanley Jordan was born in England and emigrated to Australia. He served with the 9th AIF and had been commissioned from the rank of sergeant days after landing. During his capture, Jordan received a slight flesh wound in the arm: King and Matthews were also wounded. In his diary, Creedon noted in detail his conversations with the other men, and was less than complimentary about his officer, accusing him of serious misconduct both during and after the attack. All men knew that they were not meant to give information that might be of help to the enemy: according to Creedon, Jordan was happy to answer all questions.

The questions that I remember which were asked him were these: Q. Where do you get your water from? A. We get some from the boats and some from the gullies. Q. How many men are there? A. About twenty thousand. Q. Are all your trenches covered? A. Some are covered and some are open. Q. What time do the men have their breakfast? A. Between six and seven o'clock. Q. There is a gun somewhere near your trenches on the right? A. There is one on the trenches and one— but C. Matthews interrupted and said they were everywhere. Lieut. Jordan got nettled at this and said that he was giving the information and did not want assistance. Lieut. Jordan then turned to the interpreter and said, "I will tell you everything after." No more questions were asked after this. But Lieut. Jordan started craving to the Turks for mercy saying, "Will you give me mercy and good treatment for myself and my men and I will tell you everything" – this was after they [the Turks] had told us they were sending us to Hospital.

Jordan had a comfortable time in an internment camp. In a letter he told his mother, 'I am living really well, but it is a lazy life. I study most of the day and play bridge or chess at night … The Turkish officials are exceedingly kind and courteous. For most of the time I was at their headquarters, and in Constantinople I was treated more like a guest than a prisoner.'

Jordan survived his captivity and was repatriated in November 1918. To the men captured with him, fate was not nearly so kind. Private William Allen died of dysentery, malaria and consumption in December 1916. Private John O'Callaghan died of typhoid in January 1917, as did Private Daniel Creedon the following month. Private George King died of liver failure in August 1918. Only Private Charles Matthews survived. No action was taken against Jordan after the war.

Later a Turk gave it back to me. The Turkish captain with me said: 'At this spectacle even the most gentle must feel savage, and the most savage must weep.' The dead fill acres of ground, mostly killed in the one big attack, but some recently. They fill the myrtle-grown gullies. One saw the result of machine-gun fire very clearly: entire companies annihilated – not wounded, but killed, their heads doubled under them with the impetus of their rush and both hands clasping their bayonets …

The line was not easy to settle. Neither side wanted to give its position or its trenches away. At the end Skeen agreed that the Turks had been fair. We had not been going very long when we had a message to say that the Turks were entrenching at Johnson's Jolly. Skeen had, however, just been there and seen that they were doing nothing at all. He left me at Quinn's Post, looking at the communication trench through which I had spoken to the Turks. Corpses and dead men blown to bits everywhere … A good deal of friction at first. The trenches were 10 to 15 yards apart. Each side was on the qui vive for treachery. In one gully the dead had got to be left unburied. It was impossible to bury them without one side seeing the position of the other …

When our people complained that the Turks were making loopholes, they invited me into their trench to look. Then the Turks said that we were stealing their rifles; this came from the dead land where we could not let them go. I went down, and when I got back, very hot, they took my word for it that we were not. There was some trouble because we were always crossing each other's lines. I talked to the Turks, one of whom pointed to the graves. 'That's politics,' he said.

Then he pointed to the dead bodies and said: 'That's diplomacy. God pity all of us poor soldiers.'

Throughout May and June the Anzacs repeatedly improved their lines. Trenches were deepened and linked up, while barricades were strengthened so that no one was required to run the gauntlet out in the open when moving from one place to another. Interconnecting fields of fire ensured that critical parts of the Anzac line were protected by the fire of another. Men learned the tricks of the trench trade, throwing Turkish bombs back with an astonishing agility. One soldier, having witnessed the lethal nature of firing from the parapet, developed a wooden frame enabling infantrymen to fire their rifles over the top without exposing themselves to fire.

Mining and counter-mining was undertaken and developed, sapping out towards enemy lines to frustrate Turkish attempts to detonate small mines by blowing up the enemy's galleries, or by the Anzacs detonating mines of their own under Turkish trenches. This constant effort to learn from experience ensured that the number of men killed or wounded through what was euphemistically called 'daily wastage' was reduced greatly. And when, at the end of July, the Turks once more attempted to launch a night attack at the Nek, it was comprehensively halted in its tracks.

A position of stalemate was hardly part of the original Allied script. In effect, the Turks were winning simply through battlefield inertia. Fighting, such as it was, was now merely to maintain an expensive status quo.

Such had been the fighting at Helles that the next day was left for consolidation rather than, as anticipated, rapid advance. At V Beach, the Turkish presence was still keenly felt. At 2 a.m. there had been an hour of vicious fighting in the dark before relative quiet was resumed. By the morning it was clear just how much effort the 29th Division had exerted. The first lines of Turkish trenches had been taken and pressure was still being exerted against Turkish troops in the village and the fort.

The flat, flower-spangled stretch of ground between the crest of the bank of sand on the beach and the line of yellow earth that betokened the first enemy trench was dotted with khaki figures lying in curiously symmetrical lines like corn cut with a scythe, and all terribly still. Within the trench itself we could see khaki caps, hardly visible through the high grass, and we knew that the second step had been taken. At one place, where the trench ran more at an angle to the shore, close under the wall of the village, we saw that it was almost choked with figures of men, a huddle of khaki and blue-grey amidst which bayonet blades gleamed dully, but all dead still. And then we noticed that all the faces we could see there were waxen coloured in contrast to the pink flesh tones that showed farther along the trench under the brown caps that moved sometimes; and then we understood. And after that, whenever we saw a khaki figure half hidden amidst the flowers and

Petty Officer David Fyffe, No. 3 Armoured Car Squadron, RNAS, SS *River Clyde*

long grass, we tried to see the face, because only thus could we distinguish between the quick and the dead, a uniform stillness, made necessary by the lynx-eyed snipers, making that the only method of recognition.

Soon after daybreak the advance began. Parties of men, creeping slowly in single file through the long grass, began to stream up from the sand toward the first houses of the village. Gaining the shelter of the outermost walls, they stole cautiously, rifle at the ready, alertness in the pose of every limb, up into the village until they disappeared round corners or through the huge holes that gaped in almost every wall. At first there seemed little resistance but a few minutes after the first of the parties had disappeared amid the tumbled ruins, rifles began to crack spasmodically in little gusts and outbreaks of sound, while at the entrance to the main street we saw a machine-gun section, squatting low in the grass, firing briskly at some mark farther up the street which we could not see.

Opposite: The destruction of Sedd el Bahr village was remorseless. A Tommy looks at two unburied Turks.

From the *River Clyde* it was possible to see khaki figures rushing over the horizon and jumping into trenches, the occasional flash of the sun on a bayonet or the raising of a rifle butt. Sometimes a man was seen to fall. 'I saw an officer get up from among his crouching men and begin walking along the line, apparently giving orders,' wrote Fyffe. 'Then suddenly he turned half round and fell, and his body rolled down and down the steep smooth slope like a boulder that one casts over a hill, until it came to rest beside a tree.' As the fighting moved away, Fyffe was encouraged to see Turkish infantry running helter-skelter to the rear. Later that afternoon, he was ordered ashore with his machine guns to support ongoing operations.

Then began a scene of wild confusion, for we had been told that we would not leave the ship until the next day, and consequently nothing was ready. Men were digging like terriers in the heap of baggage in the hold searching for articles of kit and equipment that had in some mysterious way gone missing. However, especially in the service, necessity knows no law, and what one could not find of one's own stuff, one made up from someone else's, and that led to complications of a somewhat violent nature when the real owner turned up thirsting for vengeance. However, by one means

Petty Officer David Fyffe, No. 3 Armoured Car Squadron, RNAS, SS *River Clyde* or another, a complete kit was at last obtained and we stood on the deck hung about with the hundred and one things that the amateur campaigner begins by considering indispensable and ends by throwing away, and feeling very like animated Christmas trees. Then the heavy Maxim guns and all their weighty accessories were slung upon our already overburdened shoulders and we staggered down the narrow gangways, stopping every moment to disentangle ourselves as the various articles that stuck out all round us caught in the rope rails and supports. Crossing the barges was ghastly work, for they were strewn with the dead among and over which we had to pick our way. From boat to boat we scrambled until we reached the last one and, jumping into the water, began to wade ashore trying not to see the awful white faces that looked up at us through the water on every side.

After landing, and walking across a beach littered with abandoned rifles and pieces of kit, Fyffe made his way up the slope towards the village, now in British hands.

Petty Officer David Fyffe, No. 3 Armoured Car Squadron, RNAS, SS *River Clyde*

We took our toilsome way up through the poppies and the yellow and white marguerites that made the whole slope one blaze of colour, and up past the walls of the village toward the shoulder of the hill. Little driblets of wounded men on their way down to the beach kept passing us on the narrow path. Men who, supported by friends on either side, hopped slowly along trying to keep one foot, swathed in blood-stained bandages, off the ground and uttering strange words when their supporters stumbled over the stones. And sometimes there were bearer-parties with a loaded stretcher that they carried with scrupulous care, and when these silent parties passed, the little group of soldiers sitting chattering and smoking by the wayside ceased their talk and gazed with pitying eyes at the still figure that lay, half covered by his overcoat on the swaying stretcher.

At last we reached our post for the night in a little orchard at the head of the village, closed in behind by the walls of the houses, but open in front to the grassy slope and the pine wood some eight hundred yards distant into which disappeared the road that led away up the peninsula.

With the landing secured, the grim task of identifying and burying the dead was undertaken. Those killed the previous day were buried alongside those killed just hours earlier, including another senior officer, Lieutenant Colonel Charles Doughty-Wylie, who had shown outstanding initiative in leading the attack through the village, only to be shot and killed at the moment of victory. He was posthumously awarded the Victoria Cross.

We set about the awful task of identifying the dead and collecting the wounded. This I will pass over. All that afternoon and throughout Monday night we continued at the work. The large burial took place at midnight under a fearful shellfire and all the time bullets were coming down on us. The moon was shining brilliantly and in a large grave we placed over 300 officers and men. We had prayers and two naval ratings sounded 'The Last Post'. Colonel Doughty-Wylie was buried with Major Grimshaw [Royal Dublin Fusiliers] where they fell and a very impressive sight there was Colonel Williams shaking the dead men's hands before they were placed in the grave. Afterwards Captain Walford was buried close to where he fell near the bend of the village above the fort.

Surgeon Peter Kelly, Royal Army Medical Corps, Attd. RNAS

Clearing the battlefield of dead on V Beach the day after the landings.

Fyffe and the other machine-gunners mounted their guns on the far edge of the village, making loopholes through which they could fire. Behind them, men worked with picks and shovels, hacking into the ground or fortifying houses. On the beach the full paraphernalia requisite to a landing was being gathered, the most essential items being ammunition and water. Without piers on which to land, nothing would be easy.

The supply of drinking water to the beaches was extremely difficult. Large tanks were established on W Beach filled with distilled water pumped from a lighter, while more 'muddy' water was taken from a spring and pumped into a trough for the animals. For two days after landing, water distribution was problematic, being taken up to the troops in kerosene cans and ammunition boxes, after which springs were located and water drawn from these.

The supply of small arms ammunition was also under severe pressure, as expenditure was high. The only available transport was fifty pack ponies of the Mounted Artillery Brigade, which had been landed early on. The animals were worked around the clock carrying water and ammunition to the front line. Even this was not enough, and men from the beach parties were sent forward carrying supplies to conveniently sited dumps to which men from the firing line were sent down to collect what was required. This process of slow resupply restricted work on the beaches until 300 mules from the Zion Mule Corps were landed, and eased matters.

Captain Albert Mure, 1/5th Royal Scots, 29th Division

On the shore I found a very tired-looking assistant beachmaster. He seemed 'all in', but he directed me alertly enough where to go and what to do. Nothing in all my brief but vigorous soldiering has impressed me more than the miraculous way in which men who look completely finished can and do go on, not only doggedly (that one expects, of course, until they drop), but vigorously and alertly.

I remarked to the assistant beachmaster, 'You seem to have had a pretty thick time.' He answered not a word. He only looked at me. It was enough. I shall remember that look while I live. There were words, and more than words, in his eyes. They seemed to say, 'I'd far rather suffer the tortures of the damned than go through that again.' I turned and went away quietly, rather sheepishly, I suspect, back over to the lighters to my pinnace to give the necessary orders, thinking hard the while. One does a good deal of vivid thinking in one's first days of actual warfare. As time goes on, one's senses get blunted for the time being; but it all comes back sharply enough afterwards. It is Providence, I take it, that steps in and does the temporary blunting; otherwise mortal men could not carry on.

Fighting, actual personal encounter or contribution to battle, is but one part of soldiering. The tangible brief 'fight' is the concentration of months of indescribably arduous and intricate preparation and transport, which is quite another part of soldiering. Things are thought out at home, munitions are made, stores gathered and packed, men trained and equipped. The simply enormous transport work is accomplished, no matter at what cost, over what distance. The awful goal of the imminent carnage reached, literally ten thousand indispensable, nerve-racking, back-breaking tasks confront and fatigue the soldier, who must work his hard way through them to his hour of supreme trial … The soldier about to plunge into the cauldron of hell that is called 'battle', with death or torture its probable end, digs a trench that he knows may be his own grave, shoulders crates of jam, carries unmanageable burdens of wire and lead, harries distraught animals, washes clothes, runs here and there on sore, blistering feet, refreshes his nerves and his eyes on festering heaps of wounded and dead, and sleeps, if he sleeps, within sound of the guns that menace him as they slaughter the comrades that shared his breakfast – and – and then goes 'over the top' in his turn.

We had by this time made considerable advance both inroad on the Peninsula and in preparation of all sorts. What we had gained, how far we had penetrated in this deadly, warded place, I knew as yet but scantily and in disjointed scraps. News filtered through, of course, but I had little leisure to listen. But of what the men in my immediate charge were doing, and the splendid spirit in which they sweated on at a job as uninteresting as it was gigantic, and as perilous as any actual battle could be, I saw and knew all. Back and forth they waded all day long, from the beach to the small boats, from the boats to the shore, unloading, carrying, stacking up, sorting munitions, food, water, stores of every sort … All day long the men worked and carried and waded, walking over the dying and the dead when they had to. Have you ever walked over dead men, still warm and quivering?

Overleaf: Setting up camp: No. 3 Armoured Car Squadron's camp just north of Sedd el Bahr. Petty Officer David Fyffe was here.

After the feint at Kum Kale, French forces landed at V Beach where they were assigned the ground on the right of the British forces. Soon they were handed control of V Beach and Sedd el Bahr fort. The French positions were the worst held by Allied forces. Not only were they constantly assailed by gunfire from the Asiatic side of the Narrows, effectively shooting them in the back, but they were handed some of the worst terrain occupied in the campaign, the Kereves Dere Ravine, from which they failed to extricate themselves, through no fault of their own, for the remainder of the campaign. By late on 27 April, Allied forces had linked up and held ground from close to S Beach on the left to the Kereves Dere on the right. The Turks had withdrawn in places, allowing the British to push forward. At the deepest point the line was now two-and-a-half miles from Helles.

Petty Officer David Fyffe, No. 3 Armoured Car Squadron, RNAS, SS *River Clyde*

All that day, Tuesday, we worked on the beach unloading stores, and next day we set off again from the village towards the firing line, taking our guns, baggage, motorcycles, stores and indeed everything necessary to our existence as a fighting force. This time, however, we were saved the terribly hard work of carrying the Maxim guns, for these were loaded upon three mules which Lieutenant Coke was cute enough to 'pinch' from a French ammunition column which innocently bivouacked outside the garden of the house we were billeted in, in the village. By the aid of the lieutenant's dog, a few judiciously placed men all walking in a pre-arranged direction, and a conveniently situated hole in the garden wall, the dark deed was done. The Frenchmen, who luckily went forward towards the firing line half an hour afterwards, did not have time to investigate the matter very thoroughly (we carefully placed a sentry at the hole in the wall to prevent any awkward trespassing) and I suppose they are still marvelling over the mysterious disappearance of those mules. Still, those purloined animals contrived to get a good bit of their own back for in the space of a few days they put two men hors de combat and much disturbed a third by the use of their hoofs at unexpected moments. A mule is the biggest hypocrite in the animal kingdom. From a front view he will wear a look of the most absolute innocence, a very cherub of a mule, but get anywhere near his stern end and, like a bolt out of a clear sky, will come the most ferocious kick that ever destroyed a man's belief in animal morality.

Our camp was in rather an exposed position, being situated on the summit of an upstanding bluff rather less than a mile behind the firing line. Here on the grassy, tree-dotted plateau which commanded a view of the entire fighting area right forward to Achi Baba, we had stacked our stores, picketed our mules, dug shelter trenches and generally established an advanced base. That night was a noteworthy one, for it marked the arrival of the boxes of bacon for which we had been sighing during the past lean week of biscuit-and-jam rations and soon thirty billycans were frizzling gaily over as many smoky fires and all the camp was full of the sweet odour of that sumptuous repast. One never really appreciates bacon until one has lived on bully beef with earth sauce, and biscuits spread with the eternal 'plum and apple' jam and flies for a week. Therefore there was jubilation in the camp. Supper over, we set ourselves to the much-needed task of trying to make ourselves look a little less like a set of assorted tramps in poor condition.

With Allied forces strung out across the toe of the Peninsula, no more time would be lost before a move was made to take the Turkish village of Krithia, two miles away, before capturing a prominent hill, Achi Baba. Preparation for this attack was poor. The 29th Division would be recommitted to the fighting alongside the French. Little account was taken of the terrain that would have to be crossed or the strength of the Turkish forces. After the severe test of the first day, and the great disappointment it encapsulated, there was a desire to make good and drive the Turks back.

Yet more back-of-the-envelope planning doomed the attack to almost certain failure. Insufficient artillery had landed on the Peninsula to support the infantry going over the top. The plan relied on the infantry to wheel while in action, an incredibly difficult manoeuvre at the best of times, but doomed when they were thrown into confusion by the presence of three gullies that ran across the line of advance. The men were exhausted and disorientated, although the Turkish soldiers facing them were hardly less tired. Nevertheless, weakened defence still held an advantage over weakened attack. When the French on the right counter-attacked and retreated, the neighbouring 88th Brigade followed suit and much of the ground gained was quickly lost. A further 3,000 Allied casualties had been added to the already heavy tally of dead and wounded.

With the arrival of Turkish reserves, any opportunity to push beyond Krithia and threaten Achi Baba was gone. The Turks now had enough men to launch a counter-attack. General Otto Liman von Sanders, commanding Turkish forces, was concerned that a daytime attack would be heavily repulsed by the massed fire of Allied naval ships lying just off the Peninsula and so it was decided to attack at night. It was a terrifying spectacle as the Turks rushed forward. And they were massacred. Success, where it existed, was against the French on the right of the line. Here Turkish troops broke through, threatening Sedd el Bahr. It was touch and go for the French troops, but they held on until daylight when devastating naval firepower brought some relief, and the Turks retreated. The French regained the ground lost. Further limited attacks were made over the following nights, but Liman conceded that it would not be possible to push the Allies into the sea and he ordered his men to 'entrench themselves as close to the enemy as possible', reducing the threat from naval bombardment. His men would now defend Achi Baba ridge. The next move had been ceded to the Allies. It was no advantage.

X marks the spot: devoid of cover, the key objective of Achi Baba looks ominous, yet tantalisingly close.

In obedience to a message, I reported for orders at Brigade Headquarters, about three hundred yards to our left front. I took an orderly with me, and was attended by a sniper. It was very annoying to be fired at without replying. That tries your nerves and your temper, if you like. I had no time to hunt snipers now, so I consigned my attentive friend to perdition, and went about my business.

At headquarters I was introduced to the General, who said my regiment had done awfully well, and that, if my lot were as good as the others, we'd be a decided acquisition. I replied that they would do their best. Then the staff captain got hold of me, and very tactfully told me that I was going to be given an honourable but not very pleasant job, which would break the men in wonderfully. And it did.

The honourable task was burying the dead. I went back at once, of course, called the officers and non-coms together, broke the grim bit of news to them, reminded them how all-important it was to take identity discs and papers off the bodies before burying them, and we got to work … It was not pleasant work, but, in small things at least, war makes philosophers of us all. I have always had an unconquerable dislike of looking at a dead body 'laid out' at home. But on active service Providence, or whatever you like to call it, seems to step in and drug you. You grow callous. One is not indifferent, but one does not think overmuch of the solemnity. I do not say that your finer senses are really blunted, but you are given a job to do, and, no matter what it is, you just do it …

It was a beautiful day. I think it was the most intensely blue of all the vivid blue days I saw at Gallipoli. The air danced and shimmered as if full of infinitely small dust of blue diamonds. Butterflies swam through it; a thousand wildflowers perfumed it. Always there in the radiant days of the brief early summer our eyes saw great patches of bloom, except where they beheld only desolation, aridity, death, and blood. Achi Baba, ever the most prominent mark in the view, loomed like a lump of awkwardness in the near distance, so shapeless that its very ugliness was picturesque. The sun went down in glory and in rainbows of fire as we worked, and the guns a little farther inland – the never-ceasing guns – belched out a venomous requiem and a reiterated threat. And so – we buried our dead.

I had to go carefully through all the papers and other belongings that

Captain Albert Mure, 1/5th Royal Scots, 29th Division

had been taken off the bodies. I think that was about the saddest task; certainly it was the hardest thing I did in the Dardanelles. I seemed to be taking a beastly liberty with the dead, and at the same time with their living kindred too!

Writing home to the relatives you did not know was trying work. It was impossible to say something fresh and different to each, and it was loathsome to repeat the same forms of regret and appreciation until they became stereotyped, and to you, at least, appeared cold and artificial. The men had all done so splendidly. And there was so little to say! There was nothing worth saying that could be said. 'The War Office regrets' is formal and perfunctory, Heaven knows, but I rather think it is the kindest of all. But I at least found even harder than writing to the men's people the scrutinising and handling of their poor little belongings. They had treasured the oddest things often, and very often the most commonplace. And the odder the thing the dead man had cherished, or the more commonplace, the more uncomfortable I felt, the more intensely guilty of desecration. The contents of some of their pockets were enough to make a fellow-corpse laugh, and again and again they were very nearly enough to make one living fellow-Scot weep.

The man we had thought the biggest blackguard and the most hardened in the regiment had carried a baby's curl folded away in a tattered bit of silver paper. A private I had put down as ignorant and common, judging him I scarcely know from what – for I do not remember having heard him speak – had on him an unfinished letter of his own. It was especially well written, Greek e's, scrupulous punctuation, and its diction was almost distinguished. There were love letters that had come from Scotland, and two that would go there unfinished. An old-fashioned prayer, written out in a cramped, ignorant hand, was signed 'Mother,' and wrapped about three battered 'fags'. A child's first letter to 'Daddy', printed, crooked, ill-spelt, looked as if it had been carried for years. Scraps of newspapers – one containing a poem, one the report of a prizefight – a knot of blue ribbon, a small magnifying glass, a pack of cards, a mouth organ (of course), three exquisite butterflies carefully pressed in an old pocketbook, a woman's ring, a snow-white curl, a lace handkerchief, a paper of peppermints, and a score of still stranger things, which I will not catalogue lest any might by odd chance be recognised, and give pain – these were some of the mementos I had to sort, and, if possible, send back to the owner's home. Almost every pocket had a photograph; most of them had several. In a dozen pockets I found the pictured face of an old woman, a severe, indomitable old woman – if her picture reported her aright – but with tender eyes; unmistakably Scots, unmistakably 'Mother'.

It was desperate work. It choked me, and I don't mind who knows it … But my saddest find of all was a pocket in which there was – nothing! Had he lived quite alone? Had no one cared? Had he not even a memory to treasure in some poor tangible token? Had he been all his life as he died – quite, quite alone?

Among the death, Mure had still noticed the beauty of the Peninsula: the astonishing light and vivid colour, the wildflowers – marigolds, poppies, daisies – and the striking perfumes. He had noticed, too, the spring butterflies that fluttered everywhere. In May nature and wildlife were in abundance.

None of us had had any sleep but there was a slight lull in the bombardment and a message came along the line to say that any man who wished to have a little shuteye could lie in, fully equipped, leaving one man in ten to keep a lookout in case the enemy made any surprise attacks. I was a lookout, the next man being about 40 yards along the trench. I could see him but suddenly he disappeared and another movement caught my eye. My sight was very strong and I detected a snake crawling over our lads who were asleep. None of them were disturbed, being exhausted. The snake was getting closer and closer to me as I stood in the trench when within about ten feet of me it suddenly stopped, reared its head two or three feet and stared at me. I kept my eye on the snake's eyes and we just stared at each other. I waited for it to get within striking distance, then like a flash it sprang, not at me but up and over the trench. It was about eight to ten feet long and as big around as my arm. I jumped forward and struck at it with my entrenching tool, only to see my blow fall a few inches short of its tail and that was the last I saw of it.

Private Edward Marlow, 2nd Hampshire Regiment, 29th Division

In defending Achi Baba, the Turks had been reinforced not only with men but with eight Maxim machine guns, brought ashore by German sailors from the *Goeben*. In such a congested area as the Helles Peninsula, this was a major stimulus for the weary Turkish troops. Unaware of this development, Hamilton was keen to press again. He knew that the Turks, if permitted by Allied inactivity, could only strengthen their defences. Achi Baba remained tantalisingly out of reach. Hamilton sent for fresh troops, the 29th Indian Brigade and the inexperienced 42nd Territorial Division. The need to act now overrode the need for time to stand back, assess and plan properly.

Intelligence on enemy battery positions was poor, while the Allies still did not have enough guns ashore to support such an operation. The French would renew their attack on the right while the 29th Division, augmented by men of the Royal Naval Division, the Indian Brigade, a brigade from the 42nd Division and Australians from the 2nd Australian Brigade, would attack towards Krithia.

Once again, the attack was an unmitigated failure, compounded by further attacks the following day and the day after. The decision to continue was imposed by the need to press on, underpinned by the desire not to accept initial losses as wasted. It was the classic gambler doubling up on his losses in the hope of a change of fortune. But what was the alternative? The Allies had to advance and speed was imperative. Such a scenario played right into the hands of the defending Turks.

Below: A place of great beauty in spring and early summer, the battlefield is ablaze with wild flowers.

Private Charles Watkins, 6th Lancashire Fusiliers, 42nd Division

From the moment we set foot ashore we felt the strangeness and magnitude of the task. Unlike our brothers of the glorious 1st Battalion, we were not battle-trained. None of us had ever heard a shot fired in anger, much less been on the receiving end of a bursting shell. It was like landing a bunch of tough Boy Scouts on a battlefield. The heavy staccato of enemy machine-gun fire didn't sound a bit like the more ladylike cracks of the blank cartridges we had fired with such enthusiasm in our mock skirmishing in Egypt. But worst of all was the low raking fire of the shrapnel which tore holes in our ranks. There was consequently indescribable confusion, quite a lot of panic, and after the first shock we

did what we should have done in the first place – what we should have been told to do before landing – dodged for whatever shelter we could find in the lee of the low cliffs and crouching behind every stone and blade of grass. Looking back, I am astonished that none of us had been given the least guidance from higher authority of what to expect or what to do. Presumably we were just to land – and the rest was up to the Almighty to sort out. Matters weren't improved by the supporting guns of the ships firing too low. To be caught between enemy guns and your own is an experience that would unnerve the stoutest soldier. I have a vivid recollection of our Battalion Commander, Lord Rochdale, harassed and shaken – but not more shaken than I was – wondering how to tell the ships to lengthen their range. A rumbustious type of lord of the old school, this Lord Rochdale, whose full figure and florid complexion was already showing the strains of the Mediterranean heat. I was a lean rangy type of youth myself and the heat didn't bother me none. Eventually I found a battalion signaller and brought him along to our Battalion Commander. I often wonder if this pathetic little 'flag-waggler' ever managed to get his shaky message through to the ships, or was it just coincidence that the ships' guns mercifully lifted their sights soon after.

At this period it was very difficult to get the wounded away. The stretcher-bearers had already been pretty well knocked about, and it meant two effective soldiers' lives risked to each wounded man, in the endeavour to get them taken back. This entailed keeping the wounded till nightfall, when a few men could be spared. But this too was dangerous, for the Peninsula was a most peculiar place to walk about in at night – you never knew the minute you might go head over heels into a nullah [watercourse]. The place abounded in nullahs, cracks, and fissures.

Captain Albert Mure, 1/5th Royal Scots, 29th Division

All telephone communications with headquarters had been lost. There was no one to send back to re-establish communications, so Mure felt it was incumbent upon himself to find headquarters, for which he received permission from his commanding officer. As always, the terrain, confusing at the best of times, proved more than a match for Mure's sense of direction.

Captain Albert Mure, 1/5th Royal Scots, 29th Division

It was dark now. I took a rifle, and hopped off to the nullah, which was, I thought, about a hundred and fifty yards to our right rear. With my usual luck, the nightly fusillade and I started together. So I had to sprint lustily for about fifty yards, and then recline as flat as I could on the cold, cold ground and get my breath. Hopping is not a soldierly gait, but it was the only possible sprinting-gait in that nutmeg-grater of a place, all holes and spikes …

This was my first essay at running about in the dark. I had almost hopped my feet off, hop-hopping about the blessed peninsula, and I had grown a callus on my back (it's there yet – permanently, I think) by lying down suddenly and long on the flinty ridges of the sun-cracked earth when the bullets began to pelt; but I had done it by daylight, when I could see where I was hopping or flopping.

I did not enjoy myself a bit. The bullets were bouncing in and out of the ground all about me. Twice they scratched my boot, and I couldn't find the nullah. I was just about fed up with myself, the war, and everyone, when things took a poignant turn. A voice just in front of me shouted, 'Halt! Hands up!' I halted very slick. You usually do. But I didn't put up my hands. I wasn't long in doing so, though, when I discovered a well-pointed revolver about six inches from my stomach. My challenger proved to be an officer with whom I had come out. I had run in a semicircle, and had arrived back at the firing line, but away on our right, and at another regiment's sector.

I asked him if he could direct me to headquarters. He pointed to three lights out at sea, and told me to march on the centre one; so off I hopped once more, munching some biscuits I had commandeered, for I was infernally hungry by now. Hopping in the dark, and munching biscuits as I hopped. Not a very soldierly picture? I beg your pardon, that is just what it is. War is not all purple and plumes and stately, burnished dignity.

Meatyard's battalion had been in support. Now they were called forward to relieve the men coming out of the line.

Sergeant William Meatyard, Plymouth Battalion, RND

We advanced to relieve the front line. There were no communication trenches, and it was necessary to relieve the firing line under darkness. As we were nearing our destination, something alarmed the Turks, and they opened up a heavy rifle fire at the line we were about to relieve, and owing to their aim being high in the dark, we got it severely. We were ordered to lie down flat; this we did. As a precaution, I lay with the butt of my rifle in front of my forehead for luck.

It was a rotten suspense while we lay there, men being hit frequently and groaning, and not knowing exactly where we were. When it had eased up a bit we got going again, and in the darkness I fell in a trench, landing on something soft. I afterwards ascertained that I had landed on one of our own men who was taking a nap in the bottom of the trench, a 'rude awakening' for him.

Having reached the line we started to deepen the trenches and improve the cover before daylight came, bullets were spitting around us all the time but the casualties were few. This was our first touch of the firing line in this quarter, and it seemed rather a weird show to start off with, getting there as we did, and not knowing the exact formation of the front and the exact formation of the enemy's line, frogs croaking, wounded men out somewhere calling for help, Very lights in all directions, and also I heard a distinct bugle call 'Cease fire'.

The result of the operation had been failure, as my object remains unachieved. The fortifications and their machine guns were too scientific and too strongly held to be rushed, although I had every available man in today. Our troops have done all flesh and blood can do against semi-permanent works and they are not able to carry them. More and more munitions will be needed to do so. I fear that this is a very unpalatable conclusion, but I can see no way out of it.

General Sir Ian Hamilton, Headquarters, MEF

The 29th Division had been fought to a standstill. Survivors were exhausted beyond the comprehension of anyone who was not there. A fresh division was needed and Kitchener agreed to send the 52nd Division as reinforcements. But reinforce what? Failure, was the obvious answer. Meanwhile, the remnants of the 88th Brigade was withdrawn into 'rest', while an Australian and a New Zealand Brigade were sent to Helles in preparation for the second Battle of Krithia.

Overleaf: Forming up: the morning the 42nd Division arrived at Helles.

Captain Albert Mure, 1/5th Royal Scots, 29th Division

Good news was coming. It reached us at six that afternoon. We were to be relieved. Then the order was cancelled. That was too much. The men were just about played out. Every human creature has a breaking point. Even the steel nerve of a Titan can wear thin. They were still as game as could be, as game as they'd been from the first. But they had done enough – for a spell. Half of them, of those left to us, had had eighteen days and nights of fighting …

I had not had my boots off for twelve days, or my clothes. I thought that my shirt had grown into my flesh in more than one place, and I knew that every inch of my skin was riddled with bites. In the twelve days I had shaved twice, and had washed, in a quart or less of water, just three times. For the rest – I had merely shaken myself like a dog, and had longed for a dog's other methods of cleanliness.

'I shall never make a good soldier,' one of our subalterns said to me bitterly one day, a boy who had already done two of the bravest things that were done at the Dardanelles.

'If you're fishing for compliments, fish elsewhere,' I retorted.

'Compliments be blowed! I mean it. There are details of active service I never could assimilate, and can scarcely endure. To die for one's country is all very well, and simple enough if it comes along in your day's work. But to itch for your country, day in and night out, for three weeks on end – that takes the patriotism of a super-saint, and demands the hide of a rhinoceros.'

And I think he was right.

About eight o'clock glorious news came. A pink paper was delivered to the CO. 'The 5th Royal Scots will be relieved tomorrow morning by orders of the GOC.' Hooray! hooray! 'That can't be cancelled, can it?' 'I hope not, sir,' I said fervently. And I meant it. Further orders came saying where we were to rest, or, rather, be supposed to rest. Rest! It wasn't done in Gallipoli.

The cooks were sent off with a fatigue party that night, in order that breakfast might be ready on the battalion's arrival the next morning. It was my job to leave before the relieving, so at half past three in the morning I stepped off with an orderly. The dawn was just breaking. After the first half-mile, as it was fairly safe, I eased up and lit my pipe. I felt at peace with all the world, though all world was at war; all the world was at war, and I had cause to know that it was.

It was a lovely dawn. Everything felt inexpressibly fresh. The new day

Opposite: Above Lancashire Landing: men watch a fledging RNAS aeroplane return from a sortie over enemy lines.

was a bath. The birds were peeping and chirping. The frogs were croaking companionably. My orderly began to whistle 'Roy's Wife of Aldi-valloch'. And between the puffings of my pipe I began to hum. Out at sea the island of Imbros blinked and glistened, and it might have been the Arran hills, and we, my orderly and I, going a-maying on the west coast, so like was this to that. I have rarely been happier. I can recall no other hour so perfectly peaceful. 'There can be, I think, no other relief so complete, so satisfying to soul and to body, no other relief comparable to the reliefs from battle. We had come out of hell. But this was peace, perfect peace. We were famished, and we were going to eat abundant food in cleanliness and at leisure. We had been in deadly peril.

We were safe. I was vermin-ridden and sweat-stenched. As I walked I could feel the unclean moisture caked between my toes. My feet felt like morasses of mud. But I was going to rest and be clean. Best of all, I was going to have my fill of sleep – sleep secure, uncurtailed, uninterrupted.

It was nine that same morning when they woke me, saying that the

'Bass Pale Ale on Draught' and bombs, too. RNAS provided bombing and vital aerial reconnaissance support for ground forces.

battalion was in sight. I went to watch it coming, and the men as they came in. I was very much struck with their faces. Those who had been boys when we sailed into the Aegean were men now, adolescence scorched and destroyed in the heat of war, their young mouths set and stern from the strain of having gone through hell. Some of them I hardly recognised – and I had known them well, seen them daily. Their very being seemed changed utterly, their souls new forged, their faces forever seared …

We are beginning the third of our precious days of rest – I grudge every moment as it passes by. We are being treated well, having had little, having little to do beyond bathing in the sea, inspecting rifles, ammunition, and so on.

Second Lieutenant John Allen, 1st Essex Regiment, 29th Division

The bathing is perfect. We undress at a beach designated by a letter. The Red Cross camp runs down to it. Horse lines run along the beach – the animals are irritable through the sun; Greek islands, hilly and historic, rise out of the sea. And then you plunge into the sea and find the water infinitely fresh and cool. It is as good as Cornwall. And of course your surroundings are of intensely more interest. Officers and men continually pass you – some doing fatigues, some in equipment just off and just returning from the trenches. A jolly, big-nosed, lean priest told me the names of the islands. He ragged me for having a coloured silk handkerchief on active service. More awkward was another interview. I asked a subaltern I picked up on the road the way to the camp; when I saw the whole of him I realised he was not a subaltern but a general. He was a nice general, and forgave the casual way I had addressed him. Nobody stands on his dignity here. Every day one is more convinced that people are at their best …

I have never lost faith in human nature. Now I know, now I know I was right. I was looking through the reports of the characters of the men in my platoon. They were prepared in Mauritius, where the regiment was in August. The characters of the men are marked D, F, G, VG, E. There was no B. A soldier called Saunders is marked 'D' [Deficient] – I know better. I have seen him tending a wounded friend under fire. Let his character be judged by that.

All sides were exhausted and so undertook what soldiers do when not fighting: they used the time to reinforce positions. Communication trenches, much missed in the fighting during Second Krithia, were also begun and a sense of permanence was established, much as it was at the Anzac enclave to the north. Neither the British nor the Turks had enough artillery to make a critical difference to the campaign. The bombardments that became so devastating on the Western Front were, relatively speaking, pinpricks on Gallipoli – one torture at least that the men on the Peninsula were spared, though they were spared little else. The pressure of command on officers like Mure had been extraordinary. The death or injury of one officer had only redoubled the pressure on those who remained, as Mure ruefully acknowledged.

Captain Albert Mure, 1/5th Royal Scots, 29th Division

On coming back 'home' up the trench [one day] I met a stretcher coming down. An orderly who was walking in front told me it held Captain McLagan, the Acting CO, who had been hit in the leg by a sniper. He was quite cheery, and assured me he would be back soon. I met him a long time afterwards in Edinburgh, and he told me that all I had said to him was, 'Damn you!' – only that, in an angry tone – and had passed on indignantly. And probably it was true. I don't think I had felt sympathetic in the least. He could ill be spared. There never was a better leader.

And we needed our best at the Dardanelles. He was every inch a soldier, as full as he could be of pluck and resourcefulness. He received the DSO in the second award of honours. I saw red when I learned he was out of it even temporarily. We simply could not spare him, and for myself I was bitterly annoyed, because this made me OC Battalion, and that was just the last thing I wanted. I had quite enough to do, and more than enough to 'carry', without any additional responsibility. I am no more superior to ambition than other men are. To say that I have ever had an advance in rank without being greatly pleased would be ridiculous, and it would be grossly untrue. But my nerves were on edge just then, I was working under terrible pressure, and the constant crisis at Gallipoli was such that an older and far better soldier than I might, in sheer patriotism, have shrunk from unaccustomed authority, from new and terrible responsibilities. I loathed it at the time.

The fight for Krithia was not won and never would be. The First and Second battles for the village ushered in an impasse that for a few hundred yards either way would not be broken. Despite the best efforts of nature, the fighting was turning large tracts of land into a dust bowl. Trenches were criss-crossing the countryside, and tracks along which men and munitions moved were widening and scarring the land. Trees were cut down, horses and mules trampled the foliage. At the beaches, particularly at W Beach, the British were building a veritable port with quays along which everything needed for a campaign could be landed by a fleet of small boats. Yet it was hard for anyone close to the sea not to turn and gaze out on a beauty that belied the reality behind it and the smell that assailed their nostrils.

In the evenings we used to sit outside the dugout and gaze out to sea and watch the glorious sunsets. The calm sea, the cloudless sky and the glorious colours of the sunset, all so peaceful and so beautiful. Then we would say to each other, 'Surely there is no war'. Even the Turkish snipers had stopped sniping and the What! What! What! of the machine guns was silent. But though nature said 'Peace' man said 'War' and the silence would be broken by the distant report of Turks' [guns] in the olive plantation beyond Gaba Tepe. The whistle of the shell as it came through the air, then the explosion of the shrapnel and the patter of the bullets in the sea and on the lighters etc., and the scuttle for shelter of the naked bathers, all reminded us that we were soldiers and not artists.

Sergeant William Meatyard, Plymouth Battalion, RND

Turkish snipers rarely went off duty to appreciate a sunset, though.

Johnny arrived in our sector of the trench, bursting with eagerness and curiosity; wouldn't even wait to divest himself of his full pack but must needs stick his head over the parapet – 'I must take a look at these Turks'. Too late to hear the warning cry of one of our chaps, 'Ge down, tha silly young bugger, get down.' Before you could count three his forehead was neatly drilled. These Turkish snipers are terrific. Within 60 seconds of arriving in our trench – and Johnny now NON EST.'

Private Charles Watkins, 6th Lancashire Fusiliers, 42nd Division

Turkish snipers were typically fearless men who could remain hidden in crevices or thick bush to carry on shooting, even when trapped behind Allied lines. Few, if caught, were taken alive. And very few were as poor a shot as one sniper recalled by Colonel Forman.

Lieutenant Colonel Douglas Forman, 15th Brigade Royal Horse Artillery

In a snug valley between high banks a limpid stream ran from North to South, and roughly speaking was the line of fire of the Battery, the left gun of which was within a few paces of the left bank of the stream. Here and there from the water's edge grew alders and dwarf oaks, some of great age. And in the hollow stem of one of these veterans a Turkish sniper, passed over by the British advance, carried on his nefarious trade for days, entirely unsuspected by the cheery personnel of the Battery, who lived and slept beside their guns not twenty yards (in some cases) from his hiding place.

The Turk who, to give him his due, must have been a stout fellow, had a silencer fitted to his rifle, and his equipment consisted of bread and ammunition. Luckily he could only fire due south away from the Battery, and what is more he seems to have been an indifferent shot, as the number of people hit by day anywhere about 200 yards behind the Battery was negligible.

After things had settled down a bit, a bathing pool was made in the stream by the gunners and funnily enough it was in full view of our friend in his old tree. But his loophole was so sited that he could not fire down to the water at that point or even on to the bank just above the pool.

One of the battalions of the 42nd Division bivouacked in the open about a couple of hundred yards in rear of the Battery. Here was our friend's chance as the place was soon alive with infantrymen getting ready for breakfast. Several were killed and wounded and it really looked as if somebody in the Battery were the culprit. An indignant infantry officer came to the Battery end of the telephone and a heated altercation ensued between him and the Battery Commander in the Observation Post.

A general 'hunt the slipper' was soon in full blast and words will not describe the astonishment of these gunners when the sniper was dragged out of his hollow tree and summarily executed before their eyes.

Given the nature of the fighting, men often appeared casually indifferent to the sights surrounding them. 'I have seen men in the trenches making a fire and cooking their bacon close to the corpse of a comrade who had "gone west" not a yard away, not an hour before, and who had shared their last meal with them,' wrote Mure. No one would survive by maintaining civilian sensitivities to the suffering of others, especially those who were new or unknown. The sniping of 'Johnny', minutes after he'd entered for the first time the front-line trench, was a case in point. Black humour was often the only saving grace.

It must have been a good twenty minutes before we'd stamped Johnny firmly down in the trench floor beneath our feet. Even our platoon officer wouldn't have the job of consoling the boy's mother – he never saw the lad. Best leave it to the War Office telegram – they're marvellously non-committal.

Private Charles Watkins, 6th Lancashire Fusiliers, 42nd Division

A few minutes after we'd disposed of Johnny and shared out what precious fags he had left in his fag case, sorrowfully rifled his pockets for mementos of his short life on this earth – things like an odd photo or two, one or two letters, an illuminated penknife inscribed 'present from Blackpool' and handed these things in to our platoon sergeant – a few minutes after we'd done all this and made our usual comment about the shortness of life these days, one of Johnny's old pals from back home, one of the original gang, came seeking him. 'They tell me Johnny's here.' He was excited and bursting with eagerness at the prospect of meeting his old buddy again. There was an uncomfortable silence.

'Did tha know 'im well, lad?' asked the sergeant.

'Did ah know 'im well? Why! We was "piecers-up" together at t' Sparth Mill, Johnny and me.'

The sergeant didn't reply, but half turned his back, whistling shrilly, and fussing and fidgeting aimlessly with the bits of his kit laid out on the firing step – like a man searching for something he might have mislaid. It was one of those, 'Oh blimey, what happens now?' sort of situations, all of us feeling hellish uncomfortable, and the sergeant most of all.

But the seeker-after-Johnny persisted in his enquiries, in an eyeball-to-eyeball confrontation with the sergeant.

'Ah'm asking thee again, Sarge, where's Johnny?'

The sergeant temporised. 'Was 'e a pal o' thine?' he asked.

'Was 'e a pal o' mine? Was 'e a pal o' mine?' said the seeker-after-Johnny, impatiently. 'Didn't ah tell thee, Sarge, we was "piecers-up" together at t' Sparth Mill afore this lot. 'Appen we'll be going back to t' Sparth again too, after this lot's over.'

'Ay! Tha might, lad – tha might. But Johnny won't piece-up no more, ah'm thinking.'

'Wot tha mean, Sarge, won't piece-up no more?'

In some of life's more poignant moments the Lancastrian will often fold himself defensively in the grim witch's cloak of cruel humour. 'Well, lad, ye could say, like, as 'ow Johnny's got the sack.'

A dead Turkish sniper: his hide was located days after the landing, and close to the British camp at W Beach.

Not every man ceremoniously placed beneath a blanket on a stretcher was dead. In the 1st Royal Munster Fusiliers one private was found to have stolen a rum jar and had imbibed more than his normal rations, much more.

General Hunter-Weston, popularly known as 'Hunter Bunter', who was much given to dramatic attitudes, came round on an inspection of the trenches. The NCO in charge of his section, realising the man's condition and hearing that the General was even then on his way round, had the brilliant idea of having the man laid out on a stretcher with a blanket thrown over him. On seeing the stretcher and blanket, the General drew himself up to his full height and threw a magnificent salute, saying loudly 'Your General salutes the glorious dead'. To our consternation a voice from beneath the blanket said equally loudly 'What's the old bugger saying?' We managed to bustle Hunter Bunter round the next traverse on the plea that a sniper had it under observation, before any awkward questions could be asked.

Second Lieutenant Roy Laidlaw, 1st Royal Munster Fusiliers, 29th Division

I decided I was going to speak to the Quartermaster Major Cremen in his den on the bank of Krithia Nullah and see if I could get some extra food. The approach had to be carefully planned because the QM was a tough regular soldier and certainly wouldn't yield anything out of the store without the utmost persuasion. It was pretty well known that his soft spots were (1) commiseration about his wound he had received by being hit with the nose cap of a shrapnel shell on his arm, which wasn't bad enough to be evacuated from the Peninsula and (2) his love of cricket and visits to Old Trafford. One afternoon, I paid him a visit in his dugout and started the softening-up process. All seemed to go well and in half an hour I had got to the stage of asking for a little extra food, saying how hungry I was. 'Really, Horridge, are you so hungry?' and sent for the quartermaster sergeant. 'Mr Horridge says he is very hungry and I have told him that if he will bring a sandbag down here at one o'clock in the morning you will fill it for him.' This was great news and I went back to Cecil [a fellow officer] glowing with the excitement of a job well done. We were elated and at 4.30 we were sitting in our little hole in the ground thinking of food and how lovely it would be eating it. At five o'clock my Company Commander sent for all officers and gave us orders for a battle that was to start the next day. 'The Company will move up into the front line and the move will begin at 10 p.m. tonight.' That did it, no food … I must have been very dense because it wasn't until long afterwards I realised the joke. Of course Cremen, being the quartermaster, knew everything when I went to see him and knew I could never bring the

Lieutenant George Horridge, 1/5th Lancashire Fusiliers, 42nd Division

sandbag that night. We moved up that night in battle equipment and I slept on a muddy path on the way to the front line with my head on a stone for a pillow.

Getting food and ammunition up to the front line was a round-the-clock operation for which work one group of men, the Indian muleteers, were unsung heroes.

What blokes they were, these muleteers. The only ones who could do anything with these mules, these obstinate long-eared bastards on four legs. Little brown-skinned men from the hills of northern India, little brown men of frail physique, perpetually frightened eyes, but with guts of steel. Without these blokes many of us would have perished of hunger in the campaign, when the only means of getting food and ammunition to us in the front line was by means of pack-laden mules being led along the narrow treacherous paths cut out on the sides of the steep gullies … Day and night, these little men led their protesting mules, bringing supplies to us with clockwork regularity. Anxiously awaiting the life-saving food, rum and ammunition, we'd wait until we saw the first two or three of them appear, greet them joyfully on arrival with abuse and cusses. They'd grin delightedly, sup gratefully the hot tea we made for them, share our smokes and in broken English return in full our affectionate curses. But we well understood on another.

Not many men on the Peninsula did a lousier, more thankless and more dangerous job. Their only weapon: the rope that dangles from the mules' heads as they led charges along narrow paths. From these deadly dangerous narrow paths both mule and muleteer would occasionally hurl headlong to destruction into the sea of mud below. It's not a job that earns many VCs, in fact I doubt if any of them ever earned a medal at all.

Private Charles Watkins, 6th Lancashire Fusiliers, 42nd Division

Opposite above (caption taken from album): 'A very sad photograph. All but two of the men here were killed on Gallipoli.'

Opposite below (caption taken from album): '"Shrapnel Gully." Ten minutes after this photo was taken, all these fellows, and heaps more, were badly smashed by a burst of shrapnel.'

By the end of May, it was clear that precious little was going right at Gallipoli. Behind the tenuous bridgehead, established at such cost, the troops' lifeline relied on the ability of the navy to bombard the Turkish forces at short notice, helping in part to make up for the chronic shortage of field guns. The great warships that had sat offshore protected the troops psychologically, too: their presence was reassuring, though unfortunately not permanent.

Disaster struck at Anzac and Helles when two pre-Dreadnought battleships, the *Triumph* and *Majestic*, were sunk in quick succession by a German U-boat, with heavy loss of life. Such loss could not be sustained and the surviving battleships disappeared over the horizon, to be used only when specifically required. The lifeline would now be maintained by far smaller, shallow-draught Monitors.

Meanwhile, at home, a political storm had blown up over the failure of a short-lived British offensive at Neuve Chapelle. A shortage of ammunition was blamed for the failure to make headway, and this helped to bring down the Liberal government, which was replaced by a coalition. Unfortunately, political upheaval at home delayed an important decision whether to send more troops to Gallipoli, ensuring that three divisions requested by Hamilton for 'success' remained one division, the 52nd, which was already on its way. The pressure

The muleteers: Indian Mule Corps in Gully Ravine.

to reignite the campaign at Gallipoli was unrelenting. In discussion between Hamilton and his commander on the ground, Hunter-Weston, it became clear that Hamilton preferred to wait until the 52nd Division arrived. Hunter-Weston wanted to attack and was supported in this view by the arrival of a new French commander equally keen to renew the offensive. A Third Battle of Krithia was dreamed up. If successful, the operation might encourage Lord Kitchener to release more men to Hamilton. This was ironic, for, while the plan of attack was not without merit, it was flawed because success was incumbent from the very start upon the arrival of reinforcements.

A four-hour bombardment would be unleashed on enemy lines, followed by a pause to trick the enemy into manning the line ready to repulse an attack. The bombardment, aided by fire from the ships at sea, would then resume for a further half-hour. In support of the infantry, Rolls-Royce armoured cars would drive up the roads to Krithia, as two waves of infantry went over the top at midday. Two French divisions would attack on the right, while the 29th Division, the 42nd Division and the Royal Naval Division would go forward on a broad line between the French and the sea to the west.

The Allied bombardment was accurate, kicking up volumes of dust and obscuring the enemy lines. Turkish redoubts had been attacked before a general bombardment of the Turkish trenches. Yet no attempt was made to knock out the Turkish second lines or the gun batteries in the rear; there was simply not enough ammunition for such a sustained effort.

The battle started in a way that was pure joy to a war schizophrenic like me. I label myself thus – more in ignorance of the proper term than in self-deprecation. But what else could you call me? One part of me glorifying in the splendour of it all, and the other part … that little black goblin of fear and apprehension that every soldier keeps hidden at the bottom of his garden.

The crescent-shaped line of the light-grey painted ships of the fleet ceased their quiet languid basking in the sun. They'd been lying there still on this calm Mediterranean lake ever since the sun had dispersed the light mists and exposed them to view. Idle, lazy, painted ships, upon a painted ocean. They were so dead still, you'd think you were looking at a framed canvas on oils. But for the occasional wink and flash in the sunlight as the

Private Charles Watkins, 6th Lancashire Fusiliers, 42nd Division

ships' brass caught the sun's rays, it was like looking at a masterpiece by some naval artist.

Waiting for the bombardment to begin, we appraised this line of ships behind us. From our vantage point on the higher ground they lay there on the calm sea, like ships at anchor at a Naval Review. You sort of felt that something was missing. They should have been 'dressed over-all' – or whatever it is these naval blokes call it – y'know what I mean – strings of flags and bunting all over them from mast to mast, and the Royal Yacht steaming slowly along the line. And all the matelots hand-in-hand lining the rails, faces scrubbed clean, uniforms spotless, hat bands gleaming white, and the music of the ships' bands adding to the gaiety and splendour of the scene. And on the shore should be a joyous crowd of sightseers – glorying in the British navy.

On our own shore we had an equally appreciative crowd of sightseers, equally appreciative, albeit a mite apprehensive. Damn and blast those little black goblins at the bottom of the garden – spoiling what should have been a perfect day out. Sun shining brilliantly, sea sparkling and clear like a day at Blackpool. The brasswork on the ships continued to wink and blink in the sunlight. The pair of minesweepers continued their long leisurely crawl along the waters. As peaceful and as glorious a summer's day as you could wish to see. We should be reaching now for our bottles of pop and ginger beer, and bringing the sandwiches out, and waiting for the ice-cream man to come along – instead of taking sly sips of our rum ration to bloody well calm the nerves.

With a roar and a bang like the end of the world the big guns of the ships opened up and the shells screamed over our heads, sousing the enemy ground till the whole place shook like an earthquake. The light quick-firing guns of the smaller ships kept up a continuous firework display of flash and smoke as their lighter quick-firing guns roamed and searched the smaller enemy targets. Less frequently, the 15-inch guns of the flagship let off a broadside that rattled your very teeth.

Captain Albert Mure, 1/5th Royal Scots, 29th Division

The bombardment ceased as sharply as it had begun. The men rattled their bayonets and cheered. A yell for victory and for home went up from every throat there. Then the second spasm commenced. It was fast. It was furious.

Words pale before it. Memory sickens at it. It stopped, and up over the top went the first line. Evidently the Turk had been lying low, for now his machine guns grew very active; and a terrible stream of wounded came flowing back to us.

When the attack went in, there was considerable initial success. In front of the 29th Division, the Turkish first line of trenches was secured quickly, many of the enemy choosing to surrender or simply to turn and run. The advantage lay on this occasion with the attackers, who swarmed on to secure the second line of trenches. However, the seeds of failure were already being sown.

Below: Officers of the 1/5th Lancashire Fusiliers. Quartermaster Major Cremen is on the far right.

An armoured car came with them, spitting and puffing and lumbering along. Nothing so ugly or so awkward ever was seen outside of a zoo. The very amateur bridge that the engineers had tossed up for them was just

Captain Albert Mure, 1/5th Royal Scots, 29th Division

beside my 'phone. The flagman waved a bit of rag about three inches square, and the car made for it. She got on to the planks all right; then! – her off-hind wheel slipped over the side, and down she came on to the axle, and (incidentally) pretty well on to my head. Nothing could be done, so the naval officer in charge and the gunner climbed out. In getting out, the naval petty officer was seriously wounded.

The attack was not progressing quite up to time, but we were getting on in patches. Unfortunately the Turks were getting on in patches, too. At this point my position was about four hundred yards from a nasty looking trench of the enemy's, and they soon spotted our broken-down car. Then the fun began. A battery started to try to blow the car to blazes. They made a good start. What with this and machine-gun bullets jumping off the car at all angles, I was having a thin time. I cannot recall ever having had a thinner. To add to my trouble, my [telephone] wire was in too constant requisition. It was the only one working, and officers from other units were finding me out and wanting to use it every few minutes.

I had just written out two messages and given them to two orderlies. I felt restless, and got up, turned about aimlessly, and moved away some ten yards. That restlessness saved my life. At that moment a shell crashed into the trench and exploded precisely where I had been sitting. Frankly, it made me feel peculiar. I remember that I stumbled a bit as I walked on, thinking that if I had stayed where I was, or gone the other way, I should, by now, have been blown to little bits. I finished what I wanted to do (for my aimlessness had been but an instant's – we had no time for aimlessness then) – and went back to the trench. I met one of my orderlies, who, fortunately for him, had left immediately with the first message I had written. He had bits of shrapnel in his jaw, in his elbow, and in his back. I bound him up and packed him off. I got back into the trench, and saw what I had not seen before, for the smoke had cleared now. My other orderly lay dead, with my message still in his hand. His body and his head lay four or five feet apart. Two of my signallers were killed also, and mutilated so horribly that to describe their condition would be inexcusable. I stood for a moment and gazed at the wreckage – wreck of trench, wreck of 'phone, wreck of men, and then I sat dully down on the mud floor of the trench.

Opposite: A Rolls-Royce armoured car parked in a trench for protection. Their use during the battle for Krithia proved they were unsuitable in trench warfare.

The 42nd Division was on the right of Mure's men. These territorials had not excelled since arriving on the Peninsula. But, then, how could they? They were inexperienced and, naturally, entirely lacking in battlefield know-how. This was their first time over the top.

Private Charles Watkins, 6th Lancashire Fusiliers, 42nd Division

We brace ourselves. 'There can't be a bloody Turk alive after that lot,' one of the chaps said, in awe at the havoc and devastation in front of us. A perfectly natural mistake for any soldier to make, as we were to find out in a few minutes.

Myself, I wasn't detailed to go over the top this time. Our machine-gun section had been detailed to remain in the front line and cover the advance in a strictly restricted arc of fire. I can't say I was sorry. Any soldier who tells you he is sorry is either a psychiatric case – or just a plain bloody liar.

The guns of the ships ceased simultaneously and the momentary contrasting silence cut the air like a whiplash. This was the signal, and from our trench a sea of bayonets disappeared into the clouds of choking dust and smoke of no-man's-land. Instantaneous impressions register on the mind like a photograph, indelibly and accurately. This was the first time I was not to accompany my mates, and it gave me the opportunity to see my own self reflected in them. Desperation struggling with

Left: Turkish soldiers in the trenches.

Right: 'Johnny Turk is a doughty fighter.' Respect for the enemy was quickly gained.

Top: Preparing for battle: 1/6th Manchester Regiment walking up the Krithia Nullah towards their jumping-off point.
Bottom: Over the top: an extraordinary photograph taken at noon, showing the 1/6th Manchester Regiment racing across no-man's-land towards the Turkish trenches.

apprehension, apprehension giving way in some cases to stark terror, exultation lifting some of them above craven fear – a bit of all these things I saw in the faces of these chaps as a bit of myself in similar circumstances. But to a single man, every man-jack of them went over – many for the last time.

By the sheerest bad luck our machine-gun section was unable to give our lads even the slightest support in covering fire. Just when a stream of machine-gun bullets should have been making some of the enemy keep their heads down, our machine-gun team had been temporarily paralysed by a shell from one of the ships falling a bit short, just at the close of the bombardment. None of us received even so much as a scratch, but the proximity of the explosion was such that our bodies were numbed. Strain was such that we couldn't make our quivering bodies obey our wills – it was as if an anaesthetic had been pumped into our spines. It was a good three or four minutes before we were able to master our frail flesh and move our arms and legs again.

Private Ridley Sheldon, 1/6th Manchester Regiment, 42nd Division

I shall never forget the moment when we had to leave the shelter of the trenches. It is indeed terrible, the first step you take – right in the face of the most deadly fire, and to realise that any moment you may be shot down; but if you are not hit, then you seem to gather courage. And when you see on either side of you men like yourself, it inspires you with a determination to press forward. Away we went over the parapet with fixed bayonets – one line of us like the wind. But it was absolute murder, for men fell like corn before the sickle. I had not gone more than 20 yards beyond our first trench, about 60 yards in all, when I was shot through the left leg about five inches above the knee. At once I realised what had happened, for it seemed as though someone had taken a red-hot gimlet and suddenly thrust it right through my leg. I dropped immediately and could not go any further.

Opposite: A close shave: Sapper William Astley of the RND Engineers photographs his best pal, Sapper Kirkby, whose boot and sock were 'shot through' by shrapnel. Miraculously, Kirkby was uninjured.

The Manchesters advanced to a depth of nearly 1,200 yards and were close to the village of Krithia, but not close enough. The Lancashire Fusiliers had attacked and suffered relatively few casualties. The Naval Division on the Manchesters'

right was also doing well, but this was when reserves were needed and there were none available.

Further to the right, the French had been battered at the Kereves Dere and had made no progress whatsoever. This had the knock-on effect that the Turks were able to divert their attention to enfilading the men of the Royal Naval Division. The few reserves to hand might have been used to support the 42nd Division's progress in the centre, but instead they were used to reinforce failure on the right and on the far left, where an attack by the 29th Indian Brigade had similarly failed to penetrate Turkish positions. The Turks counter-attacked, pressing the RND back to their jumping-off trenches, enabling the enemy to put pressure on to the right flank of the 42nd Division until nightfall, when the survivors picked their way across no-man's-land to the first Turkish trench taken that day.

The next day the Turks attacked again, using the early-morning mist to hide their advance. They almost overwhelmed the depleted Manchesters, but not quite. On 6 June the Turks pressed again, across the line held by the 42nd Division, and at times it appeared that the entire line might be broken, but still the troops held on, ably supported by artillery and the arrival of the few reserves available to bolster the line.

As the British reinforced, so did the Turks. Lieutenant Ibrahim Naci left Istanbul with his regiment on 24 May and travelled in stages down the Gallipoli Peninsula to the front line, arriving in first days of June.

Lieutenant Ibrahim Naci, 3rd Battalion, 71st Regiment, 1st Ottoman Division

5 June: It was obvious that a major battle had been going on at Sedd el Bahr since yesterday because there was constant and endless artillery fire. Sedd el Bahr could be seen clearly from here. However, the distance was far and soldiers could not be distinguished …

At night, the battle became more intense. Due to the silence of the night, it could be well heard. Now there was infantry- and machine-gun fire. It went on like this until 11.00 a.m. Then it stopped. I guess this was the time of the attack. After two or three minutes it started again.

In front of Sedd el Bahr, the enemy had many troopships. Two of them were double-funnelled, huge armoured ships with a light ash-grey colour. I guess it was landing troops ….

7 June: We got ready to go to the front line. The major told us about

the holiness and importance of the mission, and how we had to fight the enemy …

We arrived at the trenches. There was a deadly silence. The captain's voice broke this cold quiet. He summoned the soldiers. Arrangements were made at 1.30 a.m. We had taken over the advanced line. Our captain also went there. The protection of the nation and the country was left to this young officer.

After half an hour, I went to examine the arrangements. I felt a sudden anxiety in my heart, which was stoic and careless just a while ago. Is this called fear? I suppose that this is the weight of the great responsibility put on my shoulders; difficult to carry out and necessary to impose a sacrifice. It was grinning at men from all corners like a traitor. With the darkness of the night every place seemed scary.

The crashing of the waves at the shore, a boat, reefs, which looked like humans or monsters, touches me deeply. Yet it was just a road near a rocky crag on which I was moving along. Falling down the cliff and smashing on the ground seemed so easy with just a slip of the foot. However, I did not stop or turn back because the mission was a matter of the country. I had so many people left behind; I had made a commitment for their protection … This wasn't the place to think about life!

Johnny Turk is a doughty fighter. The ground in front of us became littered with Turkish dead. We were all in. It had been an endless task in the daytime and at night a continuous shift of sentry duty on the fire-step – one hour on, one hour off, in turn, right through the night. So when we stumbled along the gully one night on our way to the beach on being relieved by fresh troops, we were exhausted. On our way we passed the troops relieving us – New Zealanders, just landed that day – full of starch, self-confident, brash, bronzed and healthy – not like us, wan and forlorn. One of our chaps called out as we passed, 'Give 'em hell, lads, show 'em what you can do'. They called back, cocksure and confident. 'Just wait till we get at 'em – nobody knows what we'll give 'em.' We relieved these New Zealanders in turn some ten days later. Chastened and quiet, they passed us glumly without a word.

Private Charles Watkins, 1/6th Lancashire Fusiliers, 42nd Division

Overleaf: RAMC stretcher-bearers from the South Eastern Mounted Brigade enter the Field Ambulance dressing station at Y Ravine.

Lieutenant Ibrahim
Naci, 3rd Battalion,
71st Regiment, 1st
Ottoman Division

In the afternoon we left our location to go to the disinfector. When we climbed up the slope parallel to the valley, some new graves took my attention. I moved forward and looked …

Now my heart is really shattered. Who knows how lovingly they had grown up; the bodies of these men just lying there, fed with the love and mercy of a determined mother and father. Life … Such great changes within one day. You see people who are at the peak of happiness a short while ago, swimming in the deepest phase of unfortunate disasters. A body that had been full of joy just a few hours ago becomes indifferent to the universe, to good fortune and to all his loved ones in a sad and tragic death. Who knows with what hope of return these bodies, dropped into the dark and decayed ground, went into battle.

Going into battle, fighting, combating, crushing, and destroying the cursed enemy, then getting wounded, receiving a medal, getting a promotion; he had all this in mind. Even death …

Ah! Even though he thought about death, he never thought that death would find him …

Now I am thinking. If I become a martyr, will they bury me just like this? Under some bold trees with pale leaves, and then leave me there. What about my loved ones that I left in Istanbul? What will happen to them? Ah! What will happen to my mother, my sister, and my relatives; all trembling and crying for me? … Being thrown into a pit excavated by some pickaxes on these desolate mountains, and then maybe some broken wooden planks, or maybe nothing at my head, or even being confined to getting crushed under the feet of animals …

Fortune … Will I have the same destiny? Or, will you allow me to rejoin my loved ones? Will this happen, oh Lord?

The battle was over, and as it petered out, the 52nd Division arrived. The high watermark of the British advance at Helles had been reached, though no one would have believed it. Krithia remained out of reach and Achi Baba a long-lost dream. The battle had been unmitigated hell for everyone and Captain Albert Mure had reached the end of his capacity to carry on.

The CO told me that I would get some dinner if I went down to the gully, and he kindly waited till I came back. I went to the gully, and I got some dinner; but I felt that there was something very wrong with me. I couldn't quite diagnose what it was. My spine seemed to be misplaced, and to be made of glue rather than of bone; yet I could walk all right. I went back at about half past seven, and started my usual evening's work. But I was listless. I could neither rest nor really work. Nothing interested me – nothing! At half past two I gave it up and lay down, but I couldn't sleep. What I did from four till about half past seven I have never been able to remember. Perhaps I shall some day, but I fancy not. I believe that those three or four hours of my life are dead, and for ever buried in the chalky loam of Gallipoli. At half past seven I struggled down to the gully for breakfast. It was torture to walk. It was torture to think. It was double torture to be.

Captain Albert Mure, 1/5th Royal Scots, 29th Division

I woke up at 9.30 in the morning. I was so tired because of the marches that lasted for days … I cannot get enough sleep.

I looked in the mirror. How much weight did I lose? My cheeks are hollowed, my eyes sunken into their sockets. Then a yellow ring around my eyes made me scared. God forbid!

Lieutenant Ibrahim Naci, 3rd Battalion, 71st Regiment, 1st Ottoman Division

Below: Lancashire Landing dugouts under construction. Note the growing pile of spent shell cases in the foreground.

I wrote a letter each to my older brother Fehmi and to Yakup. Since last night, the battle has become so violent. Sleeping is not an option because of the painful explosions of hundreds of cannons. A severe infantry fire continued all night long. The continuous fire of a machine gun from time to time makes itself known immediately. May God have mercy on us …

Captain Albert Mure, 1/5th Royal Scots, 29th Division

I remember chatting quite cheerfully with someone, I cannot recall with whom, as I began to eat, and then something suddenly snapped, and I collapsed into a sort of maudlin, weeping condition. I was all in. I felt that I was going silly, and that I must have a rest, if only for one day. I had been under fire for forty-two days. And during all that time I had had very little sleep, barely tasting it now and then, just enough of it to whet to stronger agony my appetite and need for it.

I did not require to tell the CO when I got back – how I did get back I do not remember; he saw at once what a plight I was in, and he packed me off immediately for three days' leave. And he gave me a note to the medical officer at the beach. I pulled myself together enough to arrange a few matters that I ought not to leave at loose ends, got my bag, and went off by myself, not wishing to see or speak to anyone.

And even now I'd rather not write of the little I remember of how I got to the beach. It was mine, my very own, and I'll keep it so. I roamed and groped about forlornly. I was dazed, and for the most part my memory had forsaken me. I remember laughing once or twice when I heard the guns go, pleased as a child. And why not? I was a child again, a stray child, alone in Gallipoli.

Lieutenant Ibrahim Naci, 3rd Battalion, 71st Regiment, 1st Ottoman Division

In the evening the major came. We sat down in front of the tent in our cloaks and coats. We talked. After having had dinner (zucchini, chickpeas and tripe soup), I sent for Hafiz to sing an ode. Now, you can hear odes, psalms everywhere. However, there were frightening sounds far away, as if they wanted to make fun of all this spiritedness and joy, this beautiful enthusiasm, to decrease its value to nothing.

The bullets resounding in the valleys, whistling through our skies, breaking the air with terrible noises, seemed like announcing to us the reality in the time of evening with its black shadows. Actually, was it not the truth? Some place beyond, there were so many people, Turkish men sacrificing their lives with the hit of each bullet. Were we not deceiving ourselves with these songs?

Ah! Nevertheless, these sounds create such an effect. Peeling scabs of wounded hearts, reviving the painful memories of unpleasant moments we want to forget.

My mind rebalanced itself partly after a time, but not my body. I hunted for the MO for whom the commanding officer had given me a chit; but I could not find him, and presently I lay down on my back, feeling absolutely helpless, and wondering peevishly if he'd find me. For two hours or more I never moved. Then I crawled back to the hospital tent. I crawled in and held out my note. An officer took it – not he to whom it was addressed – and, after a sharp glance at me, opened and read it. He directed me to another marquee. It was near enough, and I found it and lurched in. I was swaying now like a man very drunk. An officer got up quickly, and looked at me hard. I held out my note again. The officer in the other tent had written something on the envelope, but I had no curiosity as to what it was, and I hadn't glanced at it. And I believe that I could not have read then, not even very big print.

Captain Albert Mure, 1/5th Royal Scots, 29th Division

This officer never spoke, but just looked at me, wrote something on a ticket, and pinned it on my coat. Then he said regretfully that the place was full up – choked – and that I'd better rest up a bit, and come back at seven in the morning, and that then I'd be put on board a ship. I heard what he said, but it did not mean much to me. He had to tell me a second or a third time to go away until the next day, and then I did stagger out and off again. I remember distinctly that my feelings were hurt. I wanted a home. I desired to be coddled. And I was turned out, and very homeless.

Mure was fortunate to meet his battalion's acting quartermaster, who plied him with rum. In the morning Mure returned to the tent before going down to the beach for evacuation.

Captain Albert Mure, 1/5th Royal Scots, 29th Division

I went to the end of the pier and sat down, absolutely not caring one minute what became of me, and the next minute praying to God for a boat to take me off the awful place. And when you pray at the front, you pray fervently. No slack prayers go up from the firing line!

I was in a dirty mood now. I would do nothing for anyone. How long I sat on the pier I have no idea, but eventually I found myself on a pinnace. I don't remember how I got there, but probably the midshipman in charge had carried me. He was not half my size, or nearly half my age; but he was a dominant person. We scudded out to sea and soon we came alongside a tugboat. I boarded her willingly enough, and someone showed me my way down to a tiny cabin.

I sat down. And then it dawned on me that I actually was sitting on a cushioned seat. I laughed. Nearly, I wanted to cry. And for the moment I scarcely could believe it. I on a cushion! A carpet under my feet! I not in a trench. And where were the smells and the dead and the bullets? I actually was not in a trench! …

I felt the boat moving. Dulled and half dead as my senses were, my emotions were indescribable. My blood leapt in my tired veins, exultant that I had left Gallipoli; but my heart clove to the battalion – the tattered,

The wounded lie on Gully Beach awaiting evacuation.

battered remains of it, fighting and festering in the trenches, on the beach, across the nullahs. I felt a deserter …

I was pushed along to a doctor who was taking names and issuing brisk orders. I told him that he need not bother about my name, as I must get off at once, for I had only three days' leave, and feared it was nearly up. He smiled curtly, and informed me that I was not getting off until I got off at Alexandria. I began to expostulate. I was wretchedly upset. I insisted that there was nothing wrong with me, and that I must and would get off. He turned kind at that, and told me not to be ashamed of being a very ill man; that I was chewed up, body and soul; and that my cabin was 412. I really wasn't able to argue, so I went off to the cabin, and threw myself on my bunk. But I couldn't sleep – it was all so strange – and before long I got up again …

I lay late the next day. I felt indescribably ill, and I seemed to be losing my memory. In the afternoon I struggled up to have a look round. I could walk with more and more difficulty; but I got hold of a stick and hobbled about the deck. I can never forget that sight. It outtrenched the trenches. It was crueller than the firing line. Men were lying on stretchers all over the deck, just as they had been picked up after getting first aid. They were caked with mud, and with dirt that was worse than mud, and with blood. They had the growth of weeks on their sunken faces. Some were dying, and knew it. All were badly hurt, many maimed for life.

It was appalling tragedy. The great liner, beautifully appointed, was ploughing its way through a calm sea in bright sunshine, and with just a faint breeze to temper the heat. It was a boat fit for a queen's holiday. The scenery – ill as I was – thrilled me, and I was born and bred in the beauty of Scotland. It was a boat and a day and a scene for song and laughter, and high good spirits and friendliness. There was so much here to enjoy; but instead of the passengers at ease that she and the day and the place catered and called for, the boat lay low under a weight of bleeding, weltering men, over a thousand of them, humanity maimed and mutilated! Now they lay, pallid and bleeding, on the deck of a misery-packed steamer, going to Alexandria to die, or to have a dangling leg cut off, an aching wound probed and tortured, to be sick and strangled and intolerably thirsty from anaesthetics, to be patched up, if possible, and come back to the hell of battle, the purgatory of the trench.

Those who reached Alexandria alive were fortunate. Hovering between life and death, they lay packed on the decks, waiting for help. The medical facilities were inadequate to a degree that appeared scandalous to anyone who cared to look, and utterly shocked those who did. 'It was a triumph of mismanagement,' as one survivor noted.

Lieutenant Ibrahim Naci, 3rd Battalion, 71st Regiment, 1st Ottoman Division

Midnight: I woke up with the terrible resonance of bullets flying above us. The enemy's cruiser was firing. I went in front of the tent. While trembling with the sharp cold, I looked at these malicious and fierce bullets flying in the sky.

They were falling into the valley, into the muster line on our right. Sometimes they flew over us. Then they ceased. It lasted ten minutes. The one last night had lasted five minutes …

It is 5.30 in the morning; I woke up with the order 'Take your gun!' Our lieutenant has seen an aeroplane coming and he wants us to fire at it. The aeroplane approached, but turned around and went to the right. This move continued for hours. I did not care and had my tea.

I opened my notebook with the grief of an idea that came to me yesterday. I am recording my painful memories. However, I do not know if my family will read these lines? Would my diary reach them?

Captain Albert Mure, 1/5th Royal Scots, 29th Division

In the entrance hall a nurse had a look at the tab on my coat, the tab the doctor had pinned there in Gallipoli. I had never even tried to see what it said, or whether it was in English or Red Cross hieroglyphics. But the nurse understood it, and bundled me off to a ward, and handed me over to another nurse, who ushered me into a cubicle where there already was another officer who seemed to be as silly as I was.

A glass of hot milk, and off I went to bed. But I could not even doze. My cubicle mate thrashed about and muttered to himself, and I could do nothing but lie very still and wonder what we were doing in Gallipoli. In a very keen and intimate sense I was in the Peninsula still. All the time I was in the hospital, every day of my voyage home, and for weeks after that, my spirit seemed to fret and chafe in the trenches, strive and sweat in the firing lines that I knew so well. You can carry a no-longer-fit soldier's body out of the firing-line, but not his soul; his spirit stays with his unit until the expedition is over …

Hour after hour I lay fretting and striving to recall each item of my Gallipoli weeks, and often failing miserably. But later, with returning health and strength, the memory of those livid weeks came slowly back, until it was as vivid as if it had been clearly printed in large black type on very white paper. And now it seems to me that Gallipoli was but yesterday. And often the street I'm on, in Edinburgh, in London, or in Paris, seems less real to me than the broken goat paths of Gallipoli.

7.00 a.m.: The enemy attacked us the whole night. Now we are leaving. I hope the best from Lord …

    11.00 a.m.: We went into battle. Millions of cannons and guns exploded … My first corporal has been wounded.

    Farewell.

    11.15 a.m. I. Naci.

Lieutenant Ibrahim Naci, 3rd Battalion, 71st Regiment, 1st Ottoman Division

Ibrahim Naci was killed hours later. He was twenty-one years old.

As Captain Mure left the Peninsula, the 52nd Division disembarked. This division of territorial Scotsmen was commanded by Major General Granville Egerton, at fifty-six a career soldier who had fought in the Afghan War of the 1870s and the Egyptian War of 1882. He was proud to take the division overseas, although his health was not good and was about to get much worse. He landed a few days after the rest of his division.

21 June: My first day on the Gallipoli Peninsula. We landed at one in the morning; thank goodness it was peaceful on the beach; the previous day they had 216 shells on it, damage done, one man killed and four wounded, a lot of tents riddled and a few stores destroyed. Corps Headquarters not far off got 116; thirty horses killed but no other lives lost. The battery which thus fires is located on the Asiatic shore. I dossed down on the sand and slept very indifferently till 5 a.m., when I wandered to General Hunter-Weston's Headquarters on the top of the cliff. He has a wonderful underground labyrinth of small rooms dug out and connected by passages;

Major General Granville Egerton, GOC 52nd (Lowland) Division

the rooms are roofed over; he was a real Good Samaritan and gave me his own bed to sleep on till 12, and a wash and a shave. I have felt, however, very seedy and full of indigestion.

Egerton's gratitude to Hunter-Weston was short-lived. Within days his division was to be thrown into the fighting and the results were to erode all his faith in his commanding officer's judgement to prosecute the campaign.

What was the alternative to the fruitless fighting at Gallipoli? Both sides had battered themselves into near-submission, but invariably the incentive to attack rested with the Allies. After further consideration, a decision was taken by the War Council, now renamed the Dardanelles Committee, to send out three more divisions to Gallipoli, the three that Hamilton had asked for a month before.

In an effort to bring these divisions speedily to Gallipoli, peacetime liners such as Cunard's RMS *Mauritania* and RMS *Aquitania* were requisitioned. They were able to carry a division of infantry between them, and, because of their speed, they could outpace U-boats.

Hamilton had fresh plans to attack, not at Helles but north of Anzac with a new landing, at Suvla Bay, and it was to these plans that he turned.

While he was waiting for the arrival of the reinforcements, the nature of the fighting at Helles altered. Out of necessity, small-scale bite-and-hold operations were undertaken, nibbling pieces out of the enemy line, pushing and pressing the Turks at all times. This change of tactic led to a small series of attacks in late June, some more successful than others: the French, for example, would have some success against Turkish strongpoints at the Kereves Dere, but to what end? There was little to be gained by such costly efforts, other than small tactical advantages. A week after the French assault, the British attacked up Gully Ravine in an effort to overrun a series of Turkish trenches. The 29th Division was called upon again. Close by, men belonging to the 52nd Division went into action for the first time. The fighting took place in the same way as before, only on a smaller scale. Initial success in one part of the line was counter-balanced by failure elsewhere and then the inevitable Turkish counter-attack.

The attack by the 29th Division had been supported by Egerton's 156th Brigade, which suffered more than 1,300 casualties. Among them were officers

Opposite: Mud: Gallipoli had its damp days. Twenty-one-year-old Private Gilbert Claridge (left), 1/6th Manchester Regiment, in the Helles trenches. Claridge survived the war.

whom the Major General could ill afford to lose. 'The Adjutant, Captain Branwell of the 8th Scottish Rifles [has been] killed; a fine young fellow, married and with children. I had a talk to him last night.' And then followed news that Brigadier General Scott-Moncrieff, a close friend, had been shot in the head while in the front line.

I am grieved about poor Scott-Moncrieff; he had done very well in South Africa, and was permanently rather lame from bad wounds at Spion Kop. He had finished soldiering and retired to live at a pretty little old family place, Fossaway, just at the entrance to the Devon Valley on the Ochill Hills in Fife. He took me over the house one day from Bridge of Allan. This war dragged him out and he will never see Fossaway again or be laid with his forefathers.

Major General Granville Egerton, GOC 52nd (Lowland) Division

Scott-Moncrieff's body could not be recovered. A year older than Egerton, he had soldiered all his life, serving as early as the Zulu War of 1879–80. His body was among thousands lying in no-man's-land. Appeals for a temporary truce, similar to the one in May, were turned down by the British. The dead would be left to putrefy.

The British had made some gains. Then the French attacked again, two days later, and they, too, had cause for fleeting satisfaction, but none of these attacks was going to get the Allies on to Achi Baba. When a joint British/French attack was launched on 12 July to consolidate the ground won, there was little to justify it other than to straighten the lines. The small gains were assimilated into the Allied bridgehead but at tremendous cost in men and munitions.

The fighting of the previous three weeks could not be justified, according to Major General Egerton, and his rising bitterness spilled over in his diary. He was in no doubt that the losses sustained in 156 Brigade during the fighting of 28/29 June were both futile and unnecessarily heinous, and higher, he sourly recorded, than those of the entire 29th Division. Of the fighting of the 12/13 July he was equally forthright.

Major General
Granville Egerton,
GOC 52nd
(Lowland) Division

It seems to me that the fighting of this battle was premature and at the actual moment worse than unnecessary – I submit that it was cruel and wasteful. The troops on the Peninsula were tired and worn out; there were only two Infantry Brigades, the 155th and the 157th, that had not been seriously engaged. It was well known to the higher command that large reinforcements were arriving from England and a grand attack was to be made at Suvla. Was it not therefore obvious that the exhausted garrison at Helles should be given a fortnight's respite and that the fresh attacks from that position should synchronise wth those at Suvla and Anzac? I contend that the battle of 12–13 July was due to a complete want of true appreciation of the situation. If the conception of the battle was wrong, the tactics of the action were far worse. The division of the attack by two brigades on a narrow front into two phases, no less than nine hours apart, was positively wicked.

*Opposite: Utterly
exhausted: under
the blazing sun,
soldiers take what
rest they can.*

*Overleaf: A makeshift
water trough at
Suvla: supplies were
transported from as
far as the Sweet
Water Canal in Egypt.*

5 Attempted Breakout

We were hampered, hindered and buggered about by old men.
They were relics of the Boer War, rejects from France and those
troops who survived were soon to realise it.

Anonymous

————

S ir Ian Hamilton was encouraged in his preparations for an August offensive
by the dispatch of five divisions: three – the 10th, 11th and 13th – belonging
to Kitchener's New Army, and two further territorial divisions, the 53rd and
54th. In purely numerical terms, this was an impressive addition to Hamilton's
force but, as he was to discover, these were not necessarily the best-trained
troops; the best divisions were kept back for the Western Front.

Still, there was no point in accepting these men unless they were going
to be used to force the issue in the Dardanelles. If the ultimate aim was still
to take the Kilid Bahr Plateau overlooking the Narrows, then it was possible to
go another way and not through Krithia and Achi Baba. Suvla Bay, north of
Anzac, was backed by a vast plain, greater than anywhere else on the southern
Peninsula. It would therefore be far easier to land and establish a force
unrestricted by steep hills, and deep valleys and gullies. A landing here would
widen the Anzac bridgehead, allowing Hamilton's extra divisions to secure the
ground before supporting an Anzac breakout on the right.

Intelligence suggested that there were few Turks in the immediate vicinity of
Suvla. If a landing could be made at the same time as a breakout from the Anzac
bridgehead, then perhaps speed of movement and weight of numbers could
open up objectives beyond reach at Helles. The Australian and New Zealand troops
could sweep up the ridges, it was hoped, all the way on to the Sari Bair Ridge,
to capture Koja Chemen Tepe and Chunuk Bair, the original goals of 25 April.

The detritus of war picked up close to a dressing station: a man from a RAMC Field
Ambulance displays some finds.

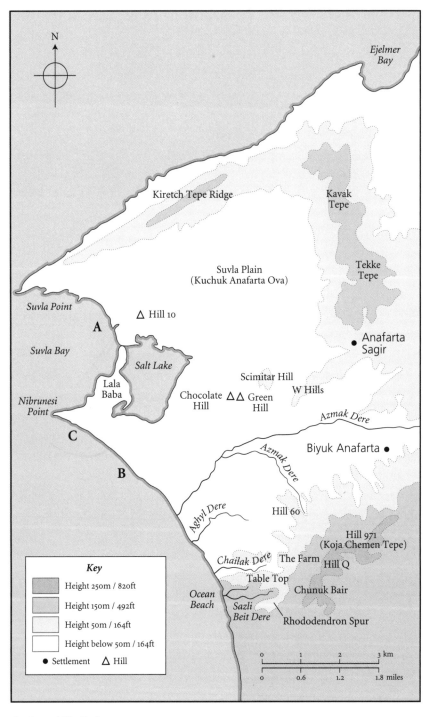

Suvla and North Anzac

It was proposed that the navy would land large numbers of men in new shallow-draught, armoured boats that could carry 500 men each and which had a ramp that dropped down to facilitate swift evacuation. The whole idea sounded plausible. However, it was vital that the Turks were not forewarned of the plan and so no proper reconnaissance of the beaches was undertaken at Suvla. The lack of Allied intelligence about where precisely the troops should disembark was a serious error of judgement.

Another lapse was in the selection of an officer to command the operation on the ground. Because Hamilton's command was of secondary importance to that of the Western Front, he was unable to procure a highly competent general for the task. He was in effect given the choice of one, Lieutenant General Frederick Stopford, aged sixty-one and another officer enjoying semi-retirement in England, where he was Lieutenant to the Tower of London. The seeds for failure were already being sown before anyone put a foot on the shore at Suvla.

General Birdwood would oversee the breakout from Anzac on 6 August. As the thrust of his troops' advance would be from the left flank of the bridgehead, so it would be worth launching a feint on the right, at Lone Pine on 400 Plateau. That evening, with Turkish forces distracted, an assault force, comprising a right and a left column, would move out, marching up North Beach to Fisherman's Hut and beyond before moving inland along the valleys. The Right Assaulting Column, comprising the New Zealand Infantry Brigade, would head up Rhododendron Ridge to attack Chunuk Bair, whilst the Left Assaulting Column, comprising the 4th Australian Brigade and an Indian brigade, would head for Hill 971 and Hill Q. Both objectives were to be captured by dawn. As the men advanced, an assault would also be made at the Nek and the Chessboard. The plan was complex enough on paper, but at night, in difficult terrain, it was asking far too much of often weakened and ill men to achieve such feats, and to a strict timetable.

When the method of attack was disclosed to me confidentially that afternoon, I gasped. It is to be remembered that Anzac is completely invested by the enemy; that no one has been able to reconnoitre the ground outside and that no one can absolutely guarantee the map. There are no villages and no inhabitants to help one, and the whole country seemed to be stiff with very sharp rocky cliffs, covered with thick scrub. I have a few ideas about

Major Cecil Allanson, 6th Gurkhas, 29th (Indian) Brigade

night marches, their great difficulty and the need of careful reconnaissance, but when I was told that we were to break through the opposing outpost line at 10 p.m. on the 6th, march along the sea coast for three miles then turn at right angles and attempt to get under this big ridge about two miles inland, by dawn, and covered from the sea by innumerable small hills and nullahs, I felt what one would have done to a subaltern at a promotion examination who made any such proposition. The more the plan was detailed as the time got nearer, the less I liked it, especially as in my own regiment there were four officers out of seven who had never done a night march in their lives. The one hope was that the scheme was so bold it might be successful.

As the Anzacs fought their way up the ridges to Chunuk Bair, the British were to land at Suvla Bay. They would seize the low heights of Lala Baba Hills and Hill 10 before using the advantage of speed and surprise to move on to the heights of Kiretch Tepe and Tekke Tepe. Turkish batteries near Chocolate and W Hills would be overrun. One other diversionary attack was planned. At Helles, the men would go over the top yet again to tie down Turkish forces. It was, without doubt, a thankless task asked of exhausted men. Overall success for the entire operation was predicated on everything working like clockwork. Yet everything in the campaign thus far militated against such granite-like optimism.

The plans were given to Stopford, and shortly afterwards a phalanx of staff officers went by sea to a point off Suvla Bay to be shown the lie of the land and to be told, much to their disbelief, that there were practically no Turkish trenches in the area.

Lieutenant Geoffrey Ryland, Royal Navy, HMS *Ark Royal*

Towards the end of July, the captain received orders to send me on board the destroyer *Arno* to point out to various Generals the salient features of the landscape north from Gaba Tepe, round Suvla Point into the Gulf of Xeros. I was informed that it was essential these officers should be thoroughly acquainted with the nature of the country since a new landing was projected. When I arrived on board the *Arno* a number of Generals were already there and almost immediately we weighed anchor and left Kefalo Bay and set course for Gaba Tepe. On the way across it occurred to me that if all this array of 'Red Tabs' was observed by the Turks on the deck of a destroyer steaming close inshore in the neighbourhood of Suvla Bay, it would not need great imagination on their part to conclude that another landing was to be made. I therefore reported to the captain of the *Arno* and suggested that we might induce the Generals to put on white working rig. He agreed and the Generals also fell in with the suggestion. The result was rather comic since elderly Generals, several of whom had large drooping moustaches, looked odd in sailor suits and caps, in most cases the latter being too small for them. I suppose at the age of twenty-five most people over forty-five look old, but I was shocked at the apparent age of some of these officers and wondered how they would be able to stick the very unpleasant and unhealthy conditions on the Peninsula.

Major General Egerton was one senior officer who had been feeling seedy ever since he had arrived on the Peninsula. His first weeks had been a salutary lesson in war, and now he was made aware that the men whom he passed on his early morning rounds to the front-line trenches were being asked to make a further sacrifice. He went to see them.

1 August: I got up at 4 a.m., shaved and had some hot tea, two sardines, and a piece of dry bread, and started off for the trenches with my General Staff Officer, Walshe. Though he is a very good and frightfully keen officer, he gets on my nerves, and on top of it all he is as deaf as forty posts, and I never am sure how much he hears of what I say. I knew that if I did not hustle he would be late this morning, and as it was I started to the minute, at 5 a.m., and he did not at once follow but started after me and caught me up, so we made a bad start and my temper got just stirred with a summer zephyr breeze. We started out and after about one and a half miles, we reached the well-known 'Pink Farm' so-called, I suppose, because it is a heap of shell-shattered ruins with no more pink about it than my boot has. Hereabouts the big communication trench to the trenches, known as the Eastern Mule Track, commences, and we followed this for over another mile. Each yard we went brought us nearer to rifle fire, and the frequent crack or moan of the 'over' bullet from the Turk. Shortly one comes to the reserve line of trenches running at right angles to the Mule Track; they are full of men

Major General Granville Egerton, GOC 52nd (Lowland) Division

mostly asleep, but they have had a fairly good night's rest, and some are astir and washing; just here are Battalion Headquarters. The men are all burnt brick-red by the sun, covered with a thick layer of dust and look thin, tired and haggard; this is their fourth day in the trenches; they were Dublin Fusiliers.

About 200 yards further we came to similar trenches, labelled 'support trenches', and a now narrow trench confronts us – 'Communication trench to firing line'. Up this and we come to the actual line confronting the Turks, full of men lying in every attitude where they can get cover and attempt at sleep. At short intervals are the lookout men, with their eyes glued to a periscope … So on along the front line; men here and there, sniping back at the Turks, but I am sure not doing it as well. After a perilous journey into a new sap, we dipped down into the big ravine called 'Gully Ravine', that here divides the ground. The ravine for the first half-mile is often very unhealthy, and they have erected screens of corrugated iron and blankets to cover from view of snipers the troops passing to and fro. The number of bullet holes in the corrugated iron were sufficient to make one accelerate one's steps a bit. From several points in the trenches, I saw a number of pitiful heaps of khaki which I knew represented men of my 156th Brigade who fell in a charge here on 28 June. These are those who fall in no-man's-land, and are described as 'missing'. I happen to know, though none of my staff do, that from these trenches in a few days' time the 29th Division are again going to attack, followed by the 42nd Division. We are to keep the minds of the Turks here employed, whilst reinforcements are engaged elsewhere – where, is the deepest secret, but at Headquarters yesterday some distant localities were mentioned, which astonished me rather, and left me wondering.

Ryland's observation on the *Arno* that many of the senior officers might not stand up to the harsh conditions on Gallipoli was sage, perhaps more so than he realised. Yet the age of many senior officers raised a wider question about the general health of the forces on the Gallipoli Peninsula. The summer was at its height; the heat was intense and disease-spreading flies saturated everything. You did not have to be old to feel tormented and desperately ill.

There set in a steady wind from the north-east which blew all day down the flayed rest areas of the Peninsula, raising great columns of blinding, maddening dust. It was a hot, parching wind, which in no way mitigated the scorch of the sun, and the dust it brought became a definite enemy to human peace. It pervaded everything. It poured into every hole and dugout, and filtered into every man's belongings; it formed a gritty sediment in water and tea, it passed into a man with every morsel of food he ate, and scraped and tore at his inside. It covered his pipe so that he could not even smoke with pleasure; it lay in a thick coating on his face so that he looked like a wan ghost, paler than disease had made him. It made the cleaning of his rifle a too, too frequent farce; it worked under his breeches, and gathered at the back of his knees, chafing and torturing him; and if he lay down to sleep in his hole it swept in billows over his face, or men passing clumsily above kicked great showers upon him. Sleep was not possible in the rest camps while that wind blew. But indeed there were many things which made rest in the rest camps impossible.

Few more terrible plagues can have afflicted British troops than the flies of Gallipoli. In May, by comparison, there were none. In June they became unbearable; in July they were literally inconceivable. Most Englishmen have lain down some gentle summer day to doze on a shaded lawn and found

Sub-Lieutenant Alan Herbert, Hawke Battalion, Royal Naval Division

Taking a nap: dust and the scorching sun made life abject misery for most men.

that one or two persistent flies have destroyed the repose of the afternoon; many women have turned sick at the sight of a blowfly in their butcher's shop. Let them imagine a semi-tropical sun in a place where there is little or no shade, where sanitary arrangements are less than primitive, where, in spite of all precautions, there are scraps of bacon and sugar and tea leaves lying everywhere in the dust, and every man has his little daily store of food somewhere near him, where there are dead bodies and the carcasses of mules easily accessible to the least venturesome fly – let them read for 'one' fly a hundred, a thousand, a million, and even then they will not exaggerate the horror of that plague.

Under it the disadvantages of a sensitive nature and a delicate upbringing were easy to see. An officer lies down in the afternoon to sleep in his hole. The flies cluster on his face. Patiently, at first, he brushes them away, with a drill-like mechanical movement of his hand; by and by he does it angrily; his temper is going. He covers his face with a handkerchief; it is distressingly hot, but at least he may have some rest. The flies settle on his hand, on his neck, on the bare part of his leg. Even there the feel of them is becoming a genuine torment. They creep under the handkerchief; there is one on his lip, another buzzing about his eye. Madly he tears off the handkerchief and lashes out, waving it furiously till the air is free. The flies gather on the walls of the dugout, on the waterproof sheet, and watch; they are waiting motionless till he lies down again. He throws his coat over his bare knees and lies back. The torment begins again. It is unendurable. He gets up, cursing, and goes out; better to walk in the hot sun or sit under the olive tree in the windy dust.

But look into the crowded ditches of the men. Some of them are fighting the same fight, hands moving and faces twitching, like the flesh of horses, automatically. But most of them lie still, not asleep, but in a kind of dogged artificial insensibility. The flies crowd on their faces; they swarm about their eyes, and crawl unmolested about their open mouths. It is a horrible sight, but those men are lucky.

Dysentery ravaged the army. Both sides suffered tortures during the summer and autumn months.

Dust and flies and the food and the water and our weakness joined forces against us, and dysentery raged among us. There were many who had never heard of the disease, and thought vaguely of the distemper of dogs. Those who had heard of it thought of it as something rather romantically Eastern, like the tsetse fly, and the first cases were invested with a certain mysterious distinction – especially as most of them were sent away. But it became universal; everybody had it, and everybody could not be sent away. One man in a thousand went through that time untouched; one in ten escaped with a slight attack. But the remainder lived permanently or intermittently in a condition which in any normal campaign would have long since sent them on stretchers to the base.

Dysentery ravaged the whole army shore. No one was free of it except, by some miracle, myself, and it caused more casualties and more evacuations from the Peninsula than anything else. We found men lying dead of it every night in the latrines. It was pitiable to see men so weak from its results.

Second Lieutenant Roy Laidlaw, 1st Royal Munster Fusiliers, 29th Division

When I was commanding a company and we went from 'rest' to relieve another unit in the trenches, none of my eighty-odd men could walk, they were so weak from dysentery, and it took us seven hours to get up to the trenches, a distance then of about three and a half miles. The men literally crawled on their hands and knees. But every man in the company came in and every one brought his rifle and ammunition!

Once in the trenches, men who apparently could not stand would drag themselves on to the fire-step and pump bullets into the enemy, if they attacked, or stand to when the order was given – and afterwards, literally collapse when it was over. The courage and sticking power of these men was superhuman.

They all looked so ill, poor devils, that it required a heart of stone to send the lighter cases, say of simple diarrhoea, back to duty. However, one had to remember the military exigencies, and my heart used to bleed as I watched some poor, diarrhoea-stricken, emaciated skeleton, with sunken lacklustre eyes and unsteady gait, accept without murmur my decision that he must return to duty, pick up his kit and slowly return to the stinking, pestilence-stricken, ill-constructed trenches.

Lieutenant Norman King-Wilson, 88th Field Ambulance, RAMC, 29th Division

Fears that the Turks might be in greater force than intelligence suggested led to alterations in the plans. To speed things up, a brigade of infantry would be taken right into Suvla Bay, but at the very point where it was believed the seabed might shoal; in other words, these men might land in relatively shallow water only to find that it became deeper again before they reached the shore. This single decision to move things along ran counter to almost every other order emanating from Stopford and his subordinates, who, the more they considered their options, saw problems and issues. Back in April, at Helles and Anzac, the plan had been for a rapid advance in the belief that the Turks would run away. In the event, the landings had been held up by Turkish preparations, high cliffs, difficult terrain and stubborn resistance. The landing at Suvla had been chosen partly because there were so few encumbrances to a landing and swift advance; but now pitfalls and problems were being imagined without evidence; suddenly, taking positions such as W Hills was no longer assumed but was to be undertaken 'if possible'. The vitality and forward momentum envisaged as a prerequisite for success was being dissipated, with no one taking a firm grip on the situation, least of all Hamilton, who failed to keep a close eye on Stopford.

There were small numbers of Turkish troops dug in near the coast to hold up any Allied landing, buying time for reinforcements to be brought up. But despite warnings from experienced officers, in particular Mustafa Kemal, senior Turkish officers had not thought it necessary to guard in force against an invasion on the northern edge of Anzac. Nevertheless, the Turks had one great advantage and that was the inherent weakness of Hamilton's strategic plans. They were overcomplicated. Furthermore, there was no proper appreciation of the state of the men being asked to attack. Disease had taken a terrible toll; as so often before, bald numbers on paper did not equate to effectiveness. As for the Kitchener Divisions due to land, there was considerable doubt among senior officers as to just what was expected of them. The 11th Division would be the first ashore, followed by the 10th Division. It was vital that officers had a clear idea of their duties.

Staff Captain Henry Goodland, 6th Royal Munster Fusiliers, 10th Division

Beyond the fact that we knew we were embarking at Mudros for somewhere on the Peninsula, no one knew exactly where. I am convinced Brigadier General Nicol [CO 30th Brigade] certainly did not, for when we arrived early in the morning in a bay crowded with shipping, he told me to find out where we were. The captain of the *Hazel*, on which ship 30th Brigade

Headquarters and the 6th Royal Munster Fusiliers were, refused to tell me anything at first, saying it was not his business, but I persuaded him to. He told me that this was Suvla Bay and pointed out to me the various landmarks: Gaba Tepe, Anzac, Achi Baba to the southwards. We had four maps of the Peninsula and he told me the right one to use.

If GHQ had any plan at all it would have appeared to have been: put the troops ashore and let them get on with it. How GHQ thought to land the whole of the 11th Division in the dark on a strange shore and, a few hours afterwards, land two brigades of the 10th Division almost on top of them, could possibly be successful passes the comprehension of even a junior officer. Units became inextricably mixed, my battalion was landed at the wrong beach; this necessitated a march of about three miles along a sandy beach in full view of the Turks who shelled us readily. My battalion lost the senior major, two captains and the adjutant killed, and twelve officers wounded. I never saw my colonel for two days, he was probably landed at a different beach.

Captain Douglas Figgis, 5th Royal Irish Fusiliers, 10th Division

Such ignorance was terrifying. Both the 11th Division and the 10th Division were utterly inexperienced. Meanwhile, it was hoped that the diversionary attack at Helles would prove successful and the Anzac breakout a triumph.

At Helles, the 29th Division attacked on the afternoon of 6 August after a brief and all-too-inadequate bombardment. The objectives were limited, success even more so as the infantry once again failed to make headway. The Turks on this occasion stayed their hand and did not counter-attack, while their reserves were sent to Anzac, precisely the move that the Helles offensive was meant to stop. The next day two brigades of the 42nd Division attacked, with sickeningly similar results. The 1/6th Lancashire Fusiliers lost many men that day, but none was regretted more than their old Boer War veteran, Captain Quartermaster William Griffiths.

All the company officers had been killed or wounded in a Turkish counter-attack, the company driven out of the newly won trench, beaten, thoroughly demoralised and ready to cut and run – like soldiers get sometimes in the

Private Charles Watkins, 1/6th Lancashire Fusiliers, 42nd Division

heat of an engagement – when out of nowhere emerges from his non-combatant duties our Captain QM, limp, walking stick, cynical grin and all. He surveys the thoroughly demoralised remains of the company angrily. 'Ready to cut and run, are you, you buggers?' 'Run from a lot of bloody Turks?' 'Lancashire lads running away!' 'Nay, never let it be said.' 'Here, Corporal, help me over the top of the trench.' 'Easy now, mind my game leg.' 'Easy now.' 'Ouch!' 'Mind my leg, blast you.' 'And now pass me my walking stick and follow me, all of yer.' And waving his walking stick high above his head, he limped smartly towards the Turkish trench followed by the now heartened and electrified remains of the company, angry and ashamed of the last few minutes. There was a brief and savage encounter and the trench was recaptured. Later, they carried in the body of the Captain QM and some bloke got a slight flesh wound in the leg going back for the Captain's walking stick, for stick and Captain were inseparable. Both Captain and stick were later buried in an improvised grave, and the grave marked with a homemade cross of biscuit-box wood.

Nothing whatsoever had been gained by the British attack, and quite why the fighting was allowed to continue for a week was, and remains, beyond comprehension.

As the 29th Division launched their attack, the Australians burst out of the Anzac bridgehead. As planned, the 1st Division made their three-pronged attack, first the diversionary move to the south at Lone Pine, then the attack to the north to seize Chunuk Bair, and, lastly, the assault in the centre towards the Nek and Chessboard.

The fighting would begin with the 1st Division attacking Lone Pine. The divisional commander made every effort to give his men the maximum amount of protection with shallow tunnels dug towards enemy lines through which the Australians could emerge, closing the distance they would have to run across no-man's-land. Those tunnels could then be opened up and used to bring up more men and evacuate the wounded. Three mines would also be detonated to provide craters in which men could shelter.

The charge over the top was fast and determined and the first Turkish trench was stormed with relative ease, men running on to the second before doubling

Opposite: Men standing in the narrow confines of the front-line trench.

back to deal with any Turks attempting to escape down communication trenches. The fighting then disintegrated into a series of individual battles as both sides fought round myriad trench traverses and down dugouts and tunnels. Inevitably, the Turkish response came, with bombs being thrown at close quarters and hand-to-hand fighting, brutal and unforgiving. Just as at Helles, Allied initial success was tempered by the determination of the Turks not to cede ground. The fighting lasted four days. The Australians had created a diversion with aplomb but at great cost to both sides. It could only be hoped that it was worthwhile.

The problem with the breakout from Anzac was always going to be the circuitous march towards the Sari Bair heights. This entailed a move of two miles north, then east under the cover of darkness, in treacherous and confusing terrain, for troops to be in position for a dawn attack. The preparation needed for such a task would have to be meticulous, the reconnaissance expert, and there was no indication that either had been given the requisite time.

When the men moved out, the advance was slow but steady. Turkish outposts that overlooked or guarded routes necessary to the advance were quickly overwhelmed. But these were easy pickings, achievements made before the stiff climb up the ridges, and before the darkness and the tricky terrain played havoc with the sense of direction and of time. The men were naturally braced for action as they pushed and pulled their way through prickly bushes, and hours passed. The moonless night, for which the offensive had been planned so as to hide the movement of troops, was now causing those same troops to doubt their guides. Halts were frequent and men already weakened by dysentery were becoming exhausted. They had not even begun to climb the various spurs ahead of them. As the night passed, so thousands became hopelessly disorientated, and even when climbs were undertaken they were to the wrong ridge. The New Zealand Brigade fared no better, despite being given what on paper looked like an easier task, a shorter route. And that was the problem. What looked straightforward on a map was deceptive. Some of the New Zealanders whose task was to climb Rhododendron Ridge were wandering around gullies at the bottom, looking up at any number of ridges that appeared indistinguishable. Commanding officers began to question whether it was sensible to carry on and at least one turned his battalion around to return to the shore. The rest of the brigade did not push on as ordered, the commanding officer taking the decision to wait until his entire force was together, unaware that one battalion had gone back. Daylight

'Angerous [sic] sniper beyond this point – turn into sap': an Anzac warning sign deters use of the shortcut to the outposts along North Beach.

alerted the Turks to the presence of the New Zealanders, and the way was soon barred to any further advance. Any chance of storming Chunuk Bair and then pressing back down the ridge to Battleship Hill was gone, if it ever existed.

With the night attack a total failure, the assault out of Anzac towards the Nek and Chessboard was also doomed.

The fighting would start as the New Zealand Brigade made its way towards Rhododendron Ridge. Preparations had in many ways mirrored those at Lone Pine: mines would be detonated at short intervals, this time under the first objective known as 'German Officer's Trench'. Tunnels had been dug to help men cross the intervening ground. At the allotted times the mines were detonated, but they had been set too deep and all three failed to make any impression on the surface. Turkish artillery responded and the shell explosions blocked the tunnels through which the infantry had been due to pass. Almost an hour after the attack had been timed to go in, the men went over the top. They were slaughtered. A second assault was ordered with the same result. A third assault was demanded but, thankfully, it was cancelled.

The determination to take 'German Officer's Trench' at all costs existed for one good and stark reason: if the Turks held it, they would be able to enfilade the Australian attacks at the Nek and the Chessboard. The simultaneous breakdown of the New Zealanders' advance ensured a catastrophe. Ironically, Birdwood, aware of the New Zealanders' slow progress, ordered the attacks at the Nek and Chessboard in the hope that his men might succeed and actually help their antipodean comrades, presumably with an advance up Battleship Hill to the top of Rhododendron Ridge. Four waves of the 3rd Light Horse Brigade would go over the top at the Nek, 600 men in all; 372 were killed or wounded.

Sergeant Cliff Pinnock, 8th Australian Light Horse, 3rd Light Horse Brigade

Above: A wooden grave marker at Ari Burnu cemetery: in memory of three 8th Australian Light Horsemen killed at the Nek on 7 August.

They were waiting ready for us and simply gave us a solid wall of lead. I was in the first line to advance and we did not get 10 yards. Everyone fell like lumps of meat. All your pals that had been with you for months and months blown and shot out of all recognition. I got mine shortly after I got over the bank and it felt like a million-ton hammer falling on my shoulder. I was really awfully lucky as the bullet went in just below the shoulder blade round by my throat and came out just a tiny way from my spine low down on the back. It was simply murder.

The first wave was followed two minutes later by the second. Then, when reports that a yellow and red signal flag carried by the first wave had been seen in the Turkish front line, a third wave was ordered. Despite protestations that nothing could be achieved, a fourth wave went. Most men were cut down within a few yards of their trench. The assault at the Nek has become one of the most infamous incidents of the entire Gallipoli campaign. Other lesser known attacks made against the trenches in front of the Chessboard achieved nothing.

The next day, 8 August, a combined force of one New Zealand and two British battalions occupied the top of Chunuk Bair, but were driven off the summit when it became clear that the Turks could call up more reserves than the

Allied battalions. Elsewhere along the ridge there was sustained fighting, but sometimes contact was by accident rather than design, as units, confused as to where they were and where they were going, ended up in fire fights. Success, when it came, was fleeting and when important heights were taken, such as Hill Q to the north of Chunuk Bair, they were lost. Trooper Clutha Mackenzie was one of those fighting to hold on to Chunuk Bair, but everywhere was in utter chaos.

From above came the incessant roar of bursting bombs and shells and rattle of musketry. At dawn the summit had been gained, but just how good or bad our position was I had not the vaguest idea. I had not heard of, nor had I seen, any progress except the taking of this summit, since Saturday morning, and had no idea as to whether the battle was progressing favourably or otherwise. What was expected of them up there to-night none knew. Each carried a pick or a shovel and two bombs. They passed the dressing stations, perched on either side on the steep slope, where hundreds of wounded lay, then over a ridge where the track stopped and out into the pitch black open. The bullets zipped past or thudded into the ground. The troop lay down while they got their bearings. A fellow close by me gave a yell and was dead. A few wounded men, limping or crawling back, passed them. Then, in extended order, they went forward again, guided by a telephone wire, keeping touch with difficulty in the scrub and the darkness. Frequently there would come from the blackness in front of their feet a warning, 'Keep clear of me, cobber, I'm wounded,' or groans and the gleam of a white bandage, and sometimes they stumbled over prone, still forms. Slowly they picked their way forward, making towards the centre of the firing, which was in a semicircle round them, the whistling bullets came from both sides as well as from in front, and the din grew fiercer. They reached at length a hollow full of wounded, then went slowly up a slope littered with equipment and dead, and, at last, topping the rise, they came upon a scene so weird and infernal that I instantly stopped and stared with awe. Lit fantastically by flickering flames, which were licking slowly through the scrub, was a small, ghastly, battle-rent piece of ground, not one hundred yards in width and rising slightly. Beyond and close on either side, it was bounded by the starry heavens, and seemed a strange, detached dreamland

Trooper Clutha Mackenzie, Wellington Mounted Rifles

where men had gone mad. The Turks lined the far edge, their ghostly faces appearing and vanishing in the eerie light, as they poured a pointblank fusillade at the shattered series of shallow holes where the remnants of the New Zealanders were fighting gallantly. Sweeping round to the left was the flashing semicircle of the enemy line, bombs exploded with a lurid glare, their murky pall drifting slowly back towards me. Shells came whirring up from the black depths behind, and burst beyond the further lip. Everywhere lay dead and dying men, mostly the former, Turkish and British. Equipment and rifles were strewn in the greatest confusion over the torn earth, and all the time the creeping flames cast weird lights upon the passing drama.

A New Zealander, a Briton and a wounded Turk make their way down to the beach. The white calico patches were worn by Allied troops as identification during the August offensive.

The Turks were calling forward significant numbers of reinforcements and, with their knowledge of the ground, distributed their men accordingly. With wearying predictability, the Turks counter-attacked weakened and demoralised Allied forces, forcing them back down the ridges so painstakingly and painfully climbed two days before. The breakout was over before it had barely begun. Meanwhile, hundreds of wounded Anzacs began crowding along the beaches, waiting for evacuation.

The condition of the wounded is indescribable. They lie in the sand in rows upon rows, their faces caked with sand and blood; one murmur for water; no shelter from the sun; many of them in saps, with men passing all the time scattering more dust on them. There is hardly any possibility of transporting them. The fire zones are desperate, and the saps are blocked with ammunition transport and mules, also whinnying for water, carrying food, etc. Some unwounded men almost mad from thirst, cursing … We have a terrible view here: lines of wounded creeping up from the hospital to the cemetery like a tide, and the cemetery is going like a live thing to meet the wounded.

We still had our swim off the beach from this position. It will be a wonderful place for tourists after the war is over. For Australians all along the flat land by the beach there are sufficient bullets to start a lead factory. Then searching among the gullies will give good results. We came across the Turkish Quartermasters' store, any quantity of coats and boots and bully beef. The latter was much more palatable than ours.

Lieutenant Colonel Joseph Beeston, OC, 4th (Australian) Field Ambulance

While the Anzac breakout was under way, the New Army divisions landed at Suvla. Key to success was the seizure of high ground that fringed the bay and plain beyond. Taking Kiretch Tepe and Tekke Tepe ridges would require a swift advance.

Behind the bay was the dry Salt Lake. It was decided to land 34th Brigade at A Beach, and 32nd Brigade the best part of two miles way at B Beach, along with 33rd Brigade, which would act as cover. 32nd Brigade would take the low-lying Lala Baba hills close to the shore and then move off and skirt the eastern side of the Salt Lake, linking up with 34th Brigade, which would then advance on the Kiretch Tepe Ridge while 32nd Brigade would march on Chocolate Hill. It was an unnecessary detour.

When the 32nd and 33rd Brigades began to land, everything went smoothly at first and the battalions moved off to secure their first objectives. Yet landing unopposed on a gently cambered beach, even at night, was hardly a great test even for inexperienced soldiers. Even then, not everyone went to the right place.

Overleaf: After the fight, 9 August: No. 3 Outpost with 40th Field Ambulance dressing station in the shelter of the spur.

Sergeant Charles Manley, 33rd Field Ambulance, RAMC, 11th Division

When we were two miles or so from the Peninsula we were transferred to motor lighters and landed about 11 p.m. We unloaded the lighters and then a landing officer came along and told us that if we did not clear out straight away we should all be blown to hell as they had landed us at the wrong point. They had landed us by Anzac Cove. The bullets were falling all round us all the while. We then started loading up the lighter again, but before we had finished, the skipper of the lighter got that funky that he shoved off and we had to walk along the open beach for about 2 miles to Lala Baba under a heavy rifle fire. On arriving at Lala Baba we found that the infantry had just landed.

Wounded soldiers from the August attack on their way to the hospital ship.

At least most of the infantry were in the right place. So far, so reasonably straightforward, and soon the first battalion, the 6th East Yorkshire Regiment,

moved off to engage the small number of Turkish troops on the low slopes of Lala Baba. They would secure the hillocks through the deployment of overwhelming force. And then nothing. It was as though that first engagement had been victory enough. In the inky darkness, gunfire could be heard, and so, to avoid the risk of confusion, 32nd Brigade sat tight to wait until daylight and did not move on for its rendezvous with 34th Brigade. In one sense it did not have to; the 34th Brigade was coming to them.

The 34th Brigade was having difficulties and, unfortunately, not at A Beach. Not only did transferring from the destroyers to the landing craft prove problematic in the dark, but when the craft headed off towards the shore they were the best part of a mile south of the intended place of disembarkation. The midshipmen who took the men in were heading directly towards that part of the beach opposite Lala Baba identified by the navy as one that would in all likelihood shoal. Sure enough, the lighters ran aground on sandbanks as much as a hundred yards from the shore.

The officer in charge of the lighter gave out some orders to a junior officer who was standing at the gangway ready to lower it for disembarkation. Up to this point we were all inwardly congratulating ourselves that we had a very easy task and that we would not be discovered landing. We had a very rude awakening! The officer gave his orders in a fairly low tone, but owing to the elements they had to be repeated several times, until his voice developed into a loud bawl. He continually bawled out the name of Robertson; simultaneously with this came the enemy's fire, which seemed to come from the right.

Sergeant William Taylor, 11th Manchester Regiment, 11th Division

The Turks on Lala Baba knew the lighters were coming. How could they not? Packed into their lighters, the men of the Manchester Regiment and of the Lancashire Fusiliers could not disembark; the water was too deep. Equally, they were targets for any Turk who need only to point his rifle in the general direction of the rising confusion. In an attempt to release the lighters, men were moved to the back, taking pressure off the bows, but this failed. In the end it was decided to send some men overboard with a rope to secure a line to the shore so that the rest of the men might follow, holding on to the taut rope to keep their heads above water. No one was sure of the exact depth of the sea around the lighter, so the tallest men, without equipment, were called on to risk life and limb. The plan worked, but the men were under fire, even if they were not always under water. It was a trying experience for them: the majority could not swim and many swallowed sea water, an unpleasant experience but one that had serious consequences as the sun rose and so did the temperature.

With men soaked to the skin, a foray was made in the direction of Lala Baba in order to suppress the Turkish fire, causing casualties among the men waiting to land from the lighters. Creeping into position, the Turks were unaware of the presence of these men until it was too late, and they were overrun.

As the rest of the men came ashore, they sat on the beaches to collect themselves and to clean their choked rifle barrels of sand. Meanwhile, commanding officers, aware that they were meant to be marching on Kiretch Tepe Ridge, had to collect their thoughts. They were not where they were supposed to be and it was still night-time. Making an educated guess as to the direction they were meant to take, they set off. They were sniped at almost all the way, but at least they were going in the right general direction, passing A Beach as they went. The men began climbing across the scrub as dawn was breaking. They were wet, cold and tired, and not in the best frame of mind to engage the enemy hiding behind rocks and bushes. The fighting was hard going, and thirst became a terrible issue for men whose mouths were lined and rimmed with salt from the sea. The advance along the ridge gradually ground to a halt.

On board ship, waiting to disembark, was Major William Rettie. One battery, A, of his brigade had managed to get ashore as planned and the rest of the artillery was meant to follow at dawn.

Major William Rettie, 59th Brigade, Royal Field Artillery, 11th Division

After a hurried breakfast we stood by waiting for the lighters, but none came. As daylight increased we could see our infantry on Lala Baba, and A Battery dragging its guns up from B Beach into a position behind it, alongside a mountain battery which was already in action, eight or ten horses pulling the pieces with considerable difficulty through the heavy sand.

Our infantry (11th Division) could also be seen doubling across the narrow spit of sand at the mouth of the Salt Lake, which by the way was dry and fit to be crossed, though there was a doubt about it at the time, and halting under cover near Hill 10. They were being shelled by two Turkish field guns concealed somewhere north of that hill.

What seemed strange to us was that we could see none of our troops on the north side of the Bay where we had been informed some of the 10th Division were to be landed. We could see Turks moving about on Kiretch Tepe Sirt apparently unmolested …

Rettie could not see any of the 10th Division for good reason. Because of the shoaling off Lala Baba it was decided not to land the division at A Beach as intended but much further down the coast at B and C Beaches, where landing was known to be straightforward. Such changes taken so abruptly would inevitably cause terrible confusion. Command and control at Suvla was moving beyond the scope of senior officers and devolved by default to battalion or

Two large lighters shuttling part of the Essex Brigade, 54th (East Anglian) Division, to Suvla.

company commanders who did not know what they were meant to do. Those waiting on the ships could only gaze on.

Sergeant John Hargrave, 32nd Field Ambulance, RAMC, 10th Division

A pale pink sunrise burst across the eastern sky as our transport came steaming into the bay. The haze of early morning dusk still held, blurring the mainland and water in misty outlines. Hawk and I had slept upon the deck. Now we got up and stretched our cramped limbs.

You must understand that we knew not where we were. We had never heard of Suvla Bay – we didn't know what part of the Peninsula we had reached. The mystery of the adventure made it all the more exciting. It was to be 'a new landing by the Xth Division' – that was all we knew.

Some of us had slept, and some had lain awake all night. Rapidly the pink sunrise swept behind the rugged mountains to the left, and was reflected in wobbling ripples in the bay. We joined the host of battleships, monitors, and troopships standing out, and 'stood by'. We could hear the rattle of machine guns in the distant gloom beyond the streak of sandy shore. The decks were crowded with that same khaki crowd. We all stood eagerly watching and listening. The death-silence had come upon us. No one spoke. No one whistled.

Staff Captain Henry Goodland, 6th Royal Munster Fusiliers, 10th Division

After waiting several hours and watching the troops on shore moving about in what appeared an aimless fashion, two iron lighters arrived and put aboard a few wounded men. A long delay occurred before the order to disembark was given and it must have been 11 a.m. when we got off, and a few minutes later grounded 50 yards from shore. The fact of having to wade ashore caused much delay and confusion as the rocks were slippery and the water breast-high and men were carrying 300 rounds of SAA [small arms ammunition] in bandoliers. We got the General off in a dinghy which we used for landing the signal stores etc. There was not more than 20 feet of beach, and immediately the men began to climb the shore bank about four or five feet high the land mines began to go off. This was very noisy and inexplicable as there was no scream of shells which is what we thought was happening. Some dozen casualties occurred, feet blown off mostly, and the general alarm caused a slowing up in the men coming from the lighters who had to be roughly spoken to make them move quicker.

The morning was now well advanced with still no sign of our barges. Not a soul came near us nor answered our signallers' efforts to open communication with ship or shore.

The bell now rang for the ordinary breakfast and as it was four hours since we had fed we felt we might as well have another, so adjourned to the saloon. There we were joined by two war correspondents who had come aboard at Imbros. They were both distinctly annoyed at being unable to get ashore.

It was a strange experience to sit sipping one's coffee in this gilded apartment, gazing out at the battle going on ashore; it was as if one was a spectator at some show, so out of it did one feel in spite of those noises the navy was making all around us, and the fact that an aeroplane a short time before had passed over dropping bombs which were, luckily, all bad shots.

About noon, lighters from the south loaded with infantry passed us on their way to a shady strip on the north shore of the bay where they proceeded to discharge their cargoes. At 1 p.m. a lighter at last came alongside us and we started getting a move on, but were brought to a standstill by the arrival of a staff officer with orders that the infantry mules were to be got out first as they were urgently required, so was the artillery, but as we could not be disembarked simultaneously we had to continue waiting.

Major William Rettie, 59th Brigade, Royal Field Artillery, 11th Division

The 6th Munsters had landed with nothing more than a general order to 'Get ashore and reinforce the troops at present fighting!' In the end this became a march to reinforce the Manchester Regiment, which was in dire difficulties on Kiretch Tepe. It took the best part of four hours to reach them, by which time it was not just the Manchesters who were short of water.

During the afternoon of the 7th the lack of water began to be felt and the situation was becoming bad. I went back to the beach just before dark with all my brigade HQ details I could get together and all water bottles that could be carried. Found the lighter full of water grounded about 100 yards from shore in the little bay where the 7th Munsters had landed. Sappers were building a tank on the shore, but there wasn't a long enough hose to

Captain Henry Goodland, 6th Royal Munster Fusiliers, 10th Division

reach it from the lighter. Saw an admiral and another naval officer walking up and down the beach and asked him to lend me his little boat which he had come ashore in, to row out to the lighter with my water bottles to fill them. Found one man on the lighter who seemed so ignorant of his job that he couldn't tell me which hatch to uncover in order to bale up some water. Baled up water with my canvas bucket and a puttee and after filling all bottles rowed ashore again and had a hard job finding our brigade HQ in the dark. No water other than this was got ashore from this water lighter on the 7th. The water situation was desperate on the 8th and the first water convoy arrived on the morning of the 9th in camel tins and skins. I established a water dump by filling biscuit tins, placing it under guard, and it was less than a bottle a man per day. Great difficulty was experienced in getting the men watered who were in the front line on the ridge, and carrying parties were organised under an officer. Found a spring away to the left towards the sea which was opened out and put under a guard. A mere trickle giving two or three tins an hour.

Lack of water was becoming desperate, as Corporal Walter Mead was well aware. He was chasing up and down the beach delivering messages. Ordered to locate a casualty clearing station towards A Beach, he set off. After crossing an inlet from the sea to the Salt Lake, known as the cut, he skirted the water's edge.

Corporal Walter Mead, Royal Engineers Signals, IX Army Corps HQ

Along this beach and exposed to long-range enemy fire were lost legions of 10th and 11th Divisional troops recently landed. Added to these were the exhausted troops from Chocolate Hill seeking water. It was found halfway along the western shores of the bay being pumped ashore from tankers anchored in the bay through canvas fire hoses into large water troughs away from the vulnerable beach. Water bottles could not be filled from the troughs which were being guarded by sentries with fixed bayonets, but in between troughs and the sea came fountains of water spouting from holes made by the bayonets of thirsty troops. Parched men have no morals so the shocking waste of valuable water went on. An occasional bout of shrapnel fire scattered the troops and hastened my journey towards the fluttering red flag flying in the distance.

The wounded up on the Kiretch Tepe Sirt were in critical need of medical attention and evacuation. Sergeant John Hargrave had had a salutary introduction to Suvla Bay when the lighter just ahead of him beached and in dropping its tailboard hit a land mine, killing two men instantly. But there was no time to dwell on such things.

We manhandled all our medical equipment and stores from the hold of the lighter to the beach. We had orders to 'fall in' the stretcher-bearers, and work in open formation to the firing line.

Sergeant John Hargrave, 32nd Field Ambulance, RAMC, 10th Division

The Kiretch Tepe Sirt runs right along one side of Suvla Bay. Our searching zone for wounded lay along this ridge, which rises like the vertebrae of some great antediluvian reptile – dropping sheer down on the Gulf of Saros side, and, in varying slopes, to the plains and the Salt Lake on the other. Here again small things left a vivid impression – the crack of a rifle from the top of the ridge, and a party of British climbing up the rocks and scrub in search of the hidden Turk. The smell of human blood soaking its way into the sand from those two 'stiffies' on the beach. The sullen silence, except for the distant crackle and the occasional moan of a shell … We were all thinking: 'Who will be the first to get plugged?' We moved slowly along the ridge, searching every bush and rock for signs of wounded men.

We wondered what the first case would be – and which squad would come across it. I worked up and down the line of squads trying to keep them in touch with each other … Those we had left on the beach were busy putting up the operating marquee and other tents, and the cooks in getting a fire going and making tea. The stretcher squads worked slowly forward. We passed an old Turkish well with a stone-flagged front and a stone trough. Later on we came upon the trenches and bivouacs of a Turkish sniping headquarters. There were all kinds of articles lying about which had evidently belonged to Turkish officers: tobacco in a heap on the ground near a bent willow and thorn bivouac; part of a field telephone with the wires running towards the upper ridges of Kiretch Tepe Sirt; the remains of some dried fish and an earthenware jar or 'chattie' which had held some kind of wine; a few very hard biscuits, and a mass of brand-new clothing …

It was near here that our first man was killed later in the day. He was looking into one of these bivouacs, and was about to crawl out when a bullet went through his brain. It was a sniper's shot. We buried him in an old Turkish trench close by, and put a cross made of a wooden bully-beef crate over him.

The sun now blazed upon us, and our soaked clothes were steaming in the heat. The open fan-like formation in which we moved was not a success. We lost the officers, and continually got out of touch with each other.

At last we reached the zone of spent bullets.

'Z-z-z-z-e-e-e-e-pp! – zing!' 'S-s-s-ippp!'

'That one was just by me left ear!' said Sergeant Joe Smith, although as a matter of fact it was yards above his head. Here, among a hail of moaning spent shots, our officers called a halt, made us fall in, in close formation, and we retired – what for I do not know.

Major William Rettie, 59th Brigade, Royal Field Artillery, 11th Division

It had been my lot in 1904 to take part in the Invasion of Essex [a military exercise] by troops from Aldershot transported by sea from Southampton. We seemed to have learnt little from these manoeuvres as the same old mistakes were made, especially that of underestimating the means of conveyance from ship to shore. At Clacton we had been over four hours late in disembarking: here we were over twenty-four.

Little news could be gathered from the naval or staff officers who came aboard as to what was happening on shore, they seemed rather reticent, but as evening fell we could see A Battery shelling Chocolate Hill. This seemed to indicate that the programme on shore was behind-hand as well as that on the sea, for the objective was down for capture early in the morning. As night fell, firing died away but the scrub round the Salt Lake, which had been set on fire, blazed away merrily.

The sea during the afternoon had got up a bit and by night-time was rather rough, retarding the work of disembarkation considerably. One lighter sank during its passage to the shore and all the animals drowned, the attending men being rescued with difficulty.

Chaos was the result, as orders were matched by counter-orders and troops were marched first one way and then another. Once, units became mixed up

and then all control was lost. Lieutenant General Stopford was all at sea, literally and metaphorically, while his senior commanders on the ground, Brigadier General William Sitwell and Major General Frederick Hammersley, were consumed by the mess in front of them. It was beyond their capabilities to bring any sort of order to the near-anarchy. Small consolation prizes such as Lala Baba and Hill 10 were captured, but these were bound to fall, being close to the shore and lightly held by Turkish troops. The real objectives such as Kiretch Tepe remained in enemy hands. Chocolate Hill and Green Hill were finally taken at the end of the day, but other objectives, such as W Hills, were not. The Turks had fought well, but they had been helped by lamentable organisation in front of them.

British troops in shallow dugouts by Chocolate Hill. Everything from tin water containers, petrol tins and earthenware rum jars was utilitised to store the precious water ration.

That night was dark, with no stars. I didn't know what part of Gallipoli we were in, and the maps issued were useless. The first cases had been picked up close to the firing line, and were mostly gunshot wounds, and now – late in the evening – all my squads having worked four miles to the beach, I was trying to get my own direction back to the ambulance … I trudged on and

Sergeant John Hargrave, 32nd Field Ambulance, RAMC, 10th Division

on in the dark, stumbling over rocks and slithering down steep crags, tearing my way through thorns and brambles, and sometimes rustling among high dry grass. Queer scents, pepperminty and sage-like smells, came in whiffs. It was cold. I must have gone several miles along the Kiretch Tepe Sirt when I came to a halt and once more tried to get my bearings. I peered at the gloomy sky, but there was no star. I listened for the lap-lap of water on the beach of Suvla Bay, but I must have been too far up the ridges to hear anything. There was dead silence. When I moved a little green lizard scuttled over a white rock and vanished among the dead scrub. I was past feeling hungry, although I had eaten one army biscuit in the early morning and had had nothing since.

It was extraordinarily lonely. You may imagine how queer it was, for here was I, trying to get back to my ambulance headquarters at night on the first day of landing – and I was hopelessly lost. It was impossible to tell where the firing line began. I reckoned I was outside the British outposts

Busy camp life near West Beach, close to Suvla Point.

and not far from the Turkish lines. Once, as I went blundering along over some rocks, a dark figure bolted out of a bush and ran away up the ridge in a panic.

'Halt!' I shouted, trying to make believe I was a British armed sentry. But the figure ran on, and I began to stride after it. This led me up the ridge over very broken ground. Whoever it was (it was probably a Turkish sniper, for there were many out night-scouting), I lost sight and sound of him.

I went climbing steadily up till at last I found myself looking into darkness. I got down on my hands and knees and peered over the edge of a ridge of rock. I could see a tiny beam of light away down, and this beam grew and grew as it slowly moved up till it became a great triangular ray. It swept slowly along the top of what I now saw was a steep precipice sloping sheer down into blackness below. One step further and I should have gone hurtling into the sea. For, although I did not then know it, this was the topmost ridge of the Kiretch Tepe Sirt.

The following morning, 8 August, Major Rettie was still on board ship waiting to disembark.

Major William
Rettie, 59th
Brigade, Royal Field
Artillery, 11th
Division

Going on deck I found the unloading of the infantry transport still dragging on. There appeared to be little doing on shore. A Battery and the Mountain Battery had apparently moved forward as they were no longer to be seen on Lala Baba.

At last, about 1 p.m., we were told we might start disembarking. Going ashore with the Adjutant, we were landed at B Beach. The Turk was keeping up a desultory fire on the spot, but most of the shells seemed to be 'duds' or buried themselves in the sand and did little damage. As we searched I was struck by the restfulness of all around. There appeared to be little going on, a good many infantrymen seemed sitting about or having a bathe. The impression conveyed to my mind was that of a 'Stand fast' at some field day.

Having located the CRA (Commander, Royal Artillery) on the beach near Lala Baba and asking for orders, was told to bring the batteries into action under cover of that hillock. This was rather a shock as we had at least expected to go forward to Chocolate Hill. On expressing surprise and asking what we were waiting for, I was met with the grim reply 'For the Turks to reinforce'; and so it proved.

The Turk was not too well supplied with guns or ammunition. Had he been so, our whole force could have been speedily blown into the sea. From the nature of some of the stuff thrown at us it was evident he was ransacking his arsenals for anything in the way of a gun to shoot at us. On one occasion, when going round the front line, a young infantry officer handed me, with a query as to what it was, a small studded projectile with a head which had evidently once been red. It had a curiously familiar look, and on closer inspection I made out that it was a 7-pounder ML shrapnel, the product of our own arsenal, and bore the date, if I remember right, of 1878.

Thin Turkish forces were reinforced, including troops from the 35th Regiment, 12th Ottoman Division, who undertook a hastily arranged march to Suvla. Amongst those moving up was Lieutenant Ismail Sunata, a young platoon commander.

In the morning, unexpected news: the enemy has landed at Anafartalar. Move out immediately. Where on earth is this? I have no map. Is it towards Sedd el Bahr, or towards Ari Burnu? The first rumor was towards Ari Burnu. We'll find out. Once the shock of the first news had passed, our company gathered and began to move to the rear. It was dusk by the time the whole division and regiment had gathered. We moved out at once. Two hours later, a half-hour pause. We move out again and keep going without stopping. We move along the streambeds between the hills, along the valleys. We passed through a village. I don't know where it is. We go on at a forced march. The depression due to excitement fills me with a dark expectations. Everything I see, the trees, the forests in the mists, look frightening to me.

Lieutenant Ismail Sunata, 2nd Battalion, 35th Infantry Regiment, 12th Ottoman Division

The men tire quickly because they have marched far and have not slept enough. They move as if dragged along. Our number shrinks as we go. The troops were no longer marching in order, It was as if everyone who grabbed his gun was heading to the front. The officers exhort them, 'Come on, boys, come on, we don't have far to go,' those who still have strength keep going.

We see some hills ahead of us. Behind these we can see searchlights, as well as the lights of flares that explode in the air and split into forty or fifty pieces. Each one sheds a powerful light, falling slowly behind the hills in front of us. We advance for hours watching the play of the searchlights and the illumination rounds.

8th August: It is before noon, and the weather is quite hot. We are moving along a narrow path. But there is a lot of brush and vegetation. We can't be seen between them. There are a few places, few and far between, where we can see for some distance. There is no trace of the excitement I had felt on leaving Istanbul. The tremendous death I had imagined among all the dangers of battle, its blood and fire, its various horrors, did not occupy my mind any more. I was hurrying to reach the summit [of a hill] and see how the enemy was landing, to understand the direction of his unending efforts, to see the British fleet that had taken an imposing position in our imaginations, and satisfy my curiosity.

The commander of the company ahead kept sending back word for the men to advance without being seen. I realised we were entering the danger zone.

When I continued on to the summit, I could see the whole bay of Saros,

Soldiers drawing
water from an old
Turkish well.
Chocolate Hill is in
the background.

and the high hills of the island of Semadirek shrouded by mist in the distance. On the shore, in Suvla Bay, many transport ships were gathered, and from the large number of barges and lighters moving to and fro it appeared the enemy was proceeding apace with their landings.

In terms of warships, there are two battleships of two masts and two funnels, of about 15–20 thousand tons each, as well as one four-funnelled and one two-funnelled cruiser, and many destroyers.

Further to the south, in the direction of Ari Burnu, several cruisers are shelling a point on Koca Cimen Tepe.

The company moved out again, organising a defence line on the west slope of Tekke Tepe about 100 metres ahead of the summit, facing the sea and Suvla Bay, with the 7th Company on our right. I had thought there were prepared trenches here, but there is nothing, we are in the open. There is nothing to protect us from any fire of any kind. Fortunately the low, stunted trees and brush hide us from enemy eyes.

In front of us a tree-lined streambed descends to the Anafarta plain. From the foothills to the sea the plain extends for four or five kilometres. There is a salt lake near Suvla Bay. But the lake is dry, and the salt in its bed is white…

I saw here the destructive effect of the warships' fire. First the thundering flash of the warships' guns, like lightning. Then one sees the place where the shells fall, although one can generally tell where they are going from the moaning sound they emit in flight. Where they fall, one first sees a flash of flame, and then pieces of steel, stones, fragments of rock, earth and all kinds of things fly up into the air. At the same time a dense cloud of smoke covers the scene. If one falls close to the hill one is standing on, the hill trembles like an earthquake.

Evening approaches as we watched the enemy landing and shelling. I ate some bread. Finally the battleships fired a group bombardment against Kiretch Tepe, to our right, and ceased fire.

Nothing much happened on 8 August. It was a Sunday. Given the lack of activity, the British troops may have assumed it was being taken as a day of rest. A bit of line-straightening here and there, consolidation of what had been won, but no urgency of any kind. Hamilton, whose attention had been firmly on the Anzac breakout, was horrified by the lack of progress and immediately called on Stopford to act. A hurriedly prepared attack went ahead the following morning and in daylight. It failed.

From down below towards the village the voice of Captain Ali Bey can be heard. He is shouting and yelling, but his words can't be made out. Right at this moment the enemy discovered them. It was by now quite light. Suddenly the warships' tremendous shells began to rain down on the village. The shells must have been at least 24cm, since when they fell on the village the hill on which I was standing shook as if in an earthquake. Fragments of the exploding shells reach as far as my position. One of them landed by my left hand. If it had kept its force a little longer my left hand would have been smashed. I picked it up and looked at it, it was as hot as fire.

The skirmish line ahead had opened fire and joined the battle. Enemy bullets were whining over my head. Soon a few wounded began to pass us.

I ordered the remaining half platoon forward. But I could not advance myself. Several soldiers, from what companies I did not know, joined me. At this point I saw our Captain Suleyman Bey was moving back to the rear,

Lieutenant Ismail Sunata, 2nd Battalion, 35th Infantry Regiment, 12th Ottoman Division

wounded. My brain suddenly engaged, and I realised that as the bullets were whining over my head they were on a high trajectory. I looked at the soldiers beside me, who were more afraid than I was. 'Up, forward!' I yelled and took off. The hill is scrubby and slopes down to the sea. I try to advance with the soldiers who remain with me, but I am running too fast. My only weapon is the oak stick. I have no pistol or other weapon. I don't even know what happened to the soldiers around me.

A little later I noticed that there were only a few soldiers from my old company, the 6th, with me. I am running as fast as I can with them. The bullets are passing overhead. I am trying to get off the hill and down into the plain as soon as I can.

At this time I saw some enemy troops to my right waving a white cloth and headed towards them. Further to my right, from the top of a hillock, Lieutenant Cerkez Fehmi was shouting 'They are surrendering, take them'. Five or ten soldiers had got there ahead of me and were bayoneting them when I shouted and stopped them. They had hurt them badly.

These British are either really stupid or unprepared. In a strange country, in a streambed, they had sat down to have breakfast. Jam, biscuits,

Turkish staff officers view the North Anzac and Suvla battlefield. Although parts of the Sari Bair Ridge were captured by the Allies, they were not held and remained an important observation point for the Turks.

sugar, chocolate, butter, cheese, forks and napkins. The napkins are pure cotton. They had been surprised at breakfast.

They could not escape. Or did not. Several of them are dying. How terrible. I did not think of killing and dying any more. We have to take them prisoner. Several blows to the soldiers who have lost control of themselves. I stopped the killing. They had already taken the weapons of the others. I sent the three survivors back with two of the soldiers with me, and a note saying 'Prisoners. In the midst of all this terror I also came by a weapon this way. Luck. I had the dead ones searched. I found some maps. Four maps. A diary. A photograph. I was very saddened by the photograph. A picture of a young man and a young British girl. What a pity.'

At first I thought this was the front line, but it turned out it was not. The strange thing was, that a machine gun somewhere in front of the field where we had taken up positions was keeping our heads down. In the meantime the British threw grenades at two soldiers trying to advance down the streambed to our right. The grenade fragments hit the poor fellows' hearts, and both were killed.

I looked at the faces of our two dead soldiers. Their faces and eyes are covered with dirt, no sign of any light. Their clothes are old and ragged. In contrast the British dead wear clean clothes and good shoes. Our troops immediately put on the tunics, trousers and boots of the dead British they find. Their boots are so well made that our lot can't wear them out in a few years.

Our battalion imam buried our two dead men. In their clothes, of course. They were immediately covered with earth.

We now have names for the dead. Ours are 'martyrs'. Theirs are 'stiffs'.

The British 10th and 11th Divisions were exhausted and lacked morale when the next division, the 53rd, arrived. Their contribution to the campaign was short. The commanding officer, Major General John Lindley, had had no clue, until the last minute, as to his division's role. 'We are naturally very excited to know what our immediate future is,' he had written on 7 August. 'I have not had an idea of any kind since I left England 3 weeks today, and know no more than the most ignorant man in the Division. It seems rather funny, but I don't suppose they know from day to day what will be wanted.'

Lindley had no idea how prescient a comment that was. After landing without incident at C Beach, he was ordered at a few hours' notice to help General Hammersley's 11th Division. Lindley had his reservations about the task but nevertheless committed his troops to the fray. The men had attacked in the morning but suffered heavy casualties owing to a Turkish counter-attack.

Major General John Lindley, GOC 53rd (Welsh) Division

This was about noon and the men were very tired, it was piping hot and there was no water. I ordered a renewal of the attack about 5. This gave the men some chance but from what the Brigadier tells me I did not expect to succeed, and as a matter of fact it [the attack] was more seriously opposed than the morning attack and at 6.30 or 7 the two brigades established themselves for the night very much on the same line as the advanced line of the morning. Of course it was disappointing but all worked well and did their best ... but the men really had no chance owing to the hurried way the thing had to be done. I nearly asked Sir Frederick Stopford on Monday night to put it off for twenty-four hours but I thought he knew the circumstances and I did not like to start on the first day by any objection and he, Sir Frederick, was extremely nice about the whole thing in an interview I had with him at his Headquarters when all was over ... I fear I lost considerably yesterday. Great difficulty experienced all day of the 11th in getting in touch with the brigades. The Cheshires and the North Wales brigades are in an awful muddle owing to so many officers having been killed or wounded, and the men are lost without them.

The division never recovered from the mauling it took fighting for Scimitar Hill and W Hills. Captain Arthur Crookenden's tirade at what happened is astonishing. Whether it is right in every detail is open to question: certainly the division was not as 'well taught' as he suggests, but there is much here that was true. His discourse summed up the entire farrago that was the landing at Suvla Bay.

Captain Arthur Crookenden, Headquarters, 159th Brigade, 53rd Division

No one at Suvla seemed to care a solitary damn. One's first day in action, terribly keen to get the best out of the Terriers one had been training, ready and anxious to prove their metal, confident that they had been well taught, keyed up to concert pitch, one was absolutely amazed, baffled and finally enraged by this sort of tepid blanket of 'Fanny Annie' which hit one at every turn. It spread to the ranks like a fog and very rapidly.

Nothing can convey the atmosphere of indifference, laissez-faire and chaos into which we plunged. Whilst the battalions were trickling along the coast road at the foot of Lala Baba, and my clerk was handing out maps from a packing case to officers as they passed(!), I went up to the top of the knoll. I saw the Salt Lake (dry) covered with men advancing towards me. I saw the HQ Staff (Lindley and Hammersley) of two divisions in a trench on the forward crest – of course in full view of the enemy – this was only on a par with everything else. After examining the situation carefully I offered to capture the distant objective, provided I was given an hour with the company commanders and their maps and compasses on top of this Lala Baba knoll. I was threatened with arrest and told to send two battalions to 'report themselves to Brigadier-General Sitwell'!

'Where?'

The wounded make their way down from sodden trenches at Suvla.

'In the bush.'

'What does Brigadier General Sitwell look like?'

'I don't know.'

This is not an extract from a comic opera, but a verbatim report of two trained Staff College graduates giving and receiving orders on the battlefield. On my refusing to convey any such silly order, I was again threatened with arrest and the order was given to my Brigadier General. The 4th Cheshires and 5th Welsh went off, and we never saw them again until daylight on the 10th. Later, two more battalions (7th Cheshires and 4th Welsh) and Brigade HQ were similarly ordered to 'report to General Sitwell in the bush'.

To find Brigadier General Sitwell, the Brigade Staff advanced ahead of the second pair of battalions (7th Cheshire and 4th Welsh), in line, extended at 250 paces ... After proceeding some distance in this formation, the left-hand man found a Brigadier General, and his Staff lying on their backs resting in the shade of a rough hedge. This was Brigadier General Sitwell. He refused to give any orders, or information, and reiterated ad nauseam 'This is your show'. I nearly brained him.

The brigade had come into action with pouch ammunition, and such boxes as the men could carry off the ship in face of strenuous objections and violent abjurations from the naval landing staff. This completed our administrative arrangements. We had no transport of any kind, sort or description. No sane man imagines a division going into action with nothing but what it can carry in its hands. This is what we did.

These four battalions, less 4th Welsh, which my Brigadier General kept in reserve, eventually, as I learnt later, reached the firing line. To get there, they passed through masses of men retiring, 'escorting' wounded, and mere fugitives, on their way, and were shelled with shrapnel. Night fell, and in my search for my lost two battalions (4th Cheshires and 5th Welsh) I found myself behind the Turks, on the ridge which turned out to be our first objective for the morrow! Anyhow, I found no battalions, and about 2 a.m. along my telegraph wire came a voluminous and complicated order for an attack in cooperation with the 158th Brigade, which we had last seen in Bedford, and as far as we knew were still there! Pitch dark and no hope of getting a line to advance on till daylight! We started off as near time as we could, with the 7th Cheshires in front and the 4th Welsh in reserve. We

Opposite top: Wooden boats in tow evacuate the wounded from Suvla and North Anzac. Bottom: Shallow wooden boxes were used to hoist the wounded on to the hospital ships.

could not get them past the barrier of the entrenched line, because all our men were inextricably mixed up with the 32nd and 34th Brigades. You could not walk along the trench saying 'Come on you, and hold back you', although we tried to do it.

The 11th Division was utterly cooked. About noon the 4th Welsh bolted from the position in rear of the trench, but the 7th Cheshires did not – they were safe in the trench anyhow. The Welsh were stopped by Heard, a GSO3 on Divisional HQ with his revolver. Before 5 p.m. a Wellingtonian order came from the blue – 'The whole line will advance at 5 p.m.' At that hour no one stirred, except Brigadier General Cowan and his staff and a few brave men of all brigades in the vicinity. They ran and walked through the burning bush for 300–400 yards, and finding themselves alone were either shot down by both sides, or walked sulkily and angrily back to the trench.

The amazing thing was that no one cared a damn. The result was a nightmare of funking, bunking, skulking, hiding, thieving, abandoning arms, and miserable cowardice, such as no one ever dreamt possible in any army. Hundreds of brave men killed to no purpose.

Lieutenant Ismail Sunata, 2nd Battalion, 35th Infantry Regiment, 12th Ottoman Division

10 August: Every half a minute to a minute, the enemy is hitting our rear with shrapnel file. We occasionally stand up and scan our front. Since the enemy can clearly see the defence line to our right, where the company commander is, the troops there began to suffer casualties. Some of the bravest and best corporals and soldiers of the company were killed and wounded there.

Wounded began arriving from the platoon on our left as well. There are hills to my right and my left, the enemy is shelling these hills well. We are on a level area, with scrub to our front. If the enemy is to advance, he must stand up to do so. Thus we can see them and defend ourselves quickly. Actually, the scrub hides us from view.

The enemy also realised this and set the brush on fire in the afternoon. We first didn't understand the cause, we realised later what was going on. The wind was blowing from the sea on to the land and the smoke was coming towards us. At this moment several wounded began to arrive from our left flank. They were going to the dressing station in the gun pits behind our lines. There they were bandaged by the medical corporal and sent back.

During this fire a bullet took the upper lip of a soldier lying beside me, shooting and talking. I did not realise it until his voice changed. I didn't know whether to laugh or cry. What cruel wounds these bullets cause in battle. The buttock of one of the men coming from the left has been ripped open, one has a broken arm, another a broken leg.

The fire draws closer and closer. The wind is helping it. We are suffocating in the smoke. The heat of the flames comes with the smoke. The sun is boiling our brains. My lips are dry and cracking from thirst and from the heat. There is no water left in my canteen. I gave it to a soldier and told him to fill it. I returned to the artillery position. There the medical corporal and orderlies from the 34th regiment were eating the biscuits they had captured from the enemy. I had forgotten my hunger. Although it was well past midday I had had no thought of eating. They gave me some of their biscuits. I ate them unwillingly. For some reason they disgust me. I came to the battle line again. The fire was now 50 metres away from us. It was moving even faster on our left. Sergeant-Major Faik Efendi was over there. I don't know how he was doing. His front was also burning. The British were firing and advancing behind the fire. We could not see them for the fire, but we concluded this from the rifle fire.

Several wounded who could not walk crawled up. One of them has had his arm shattered by a bullet through the shoulder joint, he has lost a lot of blood and looks yellow. The other is wounded above the knee and in the buttock. The bullet has shattered the bone. Both are in bad shape. I quickly sent them to the dressing station in our rear. The soldier wounded in the arm, who had lost a lot of blood, is begging 'Let me die, I can't go on'. Dying like that isn't the worst, he'll be burnt alive in the flames as well. I sent him on by force. Fortunately the dressing station is close by, and is outside the brush.

I slowly began to withdraw my soldiers before the fire. We also started firing behind the fire without seeing the enemy. This apparently had some effect. Or it may have been that the burnt scrub was still hot, but the enemy can't advance much. We kept firing. We had abandoned the brush and deployed to the side. Sergeant Faik must have done the same.

At the same time I am wondering about this hullabaloo of life and death. War is neither a game, nor a sacred thing. But it is necessary in the situation we find ourselves in. Because the enemy is on the attack. Whatever the reason, we don't think about the whys and wherefores of the battle.

Captain Frank Mills, 1/6th Royal Welsh Fusiliers, 53rd Division

I do not think you have any idea of the torments everyone suffered through thirst. One can go without food for a long time, but the agonies of thirst go on increasing. As far as I could see, no adequate arrangements had been made for water, without which I have no hesitation in saying no troops can fight properly; the few wells were registered by the Turks, and were, at that time, most of them within rifle shot. The casualties at the wells were enormous, but in spite of this the torments of thirst were so great that it was impossible to keep the troops away from the wells.

Our food for a considerable time consisted of bully beef and biscuits; how the authorities ever thought men could exist on the biscuits that were issued is a marvel to me. They were as hard as bricks, and there was no water to soak them. The teeth of the men were bad, and with false teeth, as a good many of the men had, the hard biscuits were impossible. Melted bully beef is a very different thing to cold sliced bully beef, and in the stringy form it takes when melted it is almost impossible to eat it. At this vital time [August], when good food and water was most needed, this was the state of things.

The incessant heat and dust of the summer is apparent in this image taken of a New Zealand water carrier.

After attacking on 10 August, the few men I had left of my company occupied a shallow Turkish trench for nearly a week. We only had thin drill as clothing, we discarded our packs soon after landing, and never saw the dump again. The cold at night, and heat during the day, were both intense, flies were appalling, food and water was almost nonexistent. There was a small well some little way behind my trench, which I was afraid to let the men use but finally was unable to stop them using. I defy anyone to keep really thirsty men from water if it can possibly be obtained. At night they slipped out of the trench, and tying mess tins to puttees, drew up the water. In the end I had to give way to thirst myself and drink this water, luckily it was all right. I shall never forget it as it was impregnated with wild thyme ...

The cramped position of my men – the trench was only two foot six inches deep – had a bad effect on the men. Only after dark were we able to stretch our limbs and relieve ourselves, and then with the chance of being shot, for the Turks used to fire blindly all through the night. Sanitary arrangements were nonexistent and in the dark it was impossible to get men to use one spot with so many bullets flying all round. The result in a hot climate can be imagined. The nightmare of those first few days will always remain with me. It was impossible to get at some of the wounded in front of the shallow trench, the night wind used to blow from the hills, and the smell from the dead was appalling. Everyone was sweating during the day and the breeze blew fine dust which caked on everyone's face, and filled their hair. Lack of water resulted in everyone's lips cracking and turning black with congealed blood. And every time one moved one's mouth blood streamed down their chins ... I saw several men have fits and faint through lack of water.

11 August: What day was it? I think Wednesday. The day dawned and the sun rose while we dug trenches. Quiet all around. I guess the British are also tired. We gave up digging trenches during the day. We didn't want to draw the enemy's fire by digging and carrying away earth. The men were allowed to sleep in shifts. I had not slept for four nights except for brief naps. I am amazed at how I can handle this lack of sleep amid all this effort and weariness.

Lieutenant Ismail Sunata, 2nd Battalion, 35th Infantry Regiment, 12th Ottoman Division

This evening the 5th Company is to relieve us. We will be pulled back into the streambed as battalion reserve. Being relieved in a place like this, where fighting and death come quickly, is indeed a relief.

Night fell, and darkness came.

Lieutenant Sunata's battalion was withdrawn temporarily from the front line. Nevertheless, the fighting continued with little respite as the British strove to secure a bridgehead in the face of determined Turkish resistance. Tragedy was heaped upon tragedy. The 54th Division arrived next and were thrown into the

Mules carrying water up on to Walker's Ridge at Anzac. Russell's Top is in the background.

Second Lieutenant Arthur Pelly, 1/5th Norfolk Regiment, 54th Division

furnace. Nineteen-year-old Second Lieutenant Arthur Pelly of the 1/5th Norfolk Regiment had just enough time to pen a letter home. He was happy, excited and ignorant. The letter is dated 12 August.

I wish you could be with us; it is lovely; I mean the weather … We landed two days ago, and at once began a long, winding, slippery march. At 2 o'clock we lay down till 4.30 and then on we went, until flop! The first shell fell just in front of my platoon. We then dug ourselves in on very hard ground in the blazing sun, with shells – our first taste of fire – dropping round. But the Turks must be short of ammunition, and I had no casualties; the platoon next to me three. Thank God for our Navy. The Turks have as yet only small guns, and our battleships succeed in silencing them in a wonderful way, and that roar of our 12-pounders is very comforting. Two divisions landed on this place before us – one on each flank; we are in the centre opposite our objective, a big hill, but apparently the flanks are doing the work, and we are getting a bit of rest. It is lovely, frightfully hot weather, but the nights are equally frightfully cold. We carry no pack, but just a haversack, water bottle, revolver, and field glasses. Well, here have I been resting in the shade for four hours. Goodness knows when this will get posted.

Three days later, Pelly wrote again. He had been lucky.

What a lot has happened since I wrote the above. The same night [afternoon] we had the most awful smack … We were suddenly ordered out at four, and down we went into the Turks. We were opposed by a wall of bullets, and were knocked over right and left. I got too far ahead, lost my way, and, trying to find it again, was bagged by a Turkish sniper – which swarm – at very close range. The bullet broke my left lower jaw, tore my tongue in shreds, and then out through the right cheek. Then after an awful wandering, the heroes, the RAMC, got me, and by 11 o'clock they had carried me right back – six miles – to expert care on the hospital ship. I cannot speak, and eating consists of sucking milk down a tube; swallowing is quite an agony. I am not to have my jaw set till I have recovered more blood. Flies are a curse. My mouth pours saliva and a little blood still, and anything in the way of a soiled bandage the flies form fours on. That was an awful night – absolute Hell. Excellent doctors, nurses, and the padre on board. My compass, revolver, etc. were all lost.

Second Lieutenant Arthur Pelly, 1/5th Norfolk Regiment, 54th Division

Despite his extensive injuries, Pelly survived Gallipoli, dying in old age in 1966.

This latest venture had gone the way of all the others. The attack by 163rd Brigade was meant to pave the way for a large-scale attack on the 13th towards Tekke Tepe, those distant fringing hills. Mercifully, this attack was called off. An order was given to consolidate, in other words to dig in. The Turks had held the British in a small pocket, as they had at Helles and at Anzac. Nothing much would now change; anything else, any new attack, was simply froth and bubble. The campaign was over; all it needed now was for it to dawn on someone, but that was unlikely just a week after a major landing. When another attack was ordered for the 15th, nobody was surprised.

Second Lieutenant
Ivonne Kirkpatrick,
5th Royal
Inniskilling
Fusiliers, 10th
Division

The preparations for the attack having been completed, there was nothing to do but to sit down and wait. In order to fill in the time, the company mess had a large meal at 11 a.m. – my first on the Peninsula – out of a Fortnum and Mason hamper which had just arrived. Tinned fruit, bottled asparagus, potted meat, dates, biscuits and so on; everything was devoured with the utmost celerity. During the meal we discussed the coming attack and arranged what was to be done with our effects if we were killed or wounded. I estimated for three casualties but was hooted down as a prophet of evil. No one guessed that by evening no survivors would be left to carry out our complicated testamentary dispositions.

The same day as the attack went in, yet another senior officer was killed. His name was Sir William Napier, officer commanding 4th South Wales Borderers. Sir William was a retired officer who had offered his services on the outbreak of war. What made this death so poignant was that his son had gone to his father's aid. Later that day, Lieutenant Joseph Napier penned a letter to his mother.

Lieutenant Joseph
Napier, Royal Field
Artillery, 13th
Division

Dear Mater

I daresay by now you will have had the 'War Office' telegram about Pater's death: I don't know whether they send them, but I will send one myself at the first opportunity: you see I am writing the day it occurred. Anyhow I'll tell you all I know.

About 6.10 this morning, a Sergeant from 'A' Company came down the trench and told me Pater had been shot in the back. I thought at the time that it was probably an ordinary wound. But on reaching their trenches [I] climbed out under cover, and found Pater, Servant Keene and their Company Sergeant Major putting the first aid dressing round him. His head at the time was covered by his coat which had been put there to get at his body. I still supposed him more or less all right, though there was a lot of blood about, until I happened to pull the coat back from his face, when I saw that he was already dead – and looked perfectly natural. He didn't live 5 minutes after being hit and never uttered a word. He was hit somewhere in the back while walking down one of his trenches which at the point were very low (only just dug). A sniper did the work …

I know it will come as an awful blow to you, but you must try and forget it as soon as you can. He died better here than of illness or some other way in England. Quite painless was his death.

Living here as one does in the middle of dead and wounded friends, I was not so affected about it as I thought I should be. Nevertheless I feel very much that I have a loss, a something that cannot be replaced.

I don't know if I have put things somewhat crudely or severely (I hope not) as I think a frank account of such events is best, though possibly most hurting. It has made me feel more than ever how much I want to get back to England, as does everyone here – I feel that I don't mind what the cost is (bodily) if only I could get back.

The Battalion has had a rough time and very few officers remain … in fact the 13th Division almost ceases to exist.

Your loving son, Joe

The County of London Yeomanry (Sharpshooters) in a front-line trench at Suvla. Note the trench periscope.

News of the failure at Suvla spread among the troops. Nothing appeared to work and yet there was no sign that the fighting would end. Hamilton cabled Kitchener to give a report on operations and, naturally enough, to ask for more reinforcements, at least another 50,000 men to bring the campaign to a successful conclusion. The idea was a delusion, but then what else could he do, other than to place the blame for failure well and truly on the shoulders of his immediate subordinates? There would have to be wholesale changes, although Hamilton himself survived for the time being.

Major General
Granville Egerton,
GOC 52nd
(Lowland) Division

28 August: I have not written for quite a number of days in the diary; partly because after a long day visiting my advance trenches 9 to 3 p.m., I got knocked over by the sun, and captured another go of diarrhoea, and partly because things have looked so bad and I have been so depressed that I have not had the heart to write much …

Freddy Stopford, the GOC, has been sent home. Fred Shaw, commanding 13th Division, who was sent to relieve me on the night of 13 July because I was supposed to be done, has been invalided. Hammersley, 11th Division, and Lindley, 53rd Division, have both been edged out and there has been a wholesale debacle. Meanwhile I hear General Headquarters and the French are terribly disappointed at this failure, for this is all it is. If it was not for the wet weather coming, I would not so much mind, but this fills me with doubt. Joey Davies agreed with me this morning, our government has gambled on the Turk caving in before the wet season. The Turk 'au contraire' has staked his all on holding out until the wet season. He has done more than hold out.

The Turks had reinforced and they were strengthened. The British bridgehead was secure at Suvla; they were not going to be pushed into the sea, but the ground they held was overlooked by the Turks on all sides. The enemy could drop shells wherever they liked and they could look down from the heights of Kiretch Tepe and Tekke Tepe with impunity and watch any significant move the British made. The British could straighten their line, if they wished, adopt the policy of bite and hold, but there were now no wider objectives. When the 29th Division was brought round from Helles to help spearhead an attack on

Scimitar Hill and the 11th Division tackled W Hills, the question surely had to be asked as to the point. Major General Beauvoir de Lisle had been given temporary command of IX Corps on the dismissal of Stopford. Was this really much more than a senior British officer showing his commanding officer, Hamilton, that he was on top of the job, 'doing something'?

Close to Lala Baba, de Lisle kept his only reserves, the 2nd Mounted Division, dismounted territorial Yeomanry Regiments, when the attack was launched mid-afternoon, 21 August. On Scimitar Hill the advantage fluctuated according to who had immediate numerical supremacy. To help, de Lisle inexplicably sent forward his reserves straight across the dried Salt Lake in full view of the enemy and with absolutely no cover. The Turkish guns could have had no easier target and they sprayed the Salt Lake with bursts of shrapnel as the infantry walked, then doubled towards Chocolate Hill. The losses were heinous and their attack on Scimitar or W Hills had not even begun.

About 3 p.m. we moved off. It was a beautiful Saturday afternoon and as I waited for the order to advance my thoughts flew [home] to Sparkhill. I could picture the happy people getting ready to go out into the country on bikes, motor cars etc. I wondered if I should ever see Stratford Road again. I learned afterwards that my sister Winnie was enjoying herself at a wedding about the same time.

Corporal Edward Godrich, 1/1st Worcestershire Yeomanry, 2nd Mounted Division

We advanced in column of troops across an open plain. All went well till the leading Brigade got halfway. Then hell was let loose. We machine-gunners could not hurry owing to the heavy loads that we were struggling under. We soon came across several poor chaps who had finished their soldiering, they looked just as though they were asleep. I met Billy Cruse coming back with his thumb knocked off; we passed Captain Russell lying in a pool of blood from a nasty wound in his thigh; he was laughing all over his face and as we passed him he waved his hand and told us to keep 'well extended'. I remember thinking amid all the noise, what a lot of things needed picking up – caps, rifles, equipment. I shall not forget in a hurry a small fellow of the South Notts Yeomanry. He had been hit across the knuckles by a piece of shell, completely smashing his fingers. He was about seventeen or eighteen I should say, and was very upset because he had lost his rifle.

Sergeant John
Hargrave, 32nd
Field Ambulance,
RAMC, 10th
Division

The shells from the Turks set light to the dried sage, and thistle and thorn, and soon the whole place was blazing. It was a fearful sight. Many wounded tried to crawl away, dragging their broken arms and legs out of the burning bushes and were cremated alive.

It was impossible to rescue them. Boxes of ammunition caught fire and exploded with terrific noise in thick bunches of murky smoke. A bombing section tried to throw off their equipment before the explosives burst, but many were blown to pieces by their own bombs. Puffs of white smoke rose up in little clouds and floated slowly across the Salt Lake.

The flames ran along the ridges in long lapping lines with a canopy of blue and grey smoke. We could hear the crackle of the burning thickets, and the sharp 'bang!' of bullets. The sand round Suvla Bay hid thousands of bullets and ammunition pouches, some flung away by wounded men, some belonging to the dead. As the bush-fires licked from the lower slopes of the Sari Bair towards Chocolate Hill this lost ammunition exploded, and it sounded like erratic rifle fire. The fires glowed and spluttered all night, and went on smoking in the morning. I had to go up to Chocolate Hill about some sandbags for our hospital dugouts next day, and on the way up I noticed a human pelvis and a chunk of charred human vertebrae under a scorched and charcoaled thorn bush.

Temp. Chaplain
Arthur Parham,
Attd. Headquarters
2nd South Midland
Mounted Brigade

Sunday 22 August 11.00 a.m.: I start my diary again after a gap of only twenty-four hours but such hours that I feel as if nothing can ever be quite the same again. At noon yesterday the battleships and land batteries started a terrific bombardment of the enemy's position. The noise was perfectly appalling and we sat down on our beach and watched the guns belching their fire. We ate our rations at 12.30 and at 2.30 paraded to start. It was a wonderful sight, all our splendid clean young Yeomen and thousands of others – about 10,000 in all … I went about in the middle, after the brigade, with Pearson the Bucks doctor and his ambulance section. About halfway across the valley, perhaps a mile and a half from our starting place, the enemy's guns found us; high explosive, shrapnel and star shells which soon set alight the gorse and bushes with which the plain was covered. Pearson very rightly felt he must push on to keep as near the brigade as possible and would not stop to attend to the wounded who were moaning all round us. But I had no particular job except to do what I could [and] not leave these wounded to be burned alive by the gorse fire. I stopped beside a group of six, one of whom was dead, and did what we could to patch up their wounds with field dressings which each man carries.

It was awful, the fire was drawing alarmingly near so I took off my pack and left everything with George, telling him if I did not return to make his way to any ambulance station. Then I ran with the bullets whizzing all round me to where I saw some ambulance men working. All their stretchers were occupied but I turned off the comparatively slightly wounded men and took three stretchers at a run to my group of wounded near the fire. We got them all away into a little hollow and left them there. One man with the back of his head blown off must, I think, have died very soon but anyway he was not burned alive, as no doubt many were.

My splendid brigade is utterly shattered and more than half those dear boys I have lived with for nearly ten months are killed or wounded. The General is dead, only eight officers out of the whole brigade are known to be sound in body. Two officers came back to Chocolate Hill in the night untouched but absolutely mad, one like a stupid child from the shock of shells bursting over him, Phil Wroughton of the Berks. Another, Jack Young of the Bucks, who all the men say behaved magnificently and practically saved the remnants of the brigade, in raving delirium. I heard much of the terrible story from his incessant talk as I tried to quiet him to sleep.

It is all so awful I dare not think about it yet and how it is that I am still alive myself I don't know. (As I write this I am lying on my stomach in the dirt with my head in a hole in a bank while stray bullets or a sniper's, we hardly know which, whistle above us and shells with their hideous roar rush over our heads.)

The objectives set the men were beyond their capabilities, but they were in truth beyond even battle-hardened men. A third of all those engaged that day became casualties for no ostensible gain. All sense of purpose and proportion was gone. Turkish casualties were high, too, owing, in part, to their stubborn bravery and a determination not to cede ground even when of dubious strategic worth.

Major General
Granville Egerton,
GOC, 52nd
(Lowland) Division

30 August: Someone sent me two big packets last mail from Harrods; one small one contained biscuits; the other, a huge fat one which I gloated over as likely to be full of pâté de fois gras, and plovers' eggs in aspic, etc., contained about two reams of writing paper. Very useful all the same. I have no idea who the donor is – but I should have preferred the pâté.

Oh my God, what a life this is! I shall want a six months' rest cure if I survive it, and please God no more soldiering for me again. A garden and the cultivation of flowers is what I look forward to.

I got a cable yesterday from the Lord Provost of Glagow saying that his sister, Mrs Galbraith, had had one son killed here on 12 July [William Galbraith, 7th Highland Light Infantry], a second killed in the trenches a fortnight ago [David Galbraith, 7th Highland Light Infantry], and that a third son [Norman] had just arrived here, and she was terribly anxious about losing the third – could anything be done? I had already some days previously taken the matter in hand, and the whole story seemed so tragical that I had obtained sanction to send the young man to Alexandria for duty with the transport. I had ordered him out of the trenches at once, preparatory to his going today. When I sent for him yesterday, I found he had gone back to the trenches, 'to say goodbye to his friends'. Fortunately he returned safe and bar a submarine en route, and the changes and chances of this mortal life, there is a possibility of his poor mother seeing him again. [Norman was killed in France in August 1918.]

This afternoon appeared the Corps Commander, Lieutenant General Sir Francis Davies, together with Sir Ian Hamilton and his Chief Staff Officer, General Braithwaite. They all talked in a very friendly way but I told Sir Ian straight, what I had told Davies, viz.: that my division had benefited greatly by going into the trenches, but I must have fresh blood in the ranks; that all my brigadiers said they would attack if ordered to, of course, but they doubted how it would go. I do not know if I was wise but I am not going to tell lies and say that my division is fit to go anywhere, at anything. They can kick me out if they like, but I will go down an honest man. Sir Ian looked absolutely wretchedly ill. I had a few words with young Deedes, the intelligence officer, and he told me, as I guessed, that the situation at Suvla was the same as here – stalemate – damn!

Opposite: The 21 August attack across the Salt Lake shows the Yeomanry advancing under heavy Turkish shrapnel fire. A number of casualties can be seen.

The queer thing is, that when I look back upon that 'Great Failure', it is not the danger or the importance of the undertaking which is strongly impressed so much as a jumble of smells and sounds and small things. It is just these small things which no author can make up in his study at home.

The glitter of someone carrying an army biscuit tin along the mule track; the imprinted tracks of sand-birds by the blue Aegean shore; the stink of the dead; a dead man's hand sticking up through the sand; the blankets soaked each morning by the heavy dew; the incessant rattle of a

Sergeant John Hargrave, 32nd Field Ambulance, RAMC, 10th Division

machine gun behind Pear-tree Gully; the distant ridges of the Sari Bahir range shimmering in the heat of noon-day; the angry 'buzz' of the green and black flies disturbed from a jam-pot lid; the grit of sand in the mouth with every bite of food; the sullen dullness of the overworked, death-wearied troops; the hoarse dried-up and everlasting question: 'Any water?'; the silence of the Hindus of the Pack-Mule Corps; the 'S-s-s-e-e-e-o-o-o-op! – Crash!' – of the high explosives bursting in a bunch of densely solid smoke, and the slow unfolding of these masses of smoke and sand in black and khaki rolls; the snort and stampede of a couple of mules bolting along the beach with their trappings swinging and rattling under their panting bellies; the steady burning of the starlit night skies; the regular morning shelling from the Turkish batteries on the break of dawn over the gloom-shrouded hills; the faraway call of some wounded man for 'Stretchers! Stretchers!'; the naked white men splashing and swimming in the bay; the swoop of a couple of skinny vultures over the burning white sand of the Salt Lake bed to the stinking and decomposing body of a shrapnel-slaughtered mule hidden in the willow thickets at the bottom of Chocolate Hill; a torn and bullet-pierced French warplane stranded on the other side of Lala Baba – lying over at an angle like a wounded white seabird; the rush

40th Field Ambulance dressing station at No. 3 Outpost. Stretcher-bearers evacuate a casualty to the beach.

Wounded men being loaded on to boats ready to be towed from the shore. Note the hospital ship on the horizon.

for the little figure bringing in 'the mails' in a sack over his shoulder; the smell of iodine and iodoform round the hospital tents; the long wobbling moan of the Turkish long-distance shells, and the harmless 'Z-z-z-eee-e-e-o-ooop!' of their 'dud' shells which buried themselves so often in the sand without exploding; the tattered, begrimed and sunken-eyed appearance of men who had been in the trenches for three weeks at a stretch; the bristling unshaven chins, and the craving desire for 'Woodbines'; the ingrained stale blood on my hands and arms from those fearful gaping wounds, and the red-brown bloodstain patches on my khaki drill clothes; the pestering curse of those damnable Suvla Bay flies and the lice with which every officer and man swarmed.

Overleaf: Utter exhaustion: Anzacs asleep by their gun.

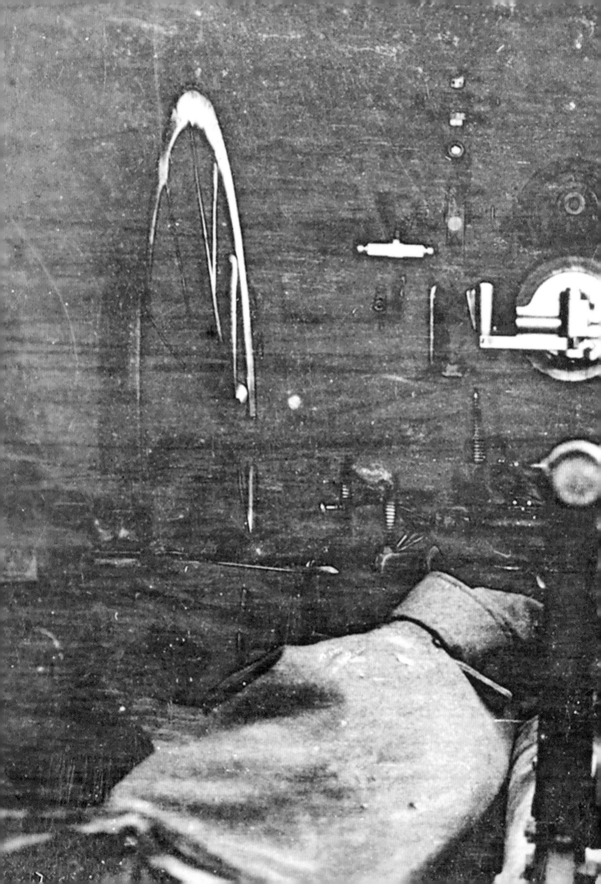

6 Sanctioning Defeat

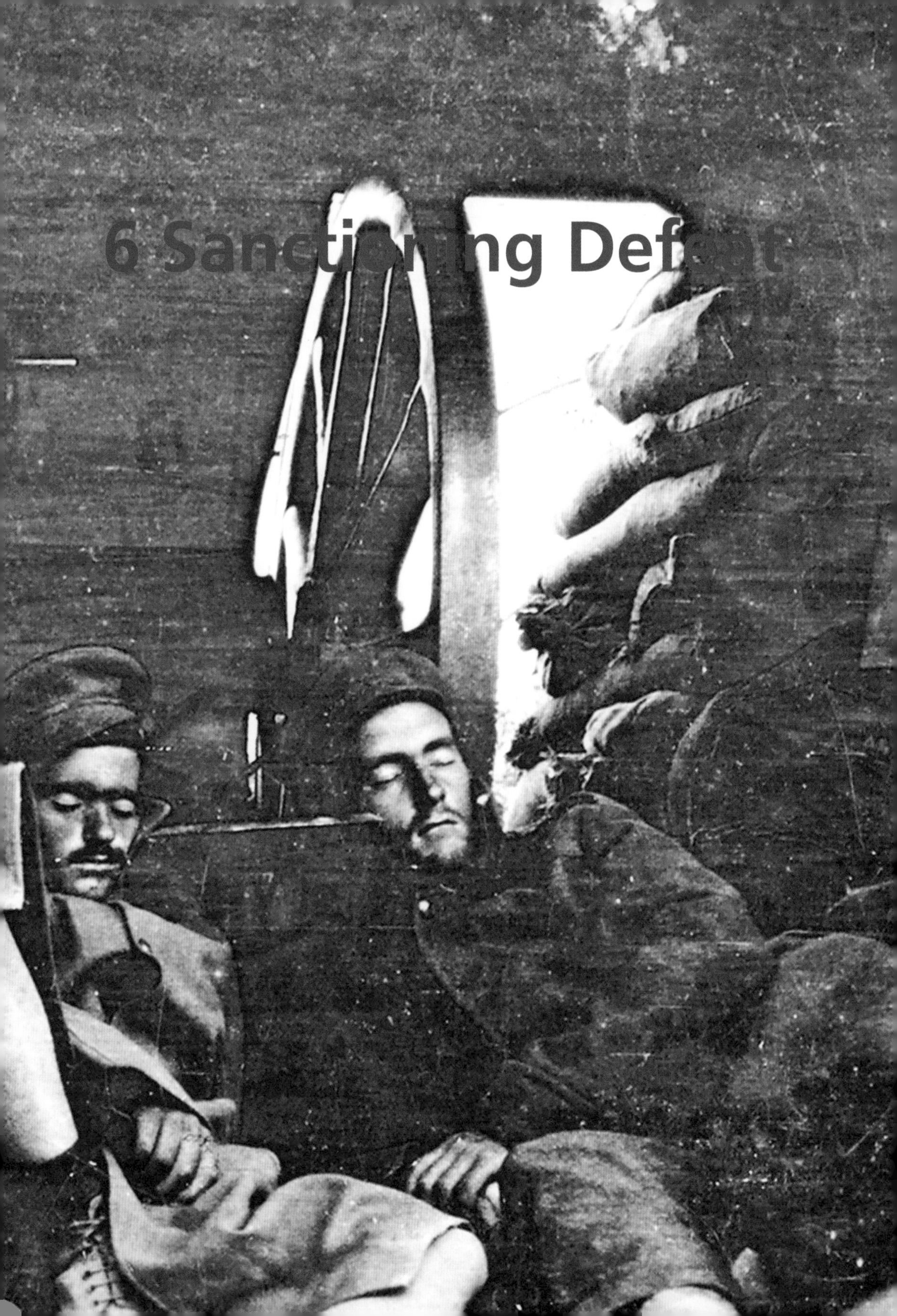

As the men left, many glances were cast over their shoulders, not, I believe, in fear that the Turks were attacking, but by way of saying goodbye to Suvla Bay and all its memories, not forgetting friends they were leaving behind. The silence was fantastic: all that could be heard was heavy breathing, the paddling of feet and an occasional stumble.

Second Lieutenant Philip Gething, 9th Royal Warwickshire Regiment, 13th Division

---

In September, the stark reality of the situation on Gallipoli would begin to sink in with everyone on or just off Suvla Bay, Anzac Cove or Helles. Winter was coming, and then what? There could be no advance when tens of thousands of men shivered and froze. Morale was fragile now; how fragile would it be in December with no prospect of relief or progress and an overwhelming sense of isolation? A belief that there was little purpose or point to the campaign permeated the trenches and the corridors of power. The first to waver openly in their commitment to the campaign were the French, whose efforts on the Western Front had far outstripped those of Britain and her Empire combined. In September, a joint Anglo-French offensive would open in France and no further French divisions would be assigned to Gallipoli, at least for the foreseeable future.

What we all feel here is that there is no leadership, no sense of anyone being at the head who is developing a plan. We are simply being butchered with no apparent result … It is impossible to suggest or describe the horror of this constant shelling or its strain upon the nerves. One moment you are apparently safe and free from danger, the next men are writhing in agony all

Temp. Chaplain Arthur Parham, Attd. Headquarters 2nd South Midland Mounted Brigade

The Royal Engineers Signal Service was responsible for maintaining telephone communication between evacuation beaches until the last possible moment.

around you and you marvel why you are yourself alive. Here we are in what is supposed to be a rest camp, in reserve behind the trenches, and in two days we have lost something like 10 per cent of our numbers. We have literally been decimated – that is, the survivors of the action last week.

Parham had arrived on Gallipoli only in mid-August and yet he was weary of the evident sense of drift. Until something was decided, the men would sit and wait and endure whatever either the Turks or nature deemed to throw at them.

Temp. Chaplain Arthur Parham, Attd. Headquarters 2nd South Midland Mounted Brigade

It is indeed a curious existence that we lead, in peril every instant, unwashed, unshaved, with filthy clothes, living in holes in the ground. Water is far too precious to be used for washing. I have not washed at all since we landed, nor shaved since Friday, and I have a stubbly red beard and need washing more than can be said! I have no clothes except what I stand up in, and they are filthy from sweat, dirt, dust and wounded men's blood. All I have with me is my haversack, containing two handkerchiefs, my emergency ration and some chocolate and sundry such things, my mess tin, Burberry [coat] and my Communion Set, which there has been no possibility of using yet. I have a handkerchief knotted round my neck, my hair is matted with dust and dirt and I am, judging by my hands, very sunburnt. In short I suppose that no tramp in England is more dirty or more disreputable.

Those fortunate enough to be billeted close to the beach had the chance of a revitalising, if hazardous, dip in the sea. Private Bernard Gill was a reinforcement sent to the 40th Field Ambulance, 13th Division.

Private Bernard Gill, 40th Field Ambulance, RAMC, 13th Division

At first we had little to do apart from attending the morning sick parades, dispensing the remedies prescribed for the patients and taking our share of the routine work of the camp. For a week or two, while stocks lasted, a rasher of prime smoked bacon was issued to each man with his breakfast rations. At dawn dozens of small fires glowed and flamed between the rows of dugouts, and the delicious smell of fried bacon floated on the breeze. Our primus stove (part of the dispensary equipment) gave us a good start in the

race to get the sizzling fat into our mouths. We made good use of our leisure: usually it was possible to have a swim some time during the day. The beach, still littered with gruesome relics of the August landings, was only a few yards from the camp. Splintered boats and pinnaces lay with broken ribs, and bathers had to be on the alert for coils of barbed wire on the bottom, empty cartridges and broken bayonets.

A lifeline home: a melancholy-looking Australian sits on a pile of mailbags. Post from home was vital to men's morale.

When the sun had but an hour to live, and the wind and the dust and the flies were already dwindling, we climbed down a cliff-path where the Indians kept their sacred but odorous goats. There was a fringe of rocks under the cliffs where we could dive. There we undressed, hot and grimy, lousy, thirsty, and tired. Along the rocks solitary Indians were kneeling towards Mecca.

Sub-Lieutenant Alan Herbert, Hawke Battalion, Royal Naval Division

Some of the old battered boats of the first landing were still nosing the shore, and at a safe distance was a dead mule. The troops did not come here but waded noisily in the shallow water; so all was quiet, save for an occasional lazy shell from Asia and the chunk-chunk of a patrol boat. The sea at this hour put on its most perfect blue, and the foothills across the Straits were all warm and twinkling in the late sun. So we sat and drank in the strengthening breeze, and felt the clean air on our contaminated flesh; and, plunging luxuriously into the lovely water, forgot for a magical moment all our weariness and disgust.

Temp. Lieutenant Colonel Marcus de la Poer Beresford, 1/4th South Wales Borderers, 13th Division

We stand to arms every morning now from 4.30 a.m. to 6 and the men get their tot of rum when there is any to give them. Heaps of digging fatigues all day. Part of our trenches was hotly shelled nearly all the afternoon. The plain we are on seems to be quite an agricultural one, and our trenches are dug in stubble fields which are divided here and there by hedges and ditches. Amongst the many trees which are dotted about are fig and mulberry trees and the covered shelter I live in has a large mulberry tree growing right over it. It is difficult to see how we could advance anywhere about here as the Turkish trenches appear to be very strong and formidable everywhere in front of us. It is very sickening the way the numbers in the battalion are going down. We are now only 249 strong out of a battalion of about 1,000 who came out, and there is no prospect of any reinforcements joining us. Sickness, deaths and wounds cause a serious daily toll. A peculiar thing about these trenches is that in some cases after you have dug down three or four feet you come to broken pieces of earthenware jugs, which must have been buried down there hundreds of years ago. I suppose they would cause great interest to those who specialised in that sort of thing, but they are too broken up to collect or piece together.

Brigade Major Cuthbert Lucas takes an early morning stretch.

Sapper Reginald Gale, 2nd Naval Brigade Signals, RND

I remember a padre rolling up one evening and we gathered round expectantly. He began by saying that the ground on which we stood was famous in ancient history. He went on talking about Helen of Troy, the

Wooden Horse, Ulysses and his battles and travels. I was fascinated. Like most boys of my social class I had left school early to earn a living and that lecture opened a new world to me. When I got home I purchased Homer's works.

One Sunday evening a padre arrived in our camp and handed out hymn books to all of us who happened to be around. It was dusk and already too dark to read, but it gave us a nice feeling to hold the books. We had no musical instrument, of course, but that was not too important because all the hymns were well-known ones and the singing went quite well. We sat around on the parapets and listened to his homely little talk. I do not remember anything he said and to what denomination he belonged I cannot say. But at least one of his congregation enjoyed that forty-five-minute service. Perhaps it was because we lived so close to the next world that we were emotional. We ended with 'Abide With Me' and the background of small arms fire no doubt added to the sincerity of our singing.

Below: A priest gives a gathering of Australian troops a blessing at Anzac.

On our red identity disc was stamped your name, initials, regiment and the initials of your own particular fancy in the religious line – like CE (Church of England), RC (Roman Catholic), OD (Other Denominations, or more tersely abbreviated by us to Odds and Sods). Besides being decorative they had a real practical value and were no end helpful to the Celestial Traffic

Private Charles Watkins, 1/6th Lancashire Fusiliers, 42nd Division

Cop busy in those early days directing the stream of traffic crowding in towards St Peter's Gate. The main road would be full of the more numerous CEs, and with the RCs and ODs being allowed to filter through now and again from the side roads. So you see, to go into battle without your identity disc would be inviting real trouble.

Being RC meant that we were of the Only True Faith, and also ensured, or so we hoped, that we could pass through those Golden Gates without to many formalities. RC meant, too, that among other things we believed in the power of our protecting saints to shield us from all harm. And if the protecting saint fell down on his job now and then and the bullet ripped into your guts, well – even a saint can slip up sometimes.

I turned to comment on this to the Lance Corporal crouched alongside me but he didn't reply. He'd just had half his lower jaw shot away with a clump of shrapnel balls. For a few brief seconds his eyes held mine in the mute agony of the badly wounded. I remember, and still with disgust, the sickening feeling of elation I got when I saw it was he and not me that had been hit. I have learned that such a reaction as was mine is a normality in human behaviour, but until I knew that, the sense of shame I first got had haunted me for many, many years. That little black devil of shame you keep trying to push down deep into the well of forgetfulness – it for ever keeps bobbing up, and it is only after the thing is explained to you properly that you feel like a man suddenly released from a dark dungeon.

At Suvla the men settled in. More trenches were dug, more dugouts, more saps, more latrines, more tracks, roads and jetties: building infrastructure was a normal response to battlefield stagnation. As men burrowed deeper, and reinforced dugouts and trenches, they made it just that little bit harder for the enemy to maim or kill. On the beach, they proved to be adept miners, hacking into sandy hillocks near Lala Baba with pick and shovel, shoring up the sides with any timber they could find and sandbagging the outside so that only a direct hit would have serious repercussions for those inside.

All day long high explosives used to sing and burst – sometimes killing and wounding men, sometimes blowing up the bully beef and biscuits, sometimes falling with a hiss and a column of white spray into the sea. It was here that the field telegraph of the Royal Engineers became a tangled spider's web of wires and cross wires. They added wires and branch wires every day, and stuck them up on thin poles. Here you could see the engineers in shirts and shorts trying to find a disconnection, or carrying a huge reel of wire. Wooden shanties sprang up where dugouts had been a day or so before. Piers began to crawl out into the bay, adding a leg and trestle and pontoon every hour. Near Kangaroo Beach was the camp of the Indians, and here you could see the dusky ones praying on prayer mats and cooking rice and 'chupatties' (sort of oatcake-pancakes).

Here they were laying a light rail from the beach up with trucks for carrying shells and parts of big guns. Here was the field post office with sacks and sacks of letters and parcels. Some of the parcels were burst and unaddressed; a pair of socks or a mouldy home-made cake squashed in a cardboard box – sometimes nothing but the brown paper, card box and string, an empty shell – the contents having disappeared. What happened to all the parcels which never got to the Dardanelles no one knows, but those which did arrive were rifled and lost and stolen. Parcels containing cigarettes had a way of not getting delivered, and cakes and sweets often fell out mysteriously on the way from England.

Kangaroo Beach was where the Australian bridge-building section had their stores and dugouts. It was one muddle and confusion of water tanks, pier planks, pontoons, huge piles of bully beef, biscuit and jam boxes. Here we came each evening with the water cart to get our supply of water, and here the water carts of every unit came down each evening and stood in a row and waited their turn. The water was pumped from the water-tank boats to the tank on shore. It was filthy water, full of dirt, and very brackish to taste. Also it was warm. During the two months at Suvla Bay I never tasted a drop of cold water – it was always sickly, lukewarm, sun-stewed.

One evening the Colonel sent me from our dugout near the Salt Lake to A Beach to make a report on the water supply. I trudged along the sandy shore. At one spot I remember the carcass of a mule washed up by the tide, the flesh rotted and sodden, and here and there a yellow rib bursting

Sergeant John Hargrave, 32nd Field Ambulance, RAMC, 10th Division

Royal Mail 'Cleared Sundays & Thursday at 5pm': the First New Zealand Battery postbox on Gallipoli.

through the skin. Its head floated in the water and nodded to and fro with a most uncanny motion with every ripple of the bay. The wet season was coming on, and the chill winds went through my khaki drill uniform. The sky was overcast, and the bay, generally a kaleidoscope of eastern blues and greens, was dull and grey.

At A Beach I examined the pipes and tanks of the water-supply system and had a chat with the Australians who were in charge. I drew a small plan, showing how the water was pumped from the tanks afloat to the standing tank ashore, and suggested the probable cause of the sand and dirt of which the CO complained. This done, I found our own ambulance water cart just ready to return to our camp with its nightly supply. Evening was giving place to darkness, and soon the misty hills and the bay were enveloped in starless gloom.

The traffic about A Beach was always congested. It reminded you of the Bank and the Mansion House crush far away in London town. Here were clanking water carts, dozens of them waiting in their turn, stamping mules and snorting horses; here were motor-transport wagons with 'WD' [War Department] in white on their grey sides; ambulance wagons jolting slowly back to their respective units, sometimes full of wounded, sometimes empty. Here all was bustle and noise. Sergeants shouting and corporals cursing; transport officers giving directions; a party of New Zealand sharpshooters in Scout hats and leggings laughing and yarning; a patrol of the REs Telegraph Section coming in after repairing the wires along the beach; or a new batch of men, just arrived, falling in with new-looking kitbags.

New troops were no longer naive about the conditions on the Peninsula, but there was still a sense of excitement at landing on what was rapidly becoming hallowed ground.

We landed where the first landing was made. I had heard about our boys charging up an almost perpendicular cliff. Tonight for the first time, I believe it. That they retained a footing on this land is marvellous. We marched around the beach (from Anzac) towards Gaba Tepe. Arrived at our battalion quarters. They are in a long deep narrow gully. The slopes are covered with small prickly bushes. Drink of coffee. Went to sleep on ground and lulled for the first time by the sound of bullets …

Packed off at 10 a.m. as fatigue party in the trenches. Climbed the northern slope, passed through numerous communication trenches and set to work navvying. Put on in three reliefs. About five o'clock both sides commenced a bombardment. Bombs, shrapnel, 75s, high explosives, bullets and old scraps of flying metal were as common as black faces in Cairo. Being just a trifle new to this I was very interested. Our guns had the best of it all the way. They are wonderful. They land shells in the Turks' trenches at times only 25 yards from ours, from miles back and only frighten us. A chip off a High Explosive smacked a chap near me. Didn't hurt him. All night our chaps pelted bombs at Abdul, poor Abdul. I would not swap him places for money. Rifle fire goes on incessantly with no other effects than to prevent either side putting up entanglements and to interest newcomers …

Sergeant Clifford Ellis, 24th Battalion, AIF

The 24th Battalion had taken up defensive positions at Lone Pine. There they remained for much of the next three months. Owing to the intensity of the fighting, the 24th exchanged front-line duties on a regular and frequent basis with its sister battalion, the 23rd. Here, the proximity of the enemy was surprising, as little as a few feet in places.

Stand to at 3.45 a.m. Fixed bayonets and equipment up. Then at about 4 a.m. a green rocket lit the hills and our guns started. Poor Abdul! But he took it philosophically. Poured in the harmless rifle fire and said nothing. Into the firing line at eleven. I was allotted a party of about a dozen under a chap by the name of Jack Mackereth. The duty of this party is to pelt bombs at Abdul, look out for any return of the compliment and guard a couple of saps. I was led along a trench where I could see through a loophole in a pile of sandbags into the Turkish trenches, just four feet away. Abdul likes this

Sergeant Clifford Ellis, 24th Battalion, AIF

handy spot for bomb pelting … I've got to convince him that he really isn't wanted there …

Bombs are neat little surprise packets that Abdul and we pitch about from side to side for mutual amusement. These have recently been responsible for a few angels. There are three chief kinds used by us. The Cricket Ball bomb – an iron case containing cordite and exploded by fuse. The Jam Tin bomb – two concentric tin cylinders, the space between the two containing resin and scraps of iron, the inner cylinder containing the explosive sent off by a fuse. The Cricket Ball bomb – a flat affair attached to a stick. This is a concussion bomb and is the champion corpse causer. These bombs are flung by hand from saps that jut out of the firing line towards the other chap's quarters. They are also flung by catapults – a Shanghai-like instrument and by trench mortars. We are more generous with these articles than Abdul…

Guarded second sap today. It's as black as pitch, just a pile of sandbags and a loophole separate us from the quarters of our friends the enemy. There is a Turkish sentry on the other side. The poor chap has a nasty cold. Some eucalyptus and puncture of lead would fix the matter up.

Private Thomas Dry, 23rd Battalion, AIF

The Turks opened up a heavy bombardment and [we] bore the brunt of it all. Shells of all descriptions were poured into us. You would feel the earth quake as a shell would bore its way into the earth. Men were ordered to take cover in the tunnels, but to what avail? A shell would come crashing through the tunnel and bury unknown numbers alive. Stretcher-bearers running past with their dead or wounded, officers giving orders, and Hell was let loose. How I escaped I don't know – shrapnel was falling by me, shells passing overhead on their deadly mission, and there I lay with never a scratch … Then came the calm. Our trenches were all knocked about. Dirt piled up like the pyramids. We had to go and dig out who we could, and gruesome game it was. Pieces of flesh, scalp, legs, tunics tattered and parts of soldiers carried away in blankets. By God, to stand by and see your own boys dug out in pieces and do nothing is almost unbearable … Many a brave man had tears in his eyes, as gazing on some friend in almost unrecognisable masses, he had but a minute before his death been joking with him. Imagine you are all sitting down to a meal with friends around you, when all of a sudden by some unseen hand the person to whom you

Opposite: A half-buried corpse, with outstretched arm, is that of a Turkish soldier. Such sights in a trench parapet were not uncommon.

are speaking drops dead by your side. Before you have recovered a head flies off another of your friends, and you then look around, and seeing nothing, you gaze on what is before you.

Lieutenant Mehmed Fasih, 47th Regiment, 16th Ottoman Division

A group of agitated soldiers approach our camp. I ask them what had happened. Mahmud Can has been hurt. He has injuries to an arm, a leg, his chest and face, and he is encrusted with sand. I run over and cut off his boots, pants and socks. The poor fellow is in bad shape, but being brave. We bandage him up and send him to the rear. His foot and arm are seriously hurt. He was hit during relief of the machine-gun crew.

After he is taken away, the captain and I go to inspect damage to our trenches. Machine-gun emplacement is below ground, at the end of a path. The gun is fired from a narrow slit facing the enemy. As if tossed in by hand, an enemy shell penetrated the position through this aperture. The carnage it caused is awful. Six dead lie there. Dismembered parts of their bodies are intermingled. Blood has drained out of bodies, and chests and arms look like wax. Shins and legs, seared by the explosion, are purple. Some bones have been stripped of flesh. The men's features are unrecognisable.

First-aid men are collecting the bits and pieces. The men's comrades have gathered and are waiting to carry their dead friends away. Alas! This is impossible … The machine-gun stand has been smashed to bits. Its various components are covered with blood and bits of human flesh. Mud is everywhere … Shredded underwear from the dead is encased in the most inaccessible parts of the gun …

As I write this in my diary, I relight and smoke the tobacco remaining in my water-pipe, and drink up what was left of my coffee when the shelling started. But the horror of what I saw remains before my eyes.

Sergeant Clifford Ellis, 24th Battalion, AIF

Abdul used to own a gun that earned the title of 'the Undertaker'. When the Undertaker killed a man, it buried him, too. The Undertaker died some time ago. The Turks captured several 75mm guns from the French and now they use them on us. We have great respect for the 75s, he's a silent worker. His shell is seen and felt as soon as heard. There are howitzers with their short barrels and high trajectories. They send along a high-explosive shell that plays pranks on pretty parapets. Machine guns that growl like a noisy motorcycle. A Hotchkiss sends along a handy shell and has a peculiar double report. Shrapnel can always be heard chuckling to itself a few seconds before it knocks the crockery about …

Roamed the beach along which the first landing was made. We discussed the incident at some length. A man couldn't run to the top of these hills in running clobber. The Australians must have charged the gullies and got inland by this means. The Turks on the ridge would retreat as they saw the danger of them being cut off from the main body. If our compatriots had been in sufficient numbers they would have gone right through … There's a ridge called 'Battleship Ridge' about a mile in front of our positions here at Lonesome [Lone] Pine. On the day of the landing companies of Australians reached the summit of this ridge but were unable to hang on for want of reinforcements. Now Abdul's artillery is on Battleship Ridge and makes us presentations ad lib. The show here is now a base for supplies. It is crowded with small but strong two-wheeled vehicles drawn by mules and driven by members of the Gurkha Army Service Corps. 'Salaam Johnnie' the Australians cry to the smiling Gurkhas. Gurkha navvies under an officer of the Royal Engineers are laying rails for trucks. Any quantity of Tommies. Jack and I made our way to the Gurkhas' dugout and strolled amongst them. Two Indians we saw having an eat-up. They offered us a thin, suspicious-looking pancake affair about the size of the bottom of a frying pan and just as tough. 'Jepartee – Very Good'. We took his word for it. All men are liars – Indians are no exception.

The paradox of fighting in such tough conditions yet being so close to the beauty of the sea and the astonishing variety of nature, was not lost on the men. At the end of the day, as the sun set, the temperature fell and the flies that plagued everyone during the day began to disappear. For a while the ambient temperature was pleasant and the opportunity to watch a glorious sunset and the brilliance of its colours gave a brief respite from misery.

The bay's changing colours were intense and wonderful. In the early morning the waves were a rich royal blue, with splashing lines of white breakers rolling in and in upon the pale-grey sand, and the seabirds skimming and wheeling overhead.

Sergeant John Hargrave, 32nd Field Ambulance, RAMC, 10th Division

At mid-day it was colourless, glaring, steel-flashing, with the sunlight blazing and everything shimmering in the heat haze. In the early afternoon, when Hawk and I used to go down to the shore and strip naked like savages, and plunge into the warm water, the bay had changed to pale blue with green ripples, and the outline of Imbros Island, on the horizon, was a long jagged strip of mauve.

Later, when the sunset sky turned lemon-yellow, orange, and deep crimson, the bay went into peacock blues and purples, with here and there a current of bottle-glass green, and Imbros Island stood clear cut against the sunset-colour, a violet-black silhouette.

Queer creatures crept across the sands and into the old Turkish snipers' trenches; long black centipedes, sand-birds – very much resembling our martin, but with something of the canary in their colour. Horned beetles, baby tortoises, mice, and green-grey lizards all left their tiny footprints on the shore.

Private Bernard Gill, 40th Field Ambulance, RAMC, 13th Division

Wandering and climbing on the rough rocky slopes behind Suvla Point I was able to forget for an hour the stress of war and enjoy peace of mind. With a few exceptions the bird life on this fabled shore was familiar. Magpies perched among the branches of the dwarf oaks; whinchats scolded from the tops of juniper bushes; redbreasts flitted in the undergrowth. Shells in flight became part of the fauna – winged creatures of the air. I learnt to recognise their varying sounds as I had learnt the call notes of birds, to estimate their height and trajectory, and to act accordingly. Sometimes they could be ignored; at other times it was necessary for me to throw myself instantly to the ground and seek cover. The birds themselves sometimes suffered casualties, especially from bursting shrapnel. One day a lark, standing on a hillock with crest erect and singing the less exuberant song of the perching bird, instead of taking to the air when I approached, ran to the shelter of a low bush. I had no difficulty in catching him and found that a wounded wing made of him a groundling instead of an aspirant at Heaven's gate. He lay in my hand unresisting but with palpitating heart, and when gently lowered to the ground made off at a great pace.

Two days later I had occasion to visit an orderly's dugout when my attention was drawn to a tapping sound that came from a biscuit tin with a perforated lid. My lark was a prisoner! 'E's 'ammering fer 'is grub', I was told. 'I soak a bit of 'ard tack in tinned milk and crumble it up.' I pointed out that he would prefer a few maggots from the carcass of a nearby stinking mule, and suggested that if the wing healed in a few days it would be a kindness to let him use it.

There were millions of flies, lice, scorpions, scorpion-spiders, chameleons, centipedes, crickets and frogs incessantly croaking at night with many other crawly creatures. We used to put a few lice in the centre of a piece of notepaper and gamble which would reach the edge first. On one occasion our chemist gave a frog an injection (in the cause of science, of course) and it jumped about ten feet into the air. Kind creatures, weren't we? In one camp under Hill 10, we would wake up to find dozens of centipedes on our blankets. They would not sting unless provoked but I have seen more than one 'sting' consisting of two rows each of 50 poison injections from their 100 legs. The doctors used to make a shallow incision along the rows of stings and rub in permanganate of potash. Sometimes we used to put a scorpion and a scorpion-spider together and see which would win. The spider usually did.

Sergeant Matthew Gray, 1/2nd Field Ambulance, RAMC, 53rd Division

Thursday 16 September: Where we are now there is a certain amount of cultivation and the ruins of small cottages and farms. The scattered trees are figs and oaks and the little fields were, I suppose, divided up by hedges but it is all so ruinous and overgrown and cut up with trenches it is difficult to make out the original lie of the land. Back towards the sea is a stretch of very poor rough land. There are a lot of tortoises in the scrub there. The only other animal I have heard of is one hare. Of birds there are swallows, rooks, partridges, magpies (or something like them) and some very pretty small birds. No vultures or carrion crows, I wish there were, for there are many poor fellows it is impossible to bury who would be best disposed of that way. It sounds horrible but it is not a question of sentiment but of sanitation. We would all do anything in the world we could to show them reverence and respect but to attempt to go and bury them would simply be to add to the number of corpses. It threatened rain in the morning and we all prepared for a wet night but fortunately it kept off.

Temp. Chaplain Arthur Parham, Attd. Headquarters 2nd South Midland Mounted Brigade

Overleaf: Trench conditions proved ideal for the proliferation of lice. Soldiers busily delousing on the beach.

Private Thomas
Dry, 23rd
Battalion, AIF

It is reckoned that Gallipoli is one of the hardest fronts to fight on. Unlike France, there are no friendly villages to get a little comfort or food, neither is there any flat country with farms. Nothing but mountains, and barren at that, save for a little scrub here and there, to say nothing of the flies with which we had to contend. These pests would be on your face, hands, down your throat, and if you were eating biscuits with jam on, it was more like biscuits and flies. We slept in dugouts, which is a place dug out of the side of the trench, with sufficient width and length to lie in with ease. The lower they are the better protection for the occupier. Here was another misery. You would turn in your sleep and knock your head or arm against the top, and the soil, being of a sandy nature, would fall down on your face, and if you happened to have your mouth open you would get it full, but we soon got used to that, and after a while got very comfortable. These are as nothing compared to the lice. For a week I did not feel them, but after that I suffered the tortures of hell, and to use the only expression, became 'Lousey'. Each day I would kill about 50, and woe to him who neglected going through himself each day. He would not sleep that night.

There was no getting rid of them. They would breed on you, and no matter how often you changed yourself, you would be just as bad the next day. My skin was red raw through scratching myself. One fellow said he had none on him. We took off his shirt, and it was swarming with them. When we showed him he said he did not know what they were before, but thought it was fleas that bit him at night. To read this you would think it impossible that we slept at night, but so hardened had we become that after we had a scratch or two we would fall asleep, and they would then do their worst. The fleas are not nearly so numerous.

It took every ounce of resilience to carry on. At Helles, Major General Egerton had been suffering from severe stomach pains and a 'buzzing in his ears' and a strong inclination to be sick. Yet he continued to do his rounds, talking to his men. He sympathised, too, with erstwhile retired officers, men in their middle age who were suffering accordingly. 'Poor Freddy Gascoigne,' wrote Egerton in his diary on the last day of August, 'this sort of thing is much worse for him than for us professionals; wife and family and dug out from an important and lucrative civil billet, after seven years of catching the 9.50 up from Peckham Rye to Wimbledon every morning.'

Egerton had held on to his command when others had been replaced, but he was not in favour with Hamilton for his outspoken views, and he knew it.

12 September: Today I went visiting the Brigade Headquarters, and then up the nullah to the Eskis [trench] line; from there up to No. 7 Sap. From No. 7, I turned along the redoubt line and made a thorough inspection of it, and talked to all the men in it. They were quite cheerful; very pleased with their mail and their small parcels which most of them had received. Two fellows were trying to brew Oxo, from a box labelled, 'Oxo in the trenches,' with some patent burning substance sent with it. Poor chaps, they looked very haggard and worn and tired; nothing but the ground and that of the hardest, and one blanket to sleep on. Every other man with, or having lately had, diarrhoea. I told them we were all pretty well fed up, but we had got to stick it.

Major General Granville Egerton, GOC 52nd (Lowland) Division

Four days later, Egerton was removed from his command and left Gallipoli. Others were following him, though not under the same cloud. Boer War veteran Baron Rochdale was another officer 'dug out' to command the 6th Lancashire Fusiliers, landing with the battalion on Gallipoli. That first day Private Charles Watson had scrambled up a low cliff alongside his forty-nine-year-old commanding officer and had noticed how 'woefully short of breath' he was, with 'sweat streaming down his face', revolver in one hand, walking stick in the other.

By rights, and at his age and physical condition he should very properly have been occupying a safe seat at the War Office or at some Headquarters Base, where he could have been and without the slightest loss of honour, instead of being on this young man's enterprise. But not for him the soft seat of war. And he stuck with us during the campaign, sharing equally our dangers and hardships until age and its infirmities finally caught up with him.

It was autumn when, with his spirit still willing, but his flesh weak, he made his undignified exit from us. Sorrowfully we watched him being hoisted, like a sack of potatoes, on to a horse's back. Wracked with

Private Charles Watkins, 6th Lancashire Fusiliers, 42nd Division

rheumatism, lumbago and the kindred illnesses of middle age, he had the greatest difficulty in clinging on to the horse being led at walking pace to the beach where a naval pinnace was waiting to cart him to the hospital ship. He deserved a more glorious exit than that.

It might have been inglorious, but it was an exit that many a man would have accepted if it meant he could leave the Peninsula, with or without dignity. As the men dug themselves further out of harm's way, so Sergeant Hargrave found himself dealing increasingly with men who were broken through illness, not injury.

Sergeant John Hargrave, 32nd Field Ambulance, RAMC, 10th Division

There were very few wounds now to attend to in the hospital dugout. Mostly we got men with sandfly fever and dysentery; men with scabies and lice; men utterly and unspeakably exhausted, with hollow, black-rimmed eyes, cracked lips and footsores; men who limped across the sandy bed, dragging their rifles and equipment in their hands; men who were desperately hungry, whose eyes held the glint of sniper-madness; men whose bodies were wasting away, the skin taut and dry like a drum, with every rib showing like the beams of a wreck, or the rafters of an old roof.

Lieutenant Mehmed Fasih, 47th Regiment, 16th Ottoman Division

I heard a soldier yell, 'Come along, you idiot! Is it death you're waiting for?' I approached the man and looked in the direction he was facing. He was shouting at a soldier lying on the ground, just below some olive trees, south of the latrines.

The fellow moved, then sat up. But he could not stand. He scratched the ground, saying he felt numb. He then collected his gear. I noticed he had underwear in his hands. He started coming towards us. The first soldier was still yelling, urging him to hurry. Under the impression he was malingering, I looked around for a stick to administer him a few whacks, but could not find any.

Moving terribly slowly, the man gradually approached. What I saw then broke my heart. He was about forty years old. A sallow, sickly private, I asked him why he had been lying on the ground.

He explained that on their way to exercises, he had suffered stomach cramps which compelled him to drop out of rank and lie down. He had soiled his underwear and showed them to us. The man displayed all the symptoms of extreme debility. He was ill, and [had] obviously been so for a long time. He had reported sick, but the doctor, certainly to please his superiors, had failed to follow his conscience and had not had the sick soldier hospitalised.

Always we were in the midst of pain and misery, hunger and death. We do not get much of the rush and glory of battle in the 'Linseed Lancers'. We deal with the wreckage thrown up by the tide of battle, and wreckage is always a sad sight – human wreckage most of all.

Sergeant John Hargrave, 32nd Field Ambulance, RAMC, 10th Division

Allied battalions were woefully understrength. The 1/4th South Wales Borderers had been in Gallipoli since mid-July. Temp. Lieutenant Colonel Marcus de la Poer Beresford's command was shrinking by the day. Once a unit of 1,000 men, by 6 October their numbers had dipped below 220 officers and men; by 10 October that number was below 200, and on 23 October the battalion comprised just 191 officers and men, the size not of even a company but of three platoons. This battalion was by no means unique.

I felt so very depressed and low-spirited, I hardly knew what to do with myself. Somehow or other, I had developed an attack of influenza which made me very weak, and I had also contracted a cough, with a splitting headache. All this, combined with the reaction, made me feel downright ill and I would have given anything to have been at home just then, for there was not a single soul to sympathise with me, or to say one loving word to me, I had to bear it all alone. Ah! No one can possibly realise what this means, unless they have gone through it all; it is an awful experience. This is one of the great drawbacks in military service; it may be all right when you are strong and well, able to rough it; but when you are feeling so bad, and longing for some gentle hand to be laid upon your burning brow, and a soothing voice to speak words of sympathy and love, then is the time you miss home and dear ones.

Private Ridley Sheldon, 1/6th Manchester Regiment, 42nd Division

Disease was no respecter of rank or profession. The Reverend Arthur Parham had been suffering for weeks. He was desperate not to leave the men to whom he gave daily communion, but in the end he had no choice.

Temp. Chaplain
Arthur Parham,
Attd. Headquarters
2nd South Midland
Mounted Brigade

Thursday 30 September: It was a perfect afternoon and it was glorious on the coast. I did not bathe though tempted to do so. I am really very seedy, frightful diarrhoea though I eat practically nothing and I suppose my kidneys are out of order somehow for I have such pains in my back I hardly know how to get about. I do hope I shall be able to stick it out.

Friday 1 October: Immediately after some bread and milk for breakfast set off to the coast to see if a day on the shore with the ambulance would do me good. I spent a very quiet day, feeling pretty seedy … To bed very tired after so much walking. One gets absurdly weak.

Saturday 2 October: I felt very seedy indeed all day, so terribly weak and prostrated. In the afternoon I walked down to the beach with the Colonel and sat there while he bathed and we stayed there till sunset before coming back. But the walk back was almost more than I could manage and I was almost fainting by the time we arrived. I just arranged for services for Berks

Sergeant John Kenyon, 9th AIF, was suffering from the effects of dysentery when this snapshot was taken. He was evacuated two days later. Awarded the DCM for gallantry on 25 April 1915, and the MM for a trench raid in June 1916, he was killed at Pozières, Somme, in July 1916, reportedly while 'fighting twelve Germans alone'.

and Bucks and then went back and had some brandy and lay down. After dinner of bread soaked in soup I was frightfully sick. The doctor says I shall have to go away for a bit.

Among the men leaving Gallipoli at the end of September was one entire division. The 10th Division was being moved to Salonika, signalling a shift in the War Office's attention away from the Peninsula. Gallipoli was not the priority it had been just weeks before.

Orders to pack up ready for a move came suddenly. The wet season was just beginning. The storm clouds were coming up over the hills in great masses of rolling banks, black and forbidding. It grew colder at night, and a cold wind sprang up during the day. Everyone was bustling about, packing the operating tent and equipment, operating table, instruments, bottles, pans, stretchers, bandages, splints, cooking dixies, bully-beef crates, biscuit tins – everything was being packed up and sorted out ready for moving. But where? No one knew. We were going to move . . . soon, very soon, it was rumoured.

Sergeant John Hargrave, 32nd Field Ambulance, RAMC, 10th Division

Within every mind a small voice asked – 'Blighty?' And then came another whiff of rumour: 'The Xth Division are going – England perhaps!' But it was too good to believe. Everyone wanted to believe it … each man in his inmost soul hoped it might be true … but it couldn't be England … and yet it might!

One night the Indian Pack-Mule Corps came trailing down with their little two-wheeled, two-muled carts and transported all our medical panniers away into the gloom, and they went towards Lala Baba. It was a good sign. Everything was gone now except our own packs and kit, and we had orders to 'Stand by' for the command to 'Fall in'. We lay about in the sand waiting – and wondering. At last towards the last minutes of midnight we got the orders to 'Fall in'. The NCOs called the 'Roll', 'numbered off' their sections and reported 'All present and correct, sir!' In a long straggling column we marched from our last encampment towards Lala Baba. The night was very dark and the sand gave under our feet. It was hard going, but every man had a gleam of hope, and trudged along heavy-laden with rolled overcoat, haversack and water bottle and stretcher, but with a light heart.

The advance party from Chocolate Hill met us at Lala Baba. Here everything was bustle and hurry. Every unit of the Xth Division was packed up and ready for embarkation. Lighters and tugs puffed and grated by the shore. Horses stamped and snorted; sergeants swore continually; officers nagged and shouted. Men got mixed up and lost their units, sections lost their way in the great crowd of companies assembled. Once Hawk loomed out of the darkness and a strong whiff of rum came with him … he disappeared again: 'See you later, Sar'nt – lookin' after things – important.'

He was full of drink, and in his hurry to look after 'things' (mostly bottles) he lost some of his own kit and my field glasses. He worked hard at getting the equipment into the lighters, notwithstanding the fact that he was 'three parts canned'. Every now and then he loomed up like some great khaki-clad gorilla, only to fade away again to the secret hiding place of a bottle. And so at last we got aboard. It was still a profound secret. No one knew whither we were going, or why we were leaving the desolation of Suvla Bay.

Searing heat would inevitably give way to cold, then colder, then freezing weather that would grip the exposed Peninsula. Blizzards would sweep in from the Mediterranean and men would need to be issued with appropriate winter clothing. Even then, conditions in small dugouts hewn out of the rocky shoreline would hardly be fit for purpose, and larger dugouts would need to be constructed. The lifeline of the men on shore, the piers that jutted out into the sea, would also need to be strengthened to withstand the gales, or they could be washed away and with their loss the entire garrison would be imperilled. With this threat in mind, stores would have to be built up in case of a natural blockade, and this posed severe and ongoing logistical problems that appeared insurmountable.

Corporal Herbert Lamb, 13th Divisional Signal Company, Royal Engineers

Monday 15th [October]: Too rough to take or land mails. Gale getting stronger … about 8 p.m. thunderstorm, lightning very vivid indeed. Terrific wind and downpour of rain. Grand climax and last straw!! Dugout flooded in two or three minutes to depth of two or three inches … Sat watching water rise. Poured down steps and through roof in several places … Baled out four buckets full of water and three biscuit tins full of mud … very rough sea indeed; has washed away a good half of the pier.

Wed 17th: Fine, wind which got stronger and more violent during the day … No bread or meat today. The wind by evening the most terrific we have had. South Eastern … The rain came on in the evening, heavy showers … The wind appalling, hard to stand against it. Sea fearfully rough. Has practically demolished pier.

By October, thoughts in London were turning towards the idea of an evacuation. What would be the casualties, Kitchener asked Hamilton, of any such withdrawal? Hamilton would not consider the idea seriously and replied that he would lose half his force. 'They would stamp our enterprise the bloodiest of tragedies!' he wrote to the Secretary of State for War. Hamilton's refusal to countenance failure proved fatal to his command. But he had already failed: the landings at Suvla and all the promises he had made as to ultimate success were hollow. His ongoing appeals for further reinforcements to bolster his position fell foul of the requirements of competing operational theatres. On 14 October the decision was taken to dismiss Hamilton, and General Sir Charles Monro, a man who believed in the primary importance of the Western Front, replaced him. As for

Deluges of rain bring more misery to men in the trenches at Suvla.

Hamilton, his career was over and he never held an active command again. He now had time to construct a defence of his command in his memoirs, *Gallipoli Diary*, published in 1920. From the beginning Hamilton had been given a nigh-impossible task, but he had hardly made the best of a bad job; indeed, his overoptimistic assessments of what was possible disguised the reality of failure for far too long.

Monro's primary task was to report back on the military situation, with all options on the table. He was advised to tell the truth, however discomforting. He left London on 23 October,

LORD KITCHENER & HIS GENERALS AT ANZAC.
— 14. 11. 15. —

arriving at Imbros five days later. On 30 October, he paid Helles, Anzac and Suvla a flying, one-day visit, reporting back to Kitchener with an assessment that could not have been more damning. The situation was untenable. Evacuation was the only solution. Monro was pilloried by Churchill: 'He came, he saw, he capitulated,' but this jibe was entirely unwarranted. The picture appeared to be clear. However, Kitchener was concerned as to how evacuation might be seen in the Middle East, with the potential loss of prestige, or, worse, the effects of a total humiliation. 'If we leave Gallipoli, the Muslim man will think he has beaten us and we shall feel the effect in Egypt, India and throughout the whole Mohammedan world,' General Henry Horne recorded him as saying. It was decided that General Horne would accompany Kitchener to the Dardanelles before a final decision was made.

Lord Kitchener with his generals at Anzac, 14 November 1915 (Kitchener, foreground, second from left). His departure from Gallipoli was followed five weeks later by the evacuation of all troops.

For three days Kitchener toured the Peninsula and came to the only sensible conclusion: Suvla and Anzac would be evacuated, and, after further consultation, so would Helles. The final decision was made by the British Cabinet: briefly, the politicians prevaricated, horrified at the thought of the casualties that might be incurred during departure. This debate over future policy in the Dardanelles was not secret; far from it. Even Turkish soldiers in front-line trenches were aware of the vacillating position of British politicians.

The postman brings the *Tasviri Efkar* [newspaper] of 12 November. Contains good news. Debate under way in House of Lords concerning eventual withdrawal of English … This news is 15 days old. It is possible that by today they have reached a decision and have started to implement it … Newspaper reports a Colonel Repington has stated that, from the military point of view, Allied forces need to be reinforced otherwise they will certainly be wiped out … It is therefore likely that, having realised nothing can be accomplished in Gallipoli, British forces here are being withdrawn to be used as reinforcements in the Balkans. In time, we shall certainly find out what is to be.

Lieutenant Mehmed Fasih, 47th Regiment, 16th Ottoman Division

After terrible storms in late October, the weather improved. Cooler weather set in and the men enjoyed what turned out to be a short Indian summer.

Temp. Lieutenant Colonel Marcus de la Poer Beresford, 1/4th South Wales Borderers, 13th Division

5 November: I took a walk along the fire trenches of the 38th Brigade on our right and could see the lie of the ground from several points of view. Walking along it was interesting to note the different occupations of the men. Some were playing cards, some cleaning rifles and ammunition, a few washing, some digging etc., and alas many could be seen with bowed head and anxious and expectant eye, while his fingers rapidly sought amongst the shirt or sock which he had taken off, for livestock of an irritating and disagreeable nature. These trenches which are next to ours were shelled with heavy high-explosive shells for about an hour before sundown and huge masses of debris and stuff were thrown high into the air. They are most horrible shells these and there is no cover which will protect you from them.

6 November: Each side shelled the other nearly all day and many heavy shells were fired. It was almost one continuous series of explosions and whizzing shells. We ask each other out here what we are gaining by all this firing, each side seems glued here simply for the purpose of inflicting loss on the other. What is the policy of our politicians at home? Out here it seems to be go as you please. It seems so disheartening to feel that things are being made a mess of at home, whilst we sit here week after week being shelled and having nothing to show for it.

Boyd's Crater: on 19 December 1915, as part of a scheme to distract Turkish attention away from the Anzac/Suvla evacuation, a British mine was exploded beneath the Turkish trenches near Gully Ravine. This photograph, taken the following day, shows the new position being consolidated, despite Turkish shelling and machine-gun fire.

The same could be said for the Anzac Bridgehead. Only low-level, remorseless attrition continued in which both sides looked to do 'something' in the name of progress. At Lone Pine, mining and countermining was much in evidence and a network of tunnels had been excavated, honeycombing the ridge.

Sun 7th [November]: Volunteered to explore a Turkish tunnel our sap had broken into while roaming underground and our heads wanted to know where it led to. Sapper Wymiss and I worked together. I carried a lead pump and together we crawled through what seemed to be like miles of awkward blackness, full of ugly corners that reached out and bumped our brain boxes. The job turned out safe enough despite a few very promising incidents. The main tunnel led out to a trench about two yards in front of the Turks' present trench, and out of which the 24th bombed our friends [the Turks] shortly after taking up our residence at Lone Pine. We stayed on guard while the sappers erected barricades and loopholes. At 11.30 we went to bed, after having been playing rabbits for nearly six hours.

Sergeant Clifford Ellis, 24th Battalion, AIF

Saturday 13th [November]: On guarding Turkish tunnel (in trenches). My post is halfway to Hades. Have to crawl, slide and perform many similar antics to arrive there. I sit behind a low barricade with a loaded revolver. Pitch dark, except for a dim light that shows where my tunnel opens into a Turk tunnel three yards away. The only noises I hear are sounds of picks and the argument of Abduls. I've come about 7,000 miles to get in touch with these Crescentiks and now they're only three yards away! A most entertaining post. Left my post at 7 p.m. Went to my dugout about twenty yards from the firing line, in support trenches. Slept about an hour. Rudely awakened by a broomstick bomb paying a visit next door. Two killed (Hardy, Bonie). One wounded (Rollings). Yours truly escaped with only a small mark above the knee. 'O Death! Where is thy sting? O War! Where is thy Glory?'

Sun 14th: Crawled down the tunnel leading to my selected post at 5 a.m. Stayed there till 7 a.m. Abdul was picking feverishly. At 11 a.m. we blew up Abdul's tunnel and as many Abduls as there happened to be in it. The tunnel leading to my post was obliterated, Hallelujah! Don't fancy playing rabbits under such conditions.

Private Thomas Dry, 23rd Battalion, AIF

The engineers work right in the firing line. They sap towards the Turks' trenches, and the Turks sap towards us. Should we hear the Turks picking we locate whereabouts they are, and try and get underneath them and blow them up, and they do the same. It is just like a race … I was in one when it was blown up, and will never forget the experience. I was only just in the mouth at the time, but the force of the charge caused me to stagger against the opposite side of the trench, and I had to feel if my nose was on and my eyes correct. They were all right. I might here say that when a sap is blown up the charge is so strong that it shakes the earth, and the feeling is just as if a huge giant tilted the earth from underneath. What I did not like about sapping was that should the Turks charge or anything else happen you were caught in a trap, being, as it were, in the bowels of the earth.

By mid-November the weather had turned again. The torment of flies might have gone, but in its place came rain and high winds, blowing great coastal clouds of dust into the air and making resupply doubly difficult. Storms were frequent, with lightning illuminating the ground and thunder reverberating along the coast. The landing piers were ripped up by the hand of God and remade by the hands of men. Then, on 26 November, as if finally to settle matters, a storm blew in such as no one had ever seen before.

The day had begun like any other: the morning was overcast, a strong wind blowing to the north-east. As the day wore on, the wind continued to pick up. Tent guy ropes became strained and the men sought to hammer in more pegs to withstand the pressures. Then it began to rain.

Private Charles Watkins 1/6th Lancashire Fusiliers, 42nd Division

By about 3 p.m. the sky started to blacken. There was an uneasy electric and irritating tension in the air. Our platoon sergeant – ever on the ball as regards the practicalities of war, told us to sheath our bayonets, 'Steel attracts lightning, tha knows, and it's best to be safe, like.'

'But wot abart mi rifle, Sarge – t'aint made o' wood, tha knows, Sarge.'

'Ay – but that's a chance tha mun take, lad, tha can't let go 'o that.'

With the dubious combination of scientific foresight and military necessity we had to be content. We cloaked up in our groundsheets, ready for the big deluge. By now it was as black as night. 'Like the end of the bloody world,' said one of our chaps, frightened, and licking his lips nervously. It certainly was eerie.

18.00 hrs: Clouds pile up a strong wind blows. Barometer predicts more rain. There are spectacular lightning bolts in the distance.

18.30 hrs: Rain now really pouring. Thunder and lightning accompany downpour.

18.50 hrs: Though downpour ends within 20 minutes, wind continues to blow. One should see what rain has done to our trenches. They are a mess. Soldiers keep slipping in the mud. Oh my God! The time for some assistance from you has come! … Work on my diary. While enemy is silent, we continue light harassing fire.

Lieutenant Mehmed Fasih, 47th Regiment, 16th Ottoman Division

Nothing holds for ever – not even an imminent storm, and the cosmic bombardment opened up with a continuous roar of thunder. The lightning flashed and played on one continuous whole. The sound – even of our own big guns' bombardments – was dwarfed into puny insignificance compared with what came out of the skies, and as if realising the futility of this competition in noise, all the guns on both sides became silent and gave up. Then the sluice gate of Heaven opened and the cold rain fell drenchingly, not in drops but literally in buckets. In less than a minute the floor of the trench was a sea of mud, ankle-deep. Ankle-deep mud was not strange to us but it was with real alarm we saw the trench itself filling fast with water. Soon it was knee-deep and we climbed on the firing step to avoid it. But it still rose higher and higher until the firing step itself disappeared from view. Little tucks in the side of the ground in the front of our trench became deep crevices under the weight of the falling rain, and the water started to stream in through them, in countless little rivers. By now the water was a good three feet high and rising fast as it was fed still more by the water swirling down from the trenches on the higher ground.

'Wot the bloody 'ell do we do now, Sarge?' somebody called out, panic-stricken. The sergeant was plainly baffled, but the issue, for once, was decided for him. 'Ah'm not stoppin' 'ere to be bloody well drownded. Ah'd rather stop a bullet,' and one of our chaps climbed up into the open in front of the trench. Quickly we all followed suit, first throwing over the

Private Charles Watkins 1/6th Lancashire Fusiliers, 42nd Division

top of the trench such possessions as we had managed to hang on to during this flooding. And the Turk, too, climbed out into the open in front of his trench.

Soon the whole line of front trenches is a line of British and Turkish troops, stood out in the open in the enforced companionship of overriding and mutual misery. Adversity sure makes strange bedfellows. By a miracle – or by some fast field-telephone work – all the big guns remained silent, As far as your eye could see in the bad visibility of the torrential rain – to the right, to the left, and in front were long lines of shivering wretched Tommies and Abduls, facing one another.

The men in trenches up on the hills and ridges at Suvla escaped the floods' worst effects as the water ran down the spurs and gullies on to the plain. Those on the plain, however, were hit by a torrent of water as the normally small streams that crossed the ground rose and burst their banks.

Lieutenant Colonel Frederick Bendell, CO 2/3rd (City of London) Battalion, the London Regiment, 29th Division

I heard a strange sound. I could have sworn it was the sea, washing on the beach! But the sea and the beach were four miles away. I stood and listened. And as I listened, in the flickering light there was a curious slapping noise in the slit outside, and a great snake of water came round the curve – breast-high – and washed me backwards into the dugout.

I was off my feet for a moment, and then, sodden and gasping, I was in the doorway again. Another moment and I was in the open air, and the horror of drowning under the dugout roof was gone. What was left was bad enough! The water was at my throat, waves of it licked my face.

I reached both hands to the top of the walls, but I could get no hold there. My fingers tore through the mud. Slowly I forced my way along the slit. If I could get to the main headquarters trench I should be better off, for this, like all trenches that faced east, had a fire-step, a broad ledge some two feet higher than the trench bottom.

I do not know how long it was before I turned the last corner. But suddenly I felt that the slit was wider. I turned round and with great difficulty got one foot up. Thank God! There was the ledge.

A great heave and I was on it – another heave and scramble and I was on the top – panting and dripping – but out of the water, out of the greasy prison walls of that horrible slit.

I stood there in the dark for a minute to get my breath. Then I called out, 'Hullo, headquarters party, is anyone here?'

Answering voices came from a few yards away, and, moving towards them, I found the MO and five or six men standing by the hedge which ran along the centre communication trench. They were all sodden and shivering, and the MO and one of the men were clearly in a bad way – the others were supporting them. The ground was covered by the water – my feet told me that – and I realised that there was a flood from the hills, and that the water must have come through the Turkish lines. They were worse off than we were! But our lot was bad enough.

Men searched for comrades washed away by the water, and those who were injured were carried down to receive medical treatment. However, the floods were just the first act in the great amphitheatre of Suvla. Almost as soon as the rain stopped, snow began to fall, and men soaked to the skin were frozen to the core by a strong northerly wind. With all their kit washed away, with any trench supplies lost to the torrent of water, there was nothing to protect them. Agonies were heaped on agonies.

Snow falls at Anzac. Looking down into Hotchkiss Gully, North Anzac

Lieutenant
Mehmed Fasih,
47th Regiment,
16th Ottoman
Division

23.00hrs [27 November]: Surprise! It is snowing. Yes, it is … flakes gently float down. Since temperature is below 0° Centigrade, snow turns to ice. Cold snap has now lasted two hours … Go out. Tour trenches. Really feel sorry for my men. If this continues, what condition are we going to be in?

00.30hrs: Leave comrades. Snowing has eased up. Communication trenches full of mud. Reach a slight incline and, since my boots are smooth, without hobnails, slip and slide for 15 metres, while clinging to side of trench, trying not to fall.

01.30hrs: Still snowing. By now it has started to powder the ground. It'll get thicker, if this continues.

02.30hrs: Am increasingly sleepy. Keep dozing off with water-pipe's mouthpiece between my lips. After issuing necessary orders to NCOs, wrap self in greatcoat and stretch out. Shoulders and knees freezing. Enemy occasionally opens fire with several rifles, just to prove his strength on the ground.

05.30hrs: Wake up …. Everything white outside. Ground covered with two fingers of snow, which is still falling. Fairly strong cold wind blows snow in our faces.

06.30hrs: Tour trenches. Conditions are terrible. Can't walk without slipping and sliding. If we have to go into action, what shall I do? My soldiers display fortitude.

Lieutenant Colonel
Frederick Bendell,
CO 2/3rd (City of
London) Battalion,
the London
Regiment, 29th
Division

No-man's-land was a lake. No attack would come over that for some time. North and south, the front trench was full of sullen brown water, and behind it was no sign of life. Only here, where the hedge joined the front trench, were there any men. Fifteen of them were there, with the company sergeant major of A [Company], a very stout fellow, who had saved several from drowning, and was cheering them up as best he could. They were all blue with cold, shivering and wild-eyed.

B Company lines ran on to higher ground, so we turned north to find them. For some way the trench was full, and the muddy water hid its dark secrets. At the extreme end of our line the slope of the ground told, and here, behind an old stone wall, we found some twenty men and three officers. They had got their machine gun in action, and I told the Company Commander that he must watch the whole front carefully, and be prepared to cover most of it. On our way back to Headquarters we saw a number of bodies of men who had obviously died of cold and exhaustion.

The men were digging when I got back. Eight of them were taking turns with two spades, and they had dug down about 4 feet in a square of 9 feet. In this hole we existed for another forty-eight hours. In the afternoon two runners got up from the Brigade. Our orders were to hang on for the present, and I learnt that the whole front was disorganised, ration parties drowned, trenches impassable, and floods everywhere in the basin.

No rations came up in all that time. We found one tin of gooseberry jam and a rum jar half full of rum and muddy water. These were shared out among the party. We had nothing dry of any kind, no matches, tobacco, paper, clothes. That evening it began to freeze and the night was bitter. The MO died in his sleep, and two other men also …

On the second day the Brigadier waded up. He stood thigh-deep in the trench to hear my gloomy report and went back with hardly a word. He had seen all that was necessary – and there was nothing to say. Moving about carefully on the top we found a number of bodies. None was wounded, all had died of cold and exposure. Two brothers of C Company had died together. The arm of one was round the other's neck, the fingers held a piece of biscuit to the frozen mouth. It seemed a strange and inexplicable thing that these men who had come there to fight, and had fought bravely, had been killed by the elements. The trenches were a foul sight. Everything was covered by a slimy scum of mud. The front trench in the southern half was unspeakably horrible; this was where the flood had been deepest and strongest.

On the third day we were withdrawn. Forty-five of us all told crawled back to a ravine near Brigade Headquarters – many on hands and knees. Forty-five out of 500. The Adjutant was killed on the way by shrapnel from a solitary shell.

It blew and froze hard last night and some of the men who have been wet through for the last 48 hours have gangrened feet and a kind of frostbite. They are going sick in dozens. There is a tremendous lot to be done and we are very hard worked. The trenches are beginning to dry but the evil done to the men is irretrievable and I wish some of the stay-at-homes could see

Overleaf: The winter conditions were terribly harsh: a snow-covered 18-pounder field gun at Anzac.

Temp. Lieutenant Colonel Marcus de la Poer Beresford, 1/4th South Wales Borderers, 13th Division

them now and realise what they are going through, and they have a good deal worse than this to go through perchance before many days are over, but I must not say more. I went down to a conference yesterday with bare legs and a pair of shoes and the General said he would give £100 for my constitution.

30 November: It is so cold and everything is so filthy dirty that I have great difficulty in keeping this diary up to date. I have not had my clothes off or washed in any way for four days. My hands and legs up to the knees are caked with mud and must remain so. It was perishingly cold last night and many men (I have heard of five of the Wiltshires and seven of the Warwickshires) were frozen to death in the trenches. Many of the men are suffering from frostbite and many others are crippled with rheumatism. We were relieved from the firing line today after being there for 47 days. We are now in reserve, but really that means very little – less sentry work and less responsibility but nearly all our men are out tonight digging a redoubt about a mile away which is urgently required. It froze again last night and our trenches are much drier, but still in an awful state. This is the most trying time I think I have ever been put in. Every man who can stand on his feet (alas, many can't) has to dig and work, things have got to that stage. Some of the men look ghastly, but if they have anything left in them, they must carry on. A tiring day with much to think about and arrange. How different most of us look to when we started from home, indeed there are few of us still here who came out originally.

1 December: Everywhere there are rifles and equipment buried by the floods. We are digging them out where we can. Thirty-two drowned Turks floated down one of the gullies. No mails have come up to us for several weeks and we are only on bully beef and biscuits again. Certainly this is the survival of the fittest. I saw some of the Welch Fusiliers going up to the trenches crying with cold and pains.

There were at least 250 British dead and 5,000 more suffering from frostbite and hypothermia. Casualty clearing stations were overwhelmed by the number of men, many crawling in on the verge of death. The storm brought home with the greatest force possible the idiocy of trying to brave out the winter weather but also, conversely, underlining how dangerous an evacuation might be when the weather was so fickle. Leaving the Peninsula would require luck as well as meticulous preparation and sound judgement, none of which had been in much evidence. In London, politicians continued to prevaricate: meeting after meeting examined and re-examined the possible scenarios. Perhaps, it was conjectured, the Salonika campaign could be closed down and the troops transferred to Gallipoli instead. The French were consulted and flatly refused to countenance a surrender of Salonika while accepting, with no alacrity, an evacuation of Gallipoli. On 7 December, the full British Cabinet met. French concerns over Salonika prevailed; Suvla and Anzac would be evacuated by 19 December.

At Gallipoli there had been a marked increase in battery and counter-battery fire, the Turks sniping with venom at the British trenches. There had also been a marked improvement in the weather, which was noted as fine and dry and then, by 8 December, as fine and warm. The weather remained good and the shelling hardly abated.

Evacuation plans envisaged either a fighting withdrawal to the beaches with fresh defensive trenches close to piers, or a withdrawal based on deception and cunning. Deception was chosen, leading the enemy to believe that Allied troops were going nowhere until the last possible moment, by which time the final troops would already be on lighters making their way to the ships.

Deception: dummies are used again, this time to give the impression of a manned trench.

An attack by the Turks during the evacuation was entirely possible, and plans were drawn up to provide two blocking forces, one holding Suvla Point and one holding Lala Baba, and much time and effort was expended ensuring that telephone cables were laid across the bay to maintain unbroken communication between the two points. Lines were also laid for communication between the troops' assembly points and the Military Landing Officer on West Beach to control the flow of troops coming down for embarkation.

In the week before final embarkation, the number of troops holding the front would be gradually decreased to the bare minimum, while

elaborate schemes were adopted to make it appear that everything was as normal. Indian muleteers continuously drove their carts, throwing up clouds of dust so that it appeared as if a consignment of stores had just arrived. Rifle and artillery fire was to cease unless the Turks attacked, in order to get the enemy used to extended periods of relative quiet, just as it would be in the last hours of the evacuation.

Where opposing lines were close, Turkish bombs thrown into the trenches would receive no reply, while ingenious booby traps were designed to keep the Turks back, and, on the parapets, rifles were set up and, through clever manipulation, were time-delayed to self-fire. Supplies that could not be evacuated were destroyed, polluted or, in some cases, buried. Then, on 18 December, the first night of the evacuation took place, leaving just 10,000 men to hold Suvla and a similar number to hold Anzac before they, too, left the following night.

Sergeant Clifford Ellis, 24th Battalion, AIF

It became apparent that something big was doing. The heads started getting rid of all surplus stores. No reinforcements were landed. Troops began to leave the Peninsula. We soon saw that these and a few other signs spelt evacuation. The feelings which this truth brought to us were very mixed. We were glad as only a battered battalion can be at the prospect of a spell. But when we contemplated the cemeteries along the shores and in Monash Gully we were anything but glad.

Private Bernard Gill, 40th Field Ambulance, RAMC, 13th Division

I was among the men assigned to the skeleton force. 'Force of skeletons' would have been a more suitable designation, for there was little flesh left on our bones by this time. The RAMC contingent was to pick up the wounded, assist the walking cases and carry the totally disabled on stretchers to the beaches where they would be embarked on the waiting boats. We considered that our chances of getting away were extremely thin. Death by shelling or drowning, or, worse, capture by the enemy and incarceration in a prisoner-of-war camp was to be our fate. We reflected gloomily that these December days, calm now and sunny, and passing so quickly, were to be our last on earth.

13 December: I may as well state at once that we have been preparing to evacuate the whole of this part of the Peninsula for many days now, supplies, carts etc. etc., and anything which can be spared has been sent away night after night, practically everything but what we stand up in. I sent away my sleeping valise and most of our cooking pots today, leaving a blanket or two and some washing kit. Fortunately the weather lately has been fine. We are entirely dependent on it as even with a slight wind it is impossible to embark. The evacuation is bound to take some time and one does not want to be held up when our forces have been greatly weakened. This is indeed a very anxious time for all of us.

19 December: I think the most anxious night I have ever had. Our line had hardly any supports to reinforce in case of attack. Surely the Turks must find out and come on, but no, they are still digging and strengthening their position. We had two or three officers' patrols out last night, all of which came in contact with Turkish patrols, which caused a good deal of firing. The engineers under cover of our patrols made the mines active and closed up the wire. At one time I feared one of our patrols had been cut off and I had to send out another to find them, which they did. We are all to leave tonight. How long the day seemed – what would happen? Would all go all

Temp. Lieutenant Colonel Marcus de la Poer Beresford, 1/4th South Wales Borderers, 13th Division

Overleaf: An evacuation barge arrives at Imbros during the early morning.

Below: Last day at Anzac, 18 December 1915: the image shows the scene at North Beach. Clearly visible are empty tents and abandoned stores, helping to create the illusion that the Anzacs were staying.

right? It seemed hardly possible. Would the weather hold? These and dozens of other possibilities could not help suggesting themselves. Another walk of inspection round the trenches. Answering endless messages. Making lots of arrangements. How dreadfully empty the trenches behind seemed. We lit numerous dummy fires where they had been before. We made men walk about the support trenches and other things to deceive [the enemy]. A German Taube had tried to fly over the lines the day before yesterday, but was driven off by five of ours who were waiting about. Had it seen anything? About 10 a.m. the Turks started firing quick High Explosive shells at the place we were going to embark at, one of which went right through the pier. There were nearly 40 of these shells. Did this mean that they knew and would shell us when we embarked? This was unpleasant to contemplate, as it would have killed hundreds. I watched this shelling from an empty trench.

Private Bernard Gill, 40th Field Ambulance, RAMC, 13th Division

We marched away silently at dusk, looking our last on the tents where we had lived and slept, played Bingo (we called it 'Housey'), aired our views on women and sang our bawdy songs. The canvas was to be left standing at the end, with lamps burning as usual, a present for Johnny Turk. It was, fortunately, a quiet evening, the sea dead calm. The isle of Imbros lay, a violet silhouette against the primrose of the sunset. The beach was crowded with troops and transport, moving silently over the loose sand. When our feet came to the firmer surface of the sea-washed shore beyond Lala Baba we halted and fell out. Now the sky was bright with stars. The bulky shape of the Peninsula, resembling a loaded camel lying down with head upraised, loomed on our left; the sea was dark and smooth, its small waves making a soft murmur. We talked in subdued tones, feeling far from happy. Our thoughts were confused: relief and guilt jostled together in our minds. We had come as invaders, fouled this legendary shore with blood and excrement and filled it with graves. Our object unattained, we were now slipping away.

About 10 p.m. came the order to fall in. We picked up our impedimenta and marched down to the nearest pier where an armour-plated lighter lay bows-on. A single plank, set at a steep angle, led from the jetty head to her deck. We filed along it, balanced precariously between sky and water, and were hustled down a broad companionway into the hold.

A single oil-lamp, hanging from a beam, burned with a smokey flame, revealing a wooden floor and balks of timber set against curved steel walls. Men came crowding in with their rifles, equipment and kitbags, and we compressed ourselves until we were packed as tight as bottles in a crate. There was no moving arm or foot. A clattering of hobnailed boots on the steel roof close above our heads told us that the deck, too, was crammed with troops. A hoarse voice shouted a command; the screw began to lash the water and the craft swayed slightly from side to side but did not move an inch. Our beetle was aground. Our discomfort increased. We sweated and swore. A cynical voice shouted, 'Thank God we've got a navy!' The irrepressible jester was among our company. He quickly set us laughing with his jokes and patter, and led us in singing the popular songs of the period. This variety entertainment came to an end when the lighter gave a sudden lurch, rolled violently and floated free on the rising tide. The motor began to hum steadily and the noise of water rippling against the steel sides of our prison informed us that at last we were under way.

Survivors photographed on their last day. Bombers from the West Kent Yeomanry pose at Y Ravine.

Sapper Thomas
Edmunds, Royal
Engineer Signals,
IX Army Corps

During the last few days the Signal Units were very busily employed in wiring up the new lines of defence. On the final night, I was assigned to a telegraph buzzer connected to one of the gates in the lines of defence. As the last few troops passed through each line, tripwires were set so as to blow up any of the enemy who were careless enough to kick them or to pick up the harmless looking boots, rifles etc. lying about, and the gate was securely fastened. The telegraphist then sent a message to Divisional Headquarters informing them that all the troops had passed his station and that he was therefore coming in. I was asked by the telegraphist, who was on the instrument communicating with the last line of defence, to relieve him while he got his kit. I did so, but evidently the fellow I had relieved was afraid that he might miss the boat in a very real sense, for he did not come back, and I was therefore compelled to remain at his set.

At about 3.30 a.m. on Monday, 20 December, all troops had been evacuated, and, acting under the instructions from the Officer-in-Charge of the Signal Office, I sent a message to the 9th Corps Headquarters, which had been transferred from A Beach on to a ship in Suvla Bay, to the effect that the evacuation was complete.

I hastily gathered up my gear, left all the candles burning brightly in the dugout as a present for Johnny Turk, and hurried down to the beach loaded with full bandolier, haversack, water bottle, mess tin, overcoat, blankets, kitbag, souvenirs, rifle and the heavy buzzer instrument. I arrived at the landing stage just as the last lighter was pushing off. Almost as soon as the lighter had left, the shore was lit up by a series of huge fires. These were the dumps of stores which it had not been possible to take away and which had therefore been soaked in petrol and fired by time fuses.

Right to the end, telephone communication was maintained between West Beach, South Pier and C Beach, until, at 2.45 a.m., lines were finally cut. An hour later, Major Crocker, the Signalling Officer for the right flank, was informed that the last boat with the GOC and staff was waiting for him so he calmly disconnected his instrument and left. He was the last man to leave Suvla. At 05.30 the GOC reported that the evacuation had been completed.

As the troops left Suvla and Anzac, an artillery bombardment and a number of small-scale attacks were made at Helles to divert Turkish attention, and a large mine was exploded.

After an hour's steady progress we slowed down and bumped gently against some obstruction. The hatches were taken off and the order was passed down to disembark. The tall side of a steamer rose above us like a cliff, and stumbling blindly through an aperture in the darkness we found ourselves on the bottom deck. A voice overheard shouted, 'Look out below, there!' and a shower of lifebelts came cascading down. I grabbed one, lay with my head pillowed on its padding, and instantly fell asleep. I awoke to see the stars fading out and the dawn glow flushing the sky. Our ship was pounding along, trailing a wake of foam, full speed for Lemnos. The Peninsula crouched low on the horizon like a cloud that would presently vanish away. Already we were far beyond range of the Turkish Artillery.

Private Bernard Gill, 40th Field Ambulance, RAMC, 13th Division

The Allies left Suvla without a hitch. At Anzac, the position had been potentially much more perilous. The Australians always held the most tenuous of positions along the tops of the ridges that overlooked their landing beaches. Had the Turks become aware of the deception and the skeleton force holding the key ridge-top positions opposite them, they could have attacked and within a matter of minutes they would have been staring down on the Anzac troops as they retreated to their boats. Very specific details written on cards had been handed to each man charged with holding the Anzac positions on the ridge as to what their role would be, before, at a given moment, they would be ordered to leave. Miners were still ordered to chip away at tunnel entrances as if mining operations were being undertaken. In fact, mines had already been dug under Turkish positions at the Nek, to be blown by engineers two hours after the last infantryman had left, thereby adding to the pretence that the Anzacs were still in position.

The atmosphere was very strained – aeroplanes were very active, anti-aircraft guns made merry and snipers were as dangerous as snakes in hot weather. It became plain that evacuation was not far distant. On the morning of the 19th Abdul sent over some more howitzers (14-inch and

Sergeant Clifford Ellis, 24th Battalion, AIF

smaller), in the afternoon he sent up a Taube. Our whole firing line for a mile or so fired at it. He went for a while but soon it was a case of 'About turn, double march'. This was the best sport since landing on the Peninsula. That night the deed was 'did'. All unnecessary men had been sent off the night before. At 9.30 I got my walking ticket. Our boots were padded with strips of a blanket. Trench floors were carpeted with blankets. We crept out like a ghost parade down through the saps to avoid abuse [from Turkish artillery]. On a transport and, once more we behold those tragic hills, standing out in the moonlight. But this time they have a very different meaning for us.

The men were to leave smartly and not to run. Officers would guide the way down in the inky darkness. The nervous strain on men who had not slept for one, two, perhaps three days was intense. It was tough, too, to leave behind fallen friends. Yet in these final hours, the fear of discovery kept men moving towards the beaches and the barges ready to take them off. Once on board, the order was given to move off, leaving stores soaked in kerosene to burn merrily while, in the distance, the Turks could still be heard firing at nothing. The evacuation of Suvla and Anzac had been achieved not with minimal casualties but with no casualties. The real loss had been in stores, mostly destroyed, but some left intact by accident or omission, to be picked over by the Turks.

Lieutenant Mehmed Fasih, 47th Regiment, 16th Ottoman Division

03.30hrs: Get up. Tea is ready. Wake up Nuri. We have tea together. The front lines are extremely quiet. No grenades.

03.35hrs: A dumdum explodes to our left. Nuri and I have tea. Battalion Commander arrives. 'Hurry! Prepare a reconnaissance patrol, consisting of ten men.' The enemy has withdrawn on the entire right part of our front. Our 19th Division has moved up and occupied his trenches.

The patrol is readied.

The problem with holding Helles was that it would be difficult to replicate the ruse. The Turks could also concentrate all their energies on the tip of the Peninsula, bringing up new, heavier artillery supplied to them since the Bulgarians had joined the Central Powers, enabling Germany to transport new and better built artillery to Turkey. Some 40,000 men remained at Helles and most were ill and tired. The two divisions holding the line were in need of rest, and so the 13th Division that had just left Suvla was reassigned to Helles to replace 42nd Division, much to the annoyance of men like Corporal Herbert Lamb who had only just got used to the pleasures of Lemnos. To the right of the British, the remaining French colonial troops clung on to the Kereves Dere.

As the British continued to assess the situation, the Turks brought up their guns from Suvla and Anzac and several Turkish divisions were made ready for an attack against Sedd el Bahr. On Christmas Eve, the Turks launched a heavy and concentrated barrage against British positions at Helles: to all intents and

Preparing for evacuation: Australians and New Zealanders sorting their kit.

purposes it must have felt to any man who was there as if the noose was tightening. It snowed on Christmas Eve and, for a few hours at least, there was relative peace.

Private Charles Watkins, 1/6th Lancashire Fusiliers, 42nd Division

On the morning of the 25th we awoke to find the whole war-scarred countryside had been blanketed overnight by a heavy fall of snow. From our high vantage point we gaze down across the main gully. The ragged terrain has been smoothed off considerably by the thick soft blanket of snow and the snow sparkles in the morning sunlight. It's beautiful to look at and you feel a lifting of the heart as you gaze over the countryside. A stainless white blanket – hiding nearly all the ravages of war – stainless – except for the pink-splashed snow near our trench, from the blood of the wounded as they had staggered back after last night's hand-grenade attack.

Down below in the gully, the apotheosis of incongruity. Incredibly, on this Devil's own playground, someone had unearthed the battalion's band instruments from their temporary storage and the bandsmen were gathered down there in the gully, their polished instruments winking and flashing in the morning's bright sun, and the strains of Christmas carols were wafted on the still morning air.

One of our chaps had a wonderful tenor voice. Back home, he used to earn a few extra shillings at weekends, singing in pubs, and he accompanied the music of the band in mellow and heart-searing voice. Accompanying the distant strains of the band he even sang – right through – all the verses of 'Once In Royal David's City' – while the rest of us stood around in silence, staring into the void of space. Hushed and overawed, we didn't dare meet the others' eyes. The magic of music. Panoramas of other earlier and happier Christmases rolled before us in a scenic flood and one of the younger boys sobbed unashamedly.

Then the music and the carols ceased. In the distance we could see the band moving off to another part of the gully, there to regale another lot of listeners with the spirit of Christmas. We sat around, quiet, for a bit – the blokes staring glumly down at their boots, scraping bits of mud off them, or twiddling with the tapes of their puttees – an awkward embarrassing spate of silence, every man deep-wrapped in his own private musings.

On 26 December the enemy shellfire continued to be heavy and the rain continued to fall. Conditions were far from pleasant and still our artillery remained strangely unresponsive. We were all very tired, but that did not stop us from doing a large amount of work on the trenches which had suffered badly during the bombardments. On this night, owing to a lack of senior NCOs, I was taking duty as Orderly NCO in attendance on the officer who was visiting sentries during the night. He was one of our most efficient and popular officers. All members of the regiment were very tired and as I followed my officer round one of the traverses he suddenly stopped; I collided with him before I could stop. On looking over his shoulder I saw the sentry on duty was standing up on the firing step with his back in the corner sound asleep. After a few seconds, my officer carried on and as he passed the sleeping sentry he stumbled roughly against him, causing him to wake up, and then carried on to the next bay where he had a few words with the sentry there. He then returned to the bay in which the sentry had been asleep and had quite a long conversation with him. I think the officer knew from the state of his own degree of fatigue that the sentry simply could not keep awake.

On the following day, the 27th, the enemy shellfire intensified and started much earlier in the day. From 10 a.m. onwards the shellfire was very heavy indeed and more accurate than previously; more shells were dropping in, or near to, the front line and by mid-afternoon we were suffering the most intense bombardment. The trenches were being very badly wrecked but, surprisingly, we did not have a large number of casualties. At one stage a pair of trousers was seen to be blown high into the air – it transpired later that they belonged to one of our officers whose dugout had been hit. Luckily this officer was not wearing them at the time.

Lance Corporal Alexander Barclay, 1/1st Ayrshire Yeomanry, Attd. 52nd Division

In London, the appointment of Haig as Commander-in-Chief and the subsequent appointment of Sir William Robertson as Chief of the Imperial General Staff, had put two confirmed 'Westerners' in positions of strategic power. Both men wanted to close down the campaign in Gallipoli, and Robertson wasted no time in putting his case for immediate and final evacuation before the Cabinet, who duly acquiesced to his wishes. On 28 December, five days after Robertson's appointment, the order was given to leave Helles.

On Gallipoli there had been every expectation that the order to evacuate would be issued and plans, remarkably similar to those carried out at Suvla and Anzac, were pursued. Once again the number of men in the line would be thinned and guns removed, leaving roughly half, 17,000 men, to be evacuated on the night of 8 January. There were subtle changes to the plan as previously conceived. There would be no discernable pattern to 'silences', in fact at intervals rapid fire would be opened by both infantrymen and artillery to confuse the Turks into believing that an attack might be imminent. On 1 January, all French troops were withdrawn, save for a few sappers and some supporting batteries. Four thin British divisions remained, the 13th, 29th, 52nd and the RND.

Sergeant John Curdie, 1/6th Highland Light Infantry, 52nd Division

We sensed something was afoot. Our engineers were particularly busy and I saw in moving around that dummies were appearing here and there, mock-ups of men and also mock-ups of mules and pretty realistic they were in a way, too.

In early January I was called in front of the commanding officer, the Adjutant, and the Regimental Sergeant Major, and I was briefed to get rid of my kit and just to carry my haversack with essentials in it. My rifle, bayonet and my boots were to be covered in sandbags, which was done there and then.

I was given a compass and an illuminated watch and it was checked for timing. I was told to move down the communication trench and find my way to W Beach. I was also given a hooded torch to make notes of when I passed particular control points which were at the intersections of support trenches and reserve lines. I was also asked to observe if there were any obstacles which I had tripped over or nearly tripped over and to pinpoint them. To observe if there were any misleading things that might have diverted me from going on a straight and narrow path and then when leaving and coming out into the open at the base of the communication trench to make my way in darkness to W Beach and time myself and make observations.

I did get to W Beach and I looked at my notes that I had written under this hooded torch. They were a bit of a jumble so I rewrote them in the shelter of the beach and returned, whereupon I was told to report to 156 Brigade Headquarters and give my account of my journey and timings, and one obstacle in particular I reported was eventually taken away. I was thanked by the Brigadier and sent on my way.

6 Jan 1916: We are engaged, as you may judge, in infernally difficult work, and on two nights the weather has played the deuce with everything. I never had more difficulty in keeping my head in my life. Dealing at night with refractory piers, refractory boats, refractory Indians, and more refractory mules, and meanwhile shells at the rate sometimes of three to the minute, from two different directions and from as many as seven guns, is just about the limit. Fortunately I don't think there will be many more days and nights of it. Meanwhile the weather has again become perfect, and Charlie Dunlop and I keep fit. There are casualties of course, continually, but Charlie and I intend to get off safely, although we do have to wait till the last boat. Hope you get this.

Lieutenant Patrick Campbell, 1/1st Ayrshire Yeomanry. Attd. 52nd Division

The Turks were naturally curious as to what was happening at Helles and on 7 January an attack was made by a Turkish division with artillery support against the extreme left flank of the British line. The assault, preceded by the detonation of two mines, was not successful; indeed, most of the Turks were easily repulsed. Only where a battalion of the 7th North Staffordshire Regiment held the line was there serious trouble, with hand-to-hand fighting in the trenches resulting in the death of the battalion's forty-six-year-old commanding officer, Lieutenant Colonel Frank Walker, and thirty-three other ranks. This was the last attack made by the Turks against the British on Gallipoli. The British had been fortunate that the Turks had not been more curious, with full evacuation just thirty-six hours away.

Overleaf: View of North Beach, highlighting the mass of stores and field hospital tents nestling in the foothills. Note the old passenger ship Milo *in the bay, which was grounded and filled with cement in late October 1915, forming a breakwater.*

Our battalion strength was down to around 160 as they were sending away men who were not completely fit. Then on the evening of 8 January the bulk of the remaining men were sent down, leaving me with Captain McCray and 19 other ranks to hold the line which almost 200 had held before. We were spread over an area close to 400 yards, one man to every 20 yards.

Sergeant John Curdie, 1/6th Highland Light Infantry, 52nd Division

Corporal Herbert Lamb, 13th Divisional Signal Company, Royal Engineers

Saturday 8th: Fine, cold, and slight frost early, hot during day. 'Z day' at last … everyone busy destroying things … lent our revolvers and ammunition for destruction of horses and mules. Hundreds being shot … everything exceptionally quiet, everything ready; some of the trenches and tracks have been strewn with salt, sugar and flour to indicate the way to the beaches and at turnings there are placed candles burning in little boxes with directions painted on calico to shine through.

The weather had held, but as the last troops began to make their way to the beaches, the wind began to pick up and there was a noticeable swell in the sea. Within hours this had increased to the point that, at W Beach, waves were smashing into the jetties and threatening to maroon the last men. Nearby, great stores of ammunition had been collected and placed into natural chambers in the cliffs and set to explode shortly after the last boat had left. Around midnight the first of these primed magazines was accidentally lit and explosions rocked the beach. If the fire had spread to the other magazines, embarkation would have been impossible. However, the danger passed and running repairs were undertaken to the piers and pontoons along which the men walked to the lighters. At Gully Beach, the weather proved too exacting and one of two lighters ran aground, forcing a rapid march by 150 men along a coastal path to W Beach.

Corporal Herbert Lamb, 13th Divisional Signal Company, Royal Engineers

9 January: At about 2 a.m. lighters came to pier, very nerve-trying as firing line had been vacated for about two hours and still Turks did not spot anything unusual; eventually got on lighters, heavy swell running, one lighter went ashore and was destroyed purposely before we left. About 3 a.m. we were taken out to HMS *Talbot*, a very difficult and dangerous job getting on board. Wind and sea rising: the sailors swung wooden ladders over on to which we had to cling for dear life as the lighter was swept at intervals away from the ship's side. We had full kit on and a roll of blankets in our hands which made it more dangerous; one man fell into sea between ship and lighter but was rescued …

The last men were embarked in rough seas between 3 a.m. and 4 a.m., with the very last, an officer, leaving half an hour later. Brigadier General James O'Dowda, the Commander of W Beach, left at 3.30 a.m., fifteen minutes after the fuses in the magazines had been lit. Detonation was expected at 4 a.m. British warships, in a last hurrah, bombarded Achi Baba for all they were worth.

I packed up my dispatch case, and leaving my office, brought up the rear of the last party. Just at that moment a GSO, very disturbed, rushed up and told me that General Maude had not yet arrived. I asked what had happened and was informed that after they had left Gully Beach General Maude discovered that his bedding roll had been left behind. He said that he was hanged if he was going to leave his bedding for the Turks, got two volunteers with a stretcher and went back for it. The time was now 3.50 a.m. and there was no sign of the missing General. I therefore sent an officer and a couple of men, who knew every inch of the beach, and gave them ten minutes to retrieve him. Fortunately they found him almost at once.

We had not gone 200 yards from the jetty when the expected terrific explosion nearly blew us out of the water. Thousands of tons of debris, rock, shell cases, bits of limber wheels, and other oddments hurtled over our heads. I could never understand how we escaped injury. The men had been battened down in the hold of the lighter and were safe, but the few of us who were on deck escaped, I imagine, because we were within the cone of the explosion, i.e. the mass of stuff fell all round us like the outside of an open umbrella. At the same time the beach was lighted up as if for a carnival, and would have delighted Mr Brock of fireworks fame. It truly was a magnificent sight.

Brigadier General James O'Dowda, GOC 38th Brigade, 13th Division

Cape Helles had no happy memories for us; not one wanted to see the place again. But what of the men we were to leave behind us there? The good comrades, who had come so gaily with us to the wars, who had fought so gallantly by our side, and who would now lie for ever among the barren rocks where they had died … No man was sorry to leave Gallipoli; but few were really glad.

Lieutenant Charles Black, 1/6th Highland Light Infantry, 52nd Division

A moment for reflection: an unknown officer of the Lanarkshire Yeomanry looks over the side of the ship.

Endpiece

No artist, no paint, no canvas can catch the utter desolation of the idle flapping in the dawn wind of the tunic of the corpse leaning grotesquely on the barbed wire. Like a monstrous Guy Fawkes doll he gibbers obscenely to the rising sun, his teeth bared in the fixed and idiotic grin of death. Only a battlefield corpse knows how to grin so idiotically at the Great Sport of War.

His mates, lying alongside him in the dew-wet grass, wait in vain for the rising sun to warm their ever-cold bones. And no artist can ever recapture the smell of decay – the frightening stench of corruption borne towards us on the morning breeze.

But in spite of all this, this bloody place of Gallipoli fascinated you. There was a 'feel' about this place that was sort of special. The glory, the pathos and the shit of war – and the feeling that what we were now doing in this Homeric contest had been done many times before in this part of the world – the feeling that we were just another generation of actors re-enacting an old familiar scene that had often been played before by earlier generations of actors on this same familiar stage. I'm bloody sure this place is haunted. Dammit – you could almost hear the clank of sword upon shield.

I once commented on this point of view to a mate of mine, but he seemed only concerned for my sanity. 'Oh! It's orlright, tha knows, mate,' he said soothingly. 'Tha's just a little bit screwy, that's all. Ere, 'ave a little sup o' this tea, an' that'll feel better'.

CHARLES WATKINS

Acknowledgements

The staff at Bloomsbury have been particularly generous in their support and practical help, especially Bill Swainson, the Senior Commissioning Editor, whose continued encouragement is much appreciated. We are also very grateful to Becky Alexander, the Managing Editor, Polly Napper, Susan Wightman, who has worked so diligently to design *Gallipoli*, Maria Hammershoy, Anya Rosenberg, Sophie Christopher, David Mann and Imogen Corke for their dedicated effort in bringing *Gallipoli* to publication. We would like to express our gratitude to the copy-editor Richard Collins for his excellent and astute editorial comments: his accuracy and precision are always impressive.

We also greatly appreciate the help, support and guidance of our excellent agent, Jane Turnbull: once again, thank you, Jane. Similarly, our warmest thanks must go to our families for their help and support: in particular to Joan van Emden, who has once again given her time and knowledge to read over and give an outside expert's eye view.

We are grateful to the following people and associations for permission to reproduce photographs, extracts from diaries, letters or memoirs: The Gallipoli Association for permission to reproduce the memories and diary extracts submitted to the Association by former veterans and members; Steve Warburton for images taken from General Lucas' album; Annie Jenkin for permission to reproduce extracts from the letters of Temp. Chaplain Arthur Parham; John Powell for permission to reproduce extracts from Sydney Powell's diary; John Dancy for permission to reproduce extended extracts from his the diary of his father, Dr Jack Dancy; Basar Eryoner for the photograph of Lieutenant Stanley Jordan. We would also like to thank the Army Medical Services Museum for their help and generosity, in particular Gail Anderson and Ceri Gage.

The authors would also like to thank the National Archives of Australia, The State Library of Victoria, Archives of the Turkish General Staff and the Army Medical Services Museum, the Great War Forum. We are also grateful to Andrew French at the Berkshire Yeomanry Museum, Haluk Oral, Mustafa Yurdal, and Ellen Thompson for their generous help. We would also like to make a special mention of the staff at the Liddle Archive, Special Collections, Leeds University, in particular Richard Davies and Fiona Gell, for their generosity and kindness, and Jonathan Wright at Pen & Sword Books for his great support.

Sources

Published memoirs

Allen, Second Lieutenant John Hugh, *Of the Gallant Company, A Memoir*, Edward Arnold, London, 1919

Atatürk, Kemal, *Atatürk Memoirs*, IWM Printed Books, 1955

Campbell, P.M., *Letters From Gallipoli*, privately published by T&A Constable, Edinburgh, 1916. Includes Brigadier General James O'Dowda's lecture notes, p.4

Bush, Eric, *Gallipoli*, George Allen & Unwin, London, 1975

Fasih, Lieutenant Mehmed, *Lone Pine (Bloody Ridge) Diary*, Denizler Kitabevi, Istanbul, 1997

Hamilton, General Sir Ian, *Gallipoli Diary*, George H. Doran Company, 1920

Hargrave, John, *At Suvla Bay*, Houghton Mifflin Co., Boston, 1917

Herbert, Alan, *The Secret Battle*, Methuen & Co., London, 1919

Herbert, Lieutenant Aubrey, *Mons, Anzac & Kut*, Hutchinson, London, 1930

Mackenzie, Clutha N., *The Tale of a Trooper*, John Lane, London, 1921

Mure, Captain Albert, *With the Incomparable 29th*, W&R Chambers, London, 1919

Naci, Ibrahim, *Farewell, A Turkish Officer's Diary of the Gallipoli Campaign*, Çanakkale, 2013

Powell, Sydney Walter, *Adventures of a Wanderer*, Hutchinson, London, 1986

Sunata, Ismail, *Geliboludan Kaftaslara*, IS Bankasi Publications

Other books

Bean, Charles, *Gallipoli Mission*, Canberra, 1949 (quoted: Major Zeki Bey)

Carlyon, L.A., *Gallipoli*, Doubleday, London, 2001 (quoted: Sergeant Cliff Pinnock)

Chambers, Stephen, *Anzac The Landing*, Pen and Sword Military, Barnsley, 2008

—, *Suvla August Offensive*, Pen and Sword Military, Barnsley, 2011

Creighton, Oswin, *With the Twenty-ninth Division in Gallipoli*, Longmans, Green & Co., London, 1916 (quoted: letters of Major George Adams, Major Harold Shaw and Staff Captain Harold Farmar)

Housman, Laurence, *Letters of Fallen Englishmen*, Victor Gollancz Ltd, London, 1930 (quoted: letters of Private Thomas Dry)

Hart, Peter, *Gallipoli*, Profile Books, London, 2011

Hart, Peter and Nigel Steel, *Defeat at Gallipoli*, Papermac, London, 1994

Liddle, Peter, *Men of Gallipoli*, Allen Lane, London, 1976 (quoted: E. Weaver, Midshipman M. Seyeux, Seaman Sauveur Payro, Seaman Ernest Bullock, General Askir Arkayan)

Purdom, C.B., *Everyman at War*, J.M. Dent, 1930 (quoted: Lieutenant Colonel Frederick Bendell)

Unpublished diaries, letters and memoirs (private collections)

Diary of Lieutenant Commander Thomas Binney, *Diary of HMS Queen Elizabeth*

Memoirs of Dr Jack Dancy, 1891–1918

Diary of Sergeant Clifford Ellis, MM

Diary of Temporary Chaplain Arthur Parham

Diary of Petty Officer David Fyffe

Letters of The Hon. Arthur Coke

Letters of Surgeon Peter Kelly

Diary of Lieutenant Edward King

Diary of Major General John Lindley

Diary of Midshipman Geoffrey Maltby

Diary of Sergeant Charles Manley

Diary of Lieutenant Harry Minchin

Letters of Corporal George Mitchell

Letters of Sapper Geoffrey Robin

Magazine of the Gallipoli Association
By kind permission, the memories of:

Major Cecil Allanson

Lance Corporal Alexander Barclay

Sapper Thomas Edmunds

Sergeant Matthew Gray

Second Lieutenant Philip Gething

Private Bernard Gill

Corporal Edward Godrich

Sergeant Matthew Gray

Lieutenant George Horridge

Private Edward Marlow

Corporal Walter Mead

Private Charles Watkins

The National Archives, Kew, London
Cabinet
Lieutenant Colonel Joseph Beeston, Cab. 45/241
Temporary Lieutenant Colonel Marcus de la Poer Beresford, Cab. 45/247
Captain Arthur Crookenden, Cab. 45/241
Diary of Major General Granville Egerton, Cab. 45/249
Memories of Lieutenant Colonel Douglas Forman, Cab. 45/220
Diary of Sapper Thomas Farrer, Cab. 45/251
Captain Douglas Figgis, Cab. 45/251
Memories of Staff Captain Henry Goodland, Cab. 45/242
Diary of Corporal Herbert Lamb, Cab. 45/256
Diary of Sergeant William Meatyard, Cab. 45/243
Memories of Frank Mills, Cab. 45/243
Diary of Captain Clement Milward, Cab. 45/243
Second Lieutenant Arthur Pelly, Cab. 45/244
Major William Rettie, 59th Brig RFA, Cab. 45/244
Account of Lieutenant Robert Seed, Cab. 45/222
Lieutenant Commander Josiah Wedgwood, Cab. 45/241

War Office
Memories of Guy Geddes, 1st Munster Fusiliers, WO 95/4310

Archives
Imperial War Museum, London. By kind permission of the Department of Documents:
IWM Docs: Captain Faik and Lieutenant Mehmet Sefik. Rayfield Papers Collection quoted by S. Aker, *The Dardanelles: The Ari Burnu Battles and 27 Regiment*
IWM Docs: Second Lieutenant Ivonne Kirkpatrick, typescript account
IWM Docs: Lieutenant Geoffrey Ryland, typescript diary
IWM Docs: Private Ridley Sheldon, typescript account
IWM Docs: Commander Edwin Unwin, typescript account, 'The Landings from the River Clyde'

The Liddle Archive: By kind permission of the Liddle Collection, Leeds University Library, with thanks to Richard Davies and Fiona Gell:
Midshipman Charles Churchill, RNMN/050; Sergeant John Curdie 1/6 HLI, Sev/01; Private Charles Duke 4th AIF, Anzac/Aust./Rec./18; Sapper Reginald Gale, RND, GS/0601; Corporal Herbert Hitch, 11th Bn AIF, Anzac/Aust./Rec./26; Second Lieutenant Roy Laidlaw, Gall. 053; Private Walter Paterson 11th Bn AIF, Anzac/Aust./075

National Army Museum: By kind permission of the National Army Museum, Chelsea, London: Sergeant William Taylor, 34th Brigade Collection

Picture credits
All photographs are taken from the authors' private collections unless otherwise stated below.

Archives of the Turkish General Staff: p. 190 (both), p. 250.
Army Medical Services Museum: By kind permission of the Army Medical Services Museum, Keogh Barracks, Ash Vale, with thanks to the Curator of Archives, Gail Anderson: p. 53, p. 119, p. 212, p. 227, p. 230, p. 232–3, p.234, p.255 (both), p. 270, p. 271, p. 279, p. 328–9.
Berkshire Yeomanry Museum: p. 209.
Ellen Thompson: p. 225, p. 296
Getty Images: p.3 (79665274), p.15 (3286500).
Imperial War Museum, London: By kind permission of the Picture Library: p.viii (Q42304), p.268 (Q70704).
The Liddle Archive: By kind permission of the Liddle Collection, Leeds University Library. With thanks to Richard Davies, Rosie Dyson and Fiona Gell: N.E. Chadwick, Gall. 019; J.N. Mankin, GS/1050; W.A. Young, Gall. 116. p. 91, p.98, p.99, p.193, p.202, p.220, p.253, p.272–3, p.282, p.310–1.
Museum Victoria, Australia: p. 144.
The National Archives of Australia: p.300.
Pen and Sword Archive: p.108, p. 146–7.
State Library of Victoria, Australia: p. 126, p. 135, p.307.
Steve Warburton: p. 102, p.103, p.278.

All maps drawn by John Gilkes.

Index

Page numbers in *italics* refer to photographs